Man Appeal

Man Appeal

Advertising, Modernism and Men's Wear

Paul Jobling

BERG

Oxford • New York

First published in 2005 by
Berg
Editorial offices:
1st Floor, Angel Court, 81 St Clements Street, Oxford, OX4 1AW, UK
175 Fifth Avenue, New York, NY 10010, USA

Berg is the imprint of Oxford International Publishers Ltd.

Library of Congress Cataloging-in-Publication Data
Jobling, Paul.
    Man appeal : advertising, modernism and men's wear / Paul Jobling.
        p. cm.
    Includes bibliographical references and index.
    ISBN 1-84520-087-X (pbk. : alk. paper) — ISBN 1-84520-086-1 (cloth :
alk. paper) 1. Advertising—Men's clothing—Great Britain—History—
20th century. I. Title.

HF6161.M38J62 2005
659.19′687′0941–dc22

2004029272

British Library Cataloguing-in-Publication Data
A catalogue record for this book is available from the British Library.

ISBN-13 978 184520 086 2 (Cloth)
ISBN-10 1 84520 086 1 (Cloth)

ISBN-13 978 184520 087 9 (Paper)
ISBN-10 1 84520 087 X (Paper)

Typeset by JS Typesetting Ltd, Porthcawl, Mid Glamorgan.
Printed in the United Kingdom by Biddles Ltd, King's Lynn.

www.bergpublishers.com

Contents

List of Figures

Acknowledgements

I should like to thank the following people for their invaluable involvement and endless support in the preparation of this book: Kathleen Rose, Kevan Rose, Marsha Meskimmon, Rachel Worth, Tracy Fowler, Lou Taylor and Kathryn Earle. Thanks also to Austin Reed for the kind permission to reproduce materials from their archives. The project came to fruition with the help of study leave during the academic year 2002–03, which was generously funded by the Arts and Humanities Research Board and the Centre for Research and Development at the University of Brighton.

Introduction

There is a powerful half-page of Southall's boots in *The Strand Magazine* for January. It strikes the eye when the pages are only being casually turned over. The advertising of this make of boots is invariably of a striking and original kind, although a little more letterpress would often improve it.

Advertising World, January 1903a

It is essential, in this age of fierce competition, to give an advertisement such an appearance from the visual and artistic standpoint that the particular community to whom it is intended to appeal must find in it something original, a feeling of freshness and of worth.

Frederick Horn, Penrose's Annual, 1935

The first half of the twentieth century was undoubtedly one of the most fecund and complex periods in both the history of advertising and the promotion of men's wear in Britain, with which this book is concerned. This was a time when vast sums of money were being dedicated to the production and circulation of advertisements promoting men's clothing; between January and September 1933, for instance, nearly £56,000 (the equivalent of just over £3 million in 2001) were spent by nine outfitters on press advertising space alone.[1] In this context, regional companies like London tailors Collett's might have a respectable, if comparatively small, advertising budget, while big national concerns like Austin Reed were responsible for the lion's share of such expenditure. Their promotional budget for this period was in excess of £2 million by today's standards, and approximates to the £3 million advertising account allocated in 2002 to Yellow Door Creative Marketing for the relaunch of the Austin Reed brand in autumn 2003.[2] Yet it was not just a question of publicity for men's wear becoming a potent economic force as the century progressed, for simultaneously a detailed discourse on advertising itself, how best to promote clothing and to whom, was also being compounded, as the two opening quotations above indicate. If, then, the advertising manager of *The Times* could assert in 1927, 'Men, generally speaking, are far better dressed since the advertising of clothes' (*Advertiser's Weekly*, 15 April 1927: 71), my task in undertaking this study was to examine how and why this should have been the case.

Pioneering work by Christopher Breward and Frank Mort has greatly illuminated and reconfigured our understanding of the relationship between masculinities and consumerism in Britain in the twentieth century, but neither author deals exclusively with advertising men's clothing and fashion, and their historical and thematic foci are, therefore, of necessity different from mine.[3] By contrast this book, which is extensively based on original archival research, is quintessentially about the representation of fashion, or the 'translation' of clothing into language and the concomitant tension between 'image-clothing' and 'written clothing' that Barthes evinces in *The Fashion System* (1967).[4] Thus, in approaching the subject of men's wear publicity as a print historian, my central aim is to deal with what D.F. McKenzie in his 1985 Panizzi Lectures at the British Library called the 'sociology of texts' (McKenzie 1986:4), and thereby to analyse how the materiality of clothing is translated into the materiality of poster and press advertising. One of the interesting things to observe on this level is how changes in the design, styling and marketing of men's wear coincided with new ideas and debates concerning the form and style of graphic design and advertising during the first half of the twentieth century. Methodologically, therefore, I have attempted to elaborate a dialectical exposition of the material in question whenever relevant, such that any technological, economic and social changes in the production and consumption of men's wear and any corresponding changes in the advertising industry can be seen to coalesce in, or give rise to, new forms and styles of clothing publicity.

We can observe this dialectic in operation in the majority of men's wear advertisements included for analysis in each of the chapters of this book, which encompasses principally promotions for suits, jackets and slacks, shirts, footwear and underwear. But suffice to state here that publicity for men's suits, which is the main focus of Chapter 5, provides a particular test case. Briefly put, during the interwar period the suit became one of the most ubiquitous and widely retailed garments, sold bespoke and ready-to-wear by a plethora of outfitters from Austin Reed to The Fifty Shilling Tailors, and worn by working, middle and upper classes alike. At the same time, the advertising industry underwent some of the most significant changes in its evolution: seminal works such as Cyril Sheldon's *Poster Advertising* (1927) and Jan Tschichold's (1930) writing on the new typography encouraged progressive agencies such as Carlton Studios, W.S. Crawford and Pritchard and Wood to espouse modernist principles of graphic communication, while their task was also aided by the rise of market research into how to reach a suitable target audience. Accordingly, promotions for Austin Reed and The Fifty Shilling Tailors both represented the suit in terms of class and social status and codified it through modern aesthetics involving the simplification of shapes and forms, photographs, sans serif typefaces, and white space. Austin Reed achieved this principally in the poster and press advertising of Tom Purvis, and The Fifty Shilling Tailors in their press campaigns with illustrations by C.B. Bowmar (Figures 18, 19 and 29). Moreover, as discussed in Chapter 6, the Utility measures and rationing that impacted on the fashion and publishing industries during the Second World War meant in turn that the suit had to be promoted according to such social and economic changes.

It can be argued, therefore, that fashion publicity has its own stylistic modes and spheres of production and consumption, and as Chapters 1 and 2 demonstrate, when it came to publicity in the press, one of the central concerns to exercise retailers and advertising agencies throughout the period 1900–45 was the need to reach an ideal target audience in terms of class, profession and age. For a long while, advertisers were left in a position of second-guessing which media would be the most appropriate ones to exploit. But newspapers and magazines slowly began to divulge their circulations and sales figures, and by the 1930s market research into class and readerships conducted by companies like Repford, J. Walter Thompson and the Incorporated Society of British Advertisers also helped retailers to corroborate their media preferences.

In addition to such economic and class considerations, of course, was the question whether men took any notice of advertisements in the first place, and it was for good reason that *Advertising World* argued in its issue of June 1911: 'Not one man in 20,000 would carefully study a page of almost microscopic particulars about a hundred or more different articles of men's wear' (*Advertising World* 1911b: 704). To this end, the tension between 'reason-why' advertising, which tended to emphasise the cost of the product and to promote it in matter-of-fact terms, and more atmospheric or suggestive forms of publicity was hotly debated. As Roland Barthes argues in his essay 'The Advertising Message' (1963), the starting point for promoting any product or service is to encode it in terms of the use value it has in our lives. But if things were always stated as baldly as this, advertisements would not satisfy our need for symbolic forms of exchange. In other words, if all suits or underwear were simply promoted in the same way, on the basis that they can be worn to keep us cool in summer or warm in winter, it would be more difficult for us to prefer one style or brand over another, or to choose which one we think satisfies most not only our individual needs, but our tastes, personalities and aspirations as well. Consequently, the invitation to buy any item becomes part of a wider signifying process that involves the product being encoded with reference to metaphors, puns, myths and dreams: 'by swathing the product in advertising language, mankind gives it meaning and thereby transforms its simple use into an experience of the mind' (Barthes 1994 [1963]: 178).

The experience of the mind to which Barthes alludes is certainly much in evidence in the majority of campaigns that are analysed in the following chapters, and it also bears much on the way that, from the start of the twentieth century, advertising was envisaged as a type of psychology, and arguably a not necessarily subtle one. This idea is addressed specifically in Chapters 2 and 4, where the impact of authors such as Walter Dill Scott and Henry Forster Adams in determining the psychology of the male consumer is addressed. Scott was at pains to point out that advertising was a form of motivation which worked on the subconscious mind, and that to be effective any advertisement must also be well conceived as a piece of design and copywriting: 'The display type and the picture which merely attract and do not instruct are in many cases worthless, for in attracting attention to themselves they divert attention from the thing being advertised' (Scott 1904f:20).

It is instructive here to observe Scott contending that design issues played a defining role in the success (or otherwise) of advertisements for men's wear, and this is another thematic leitmotiv woven into the argument of this book. Of special significance here is the interrelationship of word and image that he mentions, something which Ashley Havinden, creative director at the W.S. Crawford agency, was only too keen to amplify: 'The idea of picture and words being complementary to each other is one of the most important developments of contemporary advertising presentation' (Havinden 1935–6:15). On one level, this kind of harmony between pictures and words was bound up with debates on whether hand-drawn illustrations or photographs were the most suitable in rendering men's clothing in a persuasive atmospheric manner. Repeatedly, then, the depiction of the proverbial 'tailor's dummy' was impugned in favour of 'illustrations, which purport to represent the clothes advertised as they would look when worn' (A.H. Williams June 1912:674). And on another level, it hinged on debates concerning typographic reform. As I argue throughout the chapters in this book, this meant that the choice of a particular typeface was no mere fancy on the part of the graphic designer, but, according to Robert Braun, it was more a realisation that the balance and rhythm of any advertisement – its very emotional effects – depended on the use of serif or sans serif typeforms and the size and weight of the printed words (R. Braun 1927: 168–9). Thus different typeforms could be combined in order to give a different sense of verbal emphasis to distinct pieces of text in any advertisement. Such considerations were important whether it came to the composition of copy in newspaper and magazine publicity or when words were kept to a minimum, as was commonly the case with poster advertising. But, as Havinden and others appreciated, ideally text and image should form a holistic entity, and the designer and copywriter should collaborate in evolving the kind of visual and verbal rhetoric that afforded symbolic meaning to the garment(s) being advertised: 'The full use of the suggestion idea demands a specialised understanding of the three aspects of an advertisement – Illustration, Typography, and Copy' (Mills 1923:298).

As we shall see, this much is evident in those press and poster advertisements masterminded by Havinden for Simpson during the 1930s, or by Pritchard and Wood for Austin Reed at the same time, which are examined in Chapters 4 and 5. In particular, however, I have mobilised the press advertisements produced for Barratt shoes by Crawford's as a case study in Chapters 4 and 6 in order to examine the symbiotic relationship of text and image in men's wear advertising between 1920 and 1945. Illustrated by Andrew Johnson and with copy by G.H. Saxon Mills elaborating a series of fictive conversations between Mr Barratt and different kinds of male clients, the 'Walk the Barratt Way' campaign broke new ground in both its form and content and was one of the longest running promotions of its kind (Figures 8, 9 and 34). The arresting captions were set in modernist Gill Sans, while the main copy of some 300 words was set in a contrasting serif typeface called Mono Plantin. But the overall effect was not cluttered and the narrative thrust of the copy complemented the milieu or theme suggested by Johnson's illustrations and the opening captions. Typography was also used expressively in the copy of each advertisement and some words in phrases such as 'But – look at the way the *toes turn-up!*' were given prosodic emphasis in order to mimic the pace and rhythm of actual speech patterns (Figure 9). Furthermore, the use of dialogue rather than hard-sell tactics in the advertisements interpellates the reader to think about the benefits of the product being promoted, so that the imaginary clients who converse with Mr Barratt about their feet could also be somebody like the real 'you' who reads the copy.

Yet the campaign was not conceived to attract just anybody to Barratt Shoes, and it illuminates also the way that class could be connoted in men's wear advertising. For the performative lexis reiterated by Mr Barratt and his clients in the copy, phrases such as 'And who has ever found a pleasanter or healthier pursuit?', are based on the everyday language of the upper and middle classes, and thereby were intended to strike a chord with the company's putative ideal customer. The connotation of class through dialogic or testimonial devices such as those found in the Barratt advertisements was also very much at the heart of publicity for The Fifty Shilling Tailors, which is assessed in Chapter 5. At the same time, the style and content of some of their publicity borrowed much from the class symbolism of advertisements for Austin Reed, while campaigns for both these retailers, in common with many other companies, also represented the male body as part of what Glyn Maxwell has neatly termed an 'ornamental realm' (Maxwell 2000: 34).

In the light of so much attention having been paid to the sexual objectification of men in British advertising post-Levi 501s in 1985, it is perhaps surprising to frame the representation of men in publicity before 1945 in such a way. Nonetheless, campaigns for Austin Reed and The Fifty Shilling Tailors during the 1930s did not fight shy of depicting men as preening peacocks, solicitous of the approval of female admirers. In fact, an egregious example of such dandyism in men's wear promotions can be traced back to Pope & Bradley's series of posters, 'Le Style c'est l'Homme', which was initiated in 1911. Illustrated by William Houghton, the male figure in the posters is very much the antithesis of the 'tailor's dummy' evident in so much publicity for male dress. Rather, he is portrayed as a confident head-turner, who knowingly offers up his body for the delectation of the women who watch him stroll by in the poster as well as the male spectators who would have seen the poster as they strolled by street hoardings (Figure 5). Probably more surprising still to those of us who have encountered the erotic charge of men's underwear only since the first representation of the buff *gymnos* in Calvin Klein advertising in 1982, is the fetishistic aspect and the sexual ambiguity codified in publicity for underwear in the interwar period, which is the focus of Chapter 7. Furthermore, this chapter returns us again to the dialectical relationship between fashion, graphic communications and men's wear advertising, and is a timely reminder of the fact that even when we are dealing with the most basic – and minimal – of garments, any exploration of how clothing was promoted in Britain between 1900 and 1945 has to take account of factors as diverse as technological and social changes in clothing and retailing, the impact of class and gender politics, as well as the visual and verbal rhetoric generated by commercial artists and copywriters for the advertisements themselves.

A Note on Sources

Greenfield, O'Connell and Reid (1999) assert in their analysis of the buying habits of middle-class males in Britain in the interwar period that, 'The difficulty historians face in identifying the role of men and masculinity in consumption is in locating revealing sources' (Greenfield et al. 1999:194). Certainly, this is borne out by the fact that the majority of advertising agencies who were involved with handling many men's wear accounts between 1900 and 1945 no longer exist and along with them invaluable archival material has vanished. However, as I progressively tackled the issues in this book it became clear that there is no shortage of materials relating to men's wear advertising, and I excavated a myriad of useful sources that enabled me to investigate several cogent themes.

In the first instance, contemporaneous professional and trade literature contains a wealth of relevant information on the evolution of advertising and its relationship to the promotion of male clothing. The chief titles I have exploited to this end are the *Advertising World* (1901–40), *Advertiser's Weekly* (1913–70), *Commercial Art* (1922–31), *Advertising Display* (1926–35), *Art and Industry* (1936–58), *Penrose Annual* (1895–1982), and *MAN and his Clothes* (1926–59), the last in particular has been hitherto an unexplored rich periodical resource. These magazines cover topics as diverse as the role of instinct psychology, market research and target audiences, the role of the commercial artist and copywriter, and aesthetic debates concerning the layout of advertisements and modernism in typography and illustration. Full details of all the relevant articles that I consulted concerning these topics are provided in the Bibliography. Second, various archives such as those at the History of Advertising Trust, Austin Reed and Mass-Observation also encompass an invaluable range of primary pictorial and verbal accounts concerning men's wear advertising. The History of Advertising Trust houses in particular the archives of two of the biggest advertising agencies to have operated in the first half of the twentieth century – W.S. Crawford and London Press Exchange. Finally and not least, many examples of advertising campaigns were found in the daily and periodical press itself. Consequently, newspapers like the *Daily Mail*, *Daily Express* and *The Times*, which were mentioned regularly in *Advertising World*, *Advertiser's Weekly* and *MAN and his Clothes* since they carried a large amount of publicity for men's wear retailers and manufacturers such as Austin Reed, The Fifty Shilling Tailors, Simpson, Meridian and Wolsey, have been mobilised for the entire period covered by this study. By extension, weekly magazines with circulations in excess of 1 million copies per issue, namely the *Radio Times* and *Punch*, were particularly relevant for my analysis of men's wear publicity in the interwar period for the companies mentioned above as well as others like Barratt Shoes, while *Picture Post* was instrumental to my exploration of the impact of Utility and rationing during the Second World War.

The majority of press advertisements during the period 1900–45, whether they used photographs or hand-drawn illustrations, were printed in monochrome. Colour advertisements appeared intermittently in *Punch* and *MAN and his Clothes* at this time (see front cover and Figure 23), but it was mostly the lithographic posters for the likes of Pope & Bradley and Austin Reed that were printed more successfully in full-colour (Figures 5, 16 and 18–21). The technical and economic reasons concerning the use and frequency of different forms of reproduction are addressed principally in Chapters 2, 4 and 5.

Notes

1. In order to give the reader some kind of comparative perspective on the amounts of money that were being spent on advertising, as well as how much different items of clothing themselves cost, I have cited equivalent sums for 2001 in the footnotes of the respective chapters. These have been culled from J.J. McCusker (2003), 'The Purchasing Power of the British Pound 1264–2002', Economic History Services, http://www.eh.net/hmit/ppowerbp/

2. For example, between January and September 1933, Collett's spent £1,143 and Austin Reed spent £40,820 on press advertising (*Advertiser's Weekly*, 1933a, 1933b, 1933c, 1933d); respective 2001 equivalents are £62,973.60 and £2,248,978.38. See also, 'Austin Reed Names New Agency', *Marketing Week*, 5 September 2002, regarding Yellow Door. The first press advertisements, both featuring the same photograph of a man in a grey suit shot from the ground

upwards on the building site for Norman Foster's Swiss Re Tower, 30 St Mary Axe, London, appeared in the *Evening Standard*, 18 September 2003 (with the caption 'An Adventurous New Beginning') and British *GQ*, October 2003 (with the caption 'Adventures of a gentleman').

3. See Mort (1996), which also includes an assessment of advertising for Burton the tailor of taste during the 1950s, and Breward (1999).

4. For Barthes, however, it is written clothing (*le vêtement écrit*) that takes precedence over image-clothing (*le vêtement-image*) since, as he argues, words seem to proffer a purer reading of the fashion text than pictures. As we shall see, such logocentrism is not necessarily the case in many of the men's advertisements included in this book, which deploy a more balanced integration of word and image.

–1–

'Design is Just a Detail of our Service'

The Development of Men's Wear Advertising as a Social and Economic Force between 1900 and 1914

To sell clothing to the masculine half of humanity is a business by itself. Men usually have very definite ideas of their own, both as to the style of clothing in general, and for themselves in particular.

(*Advertising World*, July 1912)

The earliest forms of fashion publicity that originated in Britain in the eighteenth century overlapped with the rise of urban culture and shopping and embraced diverse forms of promotion, some of which we might not strictly recognise today as advertising. In the first instance the majority of retailers regarded the creation of an enticing shop façade and interior as sufficient means for attracting and establishing a suitable clientele, a convention that was to persist throughout the nineteenth and twentieth centuries. By 1910, however, men's wear retailers were being advised to 'have care as to what departments are shown together' in their window displays (*The Outfitter* 1910: 34). During the eighteenth century such forms of display would subsequently be complemented by the circulation of handbills and trade cards, and to a lesser extent by press advertising, all of which were used to reinforce the reputation of the shop in question rather than to publicise the sale of particular wares. In the issue of the *London Evening Post* for 2–4 April 1741, for example, the haberdasher John Stanton placed an advertisement, not to tell the public about the goods he sold but to inform them of a change of trading address. Otherwise, newspaper advertisements were occasionally used by large-scale retailers and manufacturers to promote both new and second-hand goods at fixed prices, and from the 1760s tailors also began to advertise different items of male and female clothing. The emphasis of such publicity was the printed word and the general format was the list, enumerating the items on offer and how much they cost. In contrast, more alluring pictorial representations of the latest fashions were available as engraved or etched plates by the late eighteenth and early nineteenth centuries. These were displayed for sale in print sellers' windows and were also incorporated into volumes such as Heideloff's *Gallery of Fashion* (1794–1802) and intermittently in magazines such as the *Lady's Magazine*.[1]

From the 1830s onwards, wood engraving began to supplant intaglio methods of reproduction and was used sporadically to illustrate flyers advertising men's tailors and outfitters like Samuel Brothers of Ludgate Hill during the 1850s and more commonly in trade weeklies such as *The Tailor and Cutter* (f. 1870). But the first quantitative and qualitative shift in the promotion of men's wear did not become evident until the end of the nineteenth century. By this time, the demands of a diverse clientele for good quality tailoring and the rise of advertising as a distinct professional practice effectively began to coalesce in terms of formative market research and media planning. Within the space of ten years or so the volume of display advertising for men's wear in the *Daily Mail*, for example, had increased almost twofold – in the issue for 14 January 1901 twelve column inches were dedicated to men's wear promotions, and twenty-two in the issue for 16 January 1911. As John Kirkwood (1911) saw it, this sharp rise in the quantity of press advertising for all kinds of products and services was due in no small measure to the mutual realisation among media and manufacturers that they had much to gain from each other economically: 'Advertisers and newspapers have recognised that their interests are identical and the result has been a vast increase in the efficiency of both' (Kirkwood 1911:134 and 137). In turn, better production values in periodical publishing led product placers to seek more advertising space in order to promote their goods, and this both subsidised the cost of newspapers and magazines and encouraged more commerce. Indeed, London men's outfitters E. Catesby & Sons were quick to realise that press advertising could be advantageously deployed to promote sales of their suits by post (*Advertising World* 1906d:563).

Yet enormous as it was at this point in time, advertising in periodicals for both the public and trade formed but one part of a much larger media machine in British material culture, which embraced a diverse range of promotional channels including posters, booklets and brochures for mail order, and showcards in shop windows.[2] From the outset, these were the staple media of many national men's wear outlets including Austin Reed and Horne Brothers, and regional traders such as Pope & Bradley, based in London, and Pettigrew & Stephens Ltd of Glasgow, which specialised in a flannel lounge suit costing 21 shillings ready to wear and 25 shillings made to measure (Figure 1).[3] Simultaneously, some men's wear retailers exploited indirect forms of advertising alongside the more usual channels. On a promotional outlay of £2,000 in 1903, for instance, J. & H. Ellis The Smart Set Tailors, founded in 1891 and owners of premises in Strand and Aldersgate Street, London, not only advertised in the *Morning Leader* and specialist magazines such as *Draper's Record*, but also ran campaigns in theatre programmes and big hotels in London to attract the passing tourist trade, as well as relying on window displays and booklets.[4] Moreover, they realised that inclusion of their name in topical press reports (the newspapers had reported on their provision of overcoats and evening dress to Boer generals visiting England), or the reporting of sports results such as the Yacht Race in their shop windows helped to promote an interest in their goods (*Advertising World* 1904a:127).

Accordingly, this chapter serves to introduce the two pivotal interdependent social and economic factors that men's wear retailers during the early twentieth century had to take into consideration in the hope of reaching as wide a public as possible with their publicity; namely, the cost of producing and placing advertisements in the most instrumental media so as to target the most appropriate male consumers in terms of class and income. But first of all, it is necessary to account for the way that these concerns simultaneously overlapped with the evolution and influence of the advertising agencies and the concomitant professionalisation of the advertising industry in Britain.

The Advertising Industry Takes Off: the Formation of the Agency System

On both sides of the Atlantic the earliest advertising agencies originated in the nineteenth century and included several of the longest surviving and largest organisations – in the United States, N.W. Ayer & Son (established in 1868) and J. Walter Thompson (1878), and in Britain, Mather & Crowther (1846) and Smith's (1877–8).[5] Until the 1890s, however, the chief function of advertising agents was usually to buy appropriate space in the press or to liaise with the printer of bills and posters on behalf of manufacturers rather than to provide design solutions or copy themselves, which were the province of either the owner or another executive of a respective company. As Pamela Walker Laird (1998: 6), in her illuminating study of early advertising in North America, attests: 'Before 1900, practitioners seldom saw their functions in any context broader than the business success of their clientele. Their claims to professional esteem they limited to how efficiently and effectively they placed messages that their clients had already created'. There were, however, a few examples of more innovative and enterprising advertising during the 1880s such as the planning of the press and poster campaigns for Pears soap by Thomas A. Barratt. This brand name was lavishly promoted both in Britain and North America by 1883 with resort to testimonials by the likes of Lillie Langtry, or by association with high art, notably the controversial use of Sir John Millais's oil painting *Bubbles* in 1886 (Loeb 1994: 96–7; Frith 1889: 421–27; Dempsey 1978:4).

By the 1890s this situation had begun to change, as the number of advertising agencies grew exponentially and they, in turn, carved out areas of creative specialisation such as copywriting and illustration in addition to buying media space. In 1892, 288 advertising agencies were listed in a business directory for New York

City in comparison to 42 in 1869 (Laird 1998:157), while in Britain numbers had increased from 6 advertising offices in 1866 to 83 advertisement agents in 1896 (Nevett 1982:100). These included C. Wilke (founded 1881), London Press Exchange (f. 1892), S.H. Benson (f. 1895), and Lee's (f. 1899). By 1903, London had a veritable advertising area of its own, with agency offices clustered around 'Printer's Land' in Strand, Fleet Street, High Holborn and Embankment. In 1908 there were 153 agencies operating in the area, such as Mather & Crowther, S.H. Benson, the Dorland Agency, Smiths, Paul E. Derrick, London Press Exchange and H. Green & Co. (*Advertising World Year Book* 1908). Many of them also held accounts for men's wear producers and retailers; for example, Mather & Crowther acted on behalf of Wolsey hosiery and underwear and the Savoy Tailor's Guild at this period in time, while Smith's promoted Curzon's the tailors.

Not all of them were to survive for very long, however, and their financial situation was quite often precarious; Lee's Advertising Agency, for instance, had been put into liquidation by 1902 because one of their main advertisers had defaulted on settling an account (*Advertising World*, September 1902:223). At the same time, advertising agencies began to develop their own expertise in originating campaigns and to organise themselves into various departments dealing with market and media research and creative matters. During the late 1880s several agencies, including Smith and Mather & Crowther, had begun to publish press directories in which they listed different types of periodicals and newspapers along with respective details concerning their price, frequency of publication and advertising rates, so that by 1914 G.W. Goodall (1914: 58) could attest, 'the agency will advise and co-operate with the advertiser at every turn and relieve him of every detail of his publicity'.[6] In point of fact it is interesting to observe how Mather & Crowther confidently toasted the diversity of their own professional remit in a tasteful company promotion in *Advertising World* (August 1909: 210). This consisted of a chiaroscuro image of a man in evening dress raising a glass of wine and the caption, 'DESIGN is just a detail of our Service – still, it's *right*' (Figure 2).

In the majority of advertising agencies, design was the province of the creative department, which usually consisted of artists, copywriters and layout people. But it was the advertising managers who masterminded and harnessed the activities of all the different specialists working for the agency. They had to demonstrate, therefore, considerable knowledge not only of the entire structure of their own organisation and the accounts it handled but also of the media industry in its entirety and what motivated human beings to purchase any particular brand.[7] Thus the seeds of the modern agency structure were sown by the end of the nineteenth century and the role of agencies as strategic profit-making organisations was later facilitated by the 1915 Finance Act that abolished the Excess Profits Duty imposed on businesses before the First World War (*Advertising Review* 1938).

Specialist courses for the training of agency personnel and companies whose expertise was the provision of advertising artwork and copy were also established at the turn of the century. The Page-Davis Advertising School opened branches in New York and Chicago in 1895 and in London four years later in order to train copywriters. Carlton Studios were established in London in 1900 with the intention, according to an advertisement in the *Advertising World* in April 1904, of furnishing 'drawings that advertise, made by artists who combine artistic ability with a knowledge of advertising value.' (Carlton was one of several studios that specialised in fashion drawing during the 1920s and 1930s and are discussed more fully in Chapter 2.) And H.E. Morgan of the printers Spottiswoode & Co. dispensed expert guidance to potential clients from their premises at 123 Oxford Street, which also housed galleries displaying 'designs for every kind of advertising' (*Advertising World* 1904f: 92). These initiatives were followed in 1911 by classes at the Polytechnic Institution in Regent Street, dealing with copywriting and the theory of advertising, taught by William Whitebrook, former literary head of staff at S.H. Benson. Certainly, by this stage of the century advertising could be regarded as a lucrative profession to follow; in a lecture delivered to students attending the Polytechnic Institution on 17 January 1911, for example, Thomas Russell cited average earnings of £500 upwards per annum and made mention of one copywriter whose annual salary was £3,500 (*Advertising World* 1911a:194).[8]

In particular, 1904 was to prove a key moment in the professionalisation of the emergent British advertising industry with the foundation of two key organisations – the Sphinx Club of London and the Association of Advertising Agents (AAA). The Sphinx Club, which came into being on 2 June 1904 after a formal ceremony in the Hotel Cecil in London, modelled itself on the original eponymous organisation formed in New York in 1896. Its thirteen founding members comprised representatives from the advertising industry, the press and manufacturers, including H. Powell Rees of the Paul E. Derrick Agency, Philip Smith of Smith's Advertising Agency, G. Wetton of the *Daily Express*, W.E. Berry of *Advertising World*, and Stephen Britton of Abbey's Effervescent Salt. Their aim was 'the bringing together socially of men engaged in the various branches of the advertising business, and the discussion of topics of practical interest to the fraternity'.[9] Smith's was also among the roster of sixty-two agencies that joined forces to constitute the Association of Advertising Agents on 21 November 1904. Other notable affiliated firms included S.H. Benson, F.E. Coe, W.L. Erwood, London Press Exchange, Mather & Crowther and C. Wilkes. In common with the Sphinx Club, the main objective of the AAA was to provide an arena for debate and exchange of ideas in order to transform advertising into a recognised and respected profession: 'We are putting ourselves in the way of establishing precedents, principles and laws . . . for the encouragement of skilled advertising . . . *i.e.* advertising that calls for the skilled efforts of experts' (*Advertising World* 1904e: 35).

By the early part of the twentieth century, therefore, advertising in Britain was showing signs of becoming a more concentrated and unified industry with identifiable social and economic aims and objectives, and these issues were stamped out in the two chief professional organs of the period, the *Advertising World* and *Advertiser's Weekly*. The latter started life on 19 April 1913 and was published by J.C. Akerman and George Warrington, and the former in December 1901 as 'An illustrated journal which no one interested in advertising – in any shape or form – can afford to be without'. It had offices in London and the United States, where it was represented until 1905 by the pioneering agency Calkins & Holden of Chicago, founded in 1902 and named after its originators, businessman Ralph Holden and design reformer Ernest Elmo Calkins. Calkins became one of the most influential polemicists for modern publicity, arguing in his seminal text, *The Business of Advertising* (1915), that the task of the advertising creative was 'to change advertising from an art to a science – or, at least, to a profession worthy of the ambition and energy of trained minds' (Calkins 1915: 8). Moreover, he saw that advertising could yield the potential to transform social and cultural patterns of existence, arguing that it 'modifies the course of a people's daily thoughts, gives them new words, new phrases, new ideas, new fashions, new prejudices and new customs' (Calkins 1915: 9).

The Role of Press Advertising and Target Audiences for Men's Wear

Much of Calkins' proselytising zeal can also be found in Britain in the editorial of the *Advertising World* and *Advertiser's Weekly* in the way that they attempted to encourage a more systematic (if not scientific) approach to how the profession operated and how it intersected with men's fashion and the media at large. Ambient forms of publicity such as posters and showcards were intermittently included in the regular reviews of contemporary advertisements in the pages of both periodicals, and the production and circulation of company brochures and pamphlets was also addressed. Austin Reed's booklet *Let Me Tell You a 'Shirt Story'* (1904), printed by Spottiswoode to promote their 'Stanaust' brand, for instance, was deemed by the *Advertising World* (1904b: 318) to have been 'the cleverest thing in shirt catalogues we have seen', while an underground poster for their Summit Shirts and Collars, designed and printed by Charles Jones & Co. of Chancery Lane, was praised for its eye-catching qualities (*Advertising World* 1913b). And in its issue of December 1911, a showcard for Viyella shirts and pyjamas, with an illustration by Mr Michael of three men wearing these garments, apparently involved in early morning discussion, came in for a similar encomium. (The image reappeared in an advertisement for Viyella entitled 'A Material Consideration' in the *Echo and Evening Chronicle*, 29 March 1915.) All of these media were overshadowed, however, by their assessment of and polemic for press advertising, which was much more problematic to monitor and regulate in terms of distribution than posters, for instance, since it necessitated a much keener awareness of the costs of production and circulation, as well as how to reach the optimum target audience for any product or service.

The details of certified magazine and newspaper circulations and advertising rates are scarce before 1920, and specific readership profiles in terms of gender, age and class were not analysed until the rise of market research in the 1930s – the Audit Bureau Circulation was incorporated in October 1931, for instance. Nonetheless, several weeklies and dailies did disclose sales (albeit unaudited ones) and advertising rates in their own promotional features. This kind of data, at the very least, would have given advertising agencies some indication of how to choose appropriate media for promoting different manufacturers' goods. For example, in 1910 the advertising rates of *Punch* were £75 per full page against a circulation of 100,000 copies weekly (*Advertising World*, December 1910: 718–19).[10] From 1913 it had also begun to offer the opportunity to advertise in colour at a rate of £120 for the back page and £100 for the inside covers.[11] By the summer of 1914, the *Daily Mirror*'s net sale was over 1 million copies and it also charged £120 for a full-page advertisement,[12] while in 1915 the *Daily Express* cited an average net sale of over 500,000 copies and advertisement rates of 18s 9d per column inch (*Advertiser's Weekly*, 4 September 1915: 156).[13]

Of the popular dailies, the *Daily Mail*, with an average net sale of 768,850 copies in 1913–14 (*Advertiser's Weekly*, 11 April 1914:533), was the only one that occasionally dedicated its entire front page to advertising at a charge of £350, and this was keenly sought after by many men's wear manufacturers (Gardner 1993: 68).[14] For instance, Saxone Shoes used the front page of the *Mail* in April 1907, Wolsey on 24 September 1912, Lockwood and Bradley, London's so-called leading tailors, on 8 April 1913, and Dunn & Co. used it on 24 April 1913 to promote straw hats. Other men's wear retailers who advertised in the *Mail* included Catesby and Sons (a back-page promotion on 6 October 1902 for an overcoat, retailing at 36s 6d, and boots at 15s),[15] and J. & H. Ellis, the Strand tailors, in 1912. Austin Reed, who had started trading in 1900, ran sporadic announcements in the *Mail* during 1907 for their 'Stanaust' shirt and also promoted it on a monthly basis in *Punch* between 1902 and 1909, but by 1910 the company temporarily suspended its use of press campaigns and concentrated instead on circularising the 7,000 customers on its subscription list every few weeks (*Advertising World* 1909b:168). It wasn't until Austin Reed began to open branches outside London that they resumed advertising in the local and national press in weeklies like *Punch*. Thus the Summit shirt collar was promoted in the *Birmingham Daily Mail* on 5 June 1913, shortly after the branch opening at 41 New Street, and also in *Punch* in the same year, while during the First World War, Summit soft collars for army and navy personnel were publicised in *Punch* in 1916.

Beyond this, of course, what has to be taken into account is whether men took any notice of advertisements anyway. It was not for nothing that *Advertising World* could claim in this regard that 'Not one man in 20,000 would carefully study a page of almost microscopic particulars about a hundred or more different articles of men's wear' (June 1911b: 674). Some critics, however, took the opposite view, arguing precisely a didactic role for advertising rather than merely espousing hard-sell tactics with the overt goal to increase sales. Charles Penwarden, for instance, saw that press advertising would be the optimum means for educating men about how to wear specific items of clothing – in this case, hats – to their best effect:

> Advertising would make the fashion by pointing out the advantages of wearing a certain hat at a certain time . . . It is not possible to increase the number of wearers of hats by advertising, but it is possible to enable the buyer to procure a more suitable article. (Penwarden 1908:578)

Penwarden does not mention which newspapers and magazines the advertiser should use and nor does he deal with the thorny issue of class. Nonetheless his comments beg a further important question: to what extent would different types of men have been disposed to spend whatever cash they had on clothes? For, as G. Wetton, the advertising manager of the *Daily Express*, realised, 'the question of circulation is not of such primary importance as whether you reach the class of people who would become purchasers of that which you have to offer' (*Advertiser's Weekly*, 25 April 1914: 50).

In 1910, Marcus Heber Smith wrote in the *Advertising World* that, broadly speaking, the men's tailoring market in Britain was constituted of three classes of clothes wearers – the 'West-Ender', who shopped exclusively in Sackville Street or Savile Row and who would pay upwards of £6 6s for a suit; 'Class B' men on fixed incomes, who were prepared to pay between £2 2s and £4 4s for a suit; and 'Class C', to which belonged men earning £2 a week or less and who bought ready-made clothing (Heber Smith 1910:423).[16] In essence, it was 'Class B' men whom the majority of retailers targeted with their advertising, since the 'West-Ender' and 'Class C' males were already predisposed in terms of income to shop where they saw fit. The archetypal middle-class male to whom retailers like Austin Reed, Pope & Bradley, J. & H. Ellis, and Samuel Brothers made an appeal in their advertising, therefore, were white-collar workers in the City of London and Civil Servants (Figure 5). From the outset, Reed himself realised that this market would have maximum potential and he emphasised especially the impact of young graduates on the men's wear trade: 'Just then we were beginning to experience the first fruits of higher education – a new type of young man was coming into the City – young men of taste and discrimination; men with a new outlook on life, and men to whom ideas appealed strongly' (Ritchie 1990:19).

In particular, it was professional males earning the golden mean of £800 per annum (who, if married, could spend £40 of that sum on clothing) that would have been the ideal target audience for such men's wear retailers (Breward 1999:81).[17] Consequently, these outlets promoted themselves in newspapers and periodicals with a predominantly middle-class readership such as the *Mail*, *The Times* and *Punch* but they never resorted to advertising in the *Daily Mirror* or the *News of the World*, which had sales in excess of 1 million copies per issue but whose readers were mostly from the working classes. Indeed, in an advertisement called 'The Compleat Salesman, Mr. Punch as Outfitter', *Punch* portrayed itself as the magazine which was read by people who 'spend more on clothes than any other section of the community' and the 'one universal medium that gets into the hands of the best people' (*Advertiser's Weekly*, 8 April 1916: 270). A similar class bias could also be expressed in the specialist periodical market. Thus J. & H. Ellis – the men's tailor that provided clothing for King George V in 1912 – had advertised a four guineas dress suit in *Society* in 1895 (*Advertising World* 1912a:37–8).[18] Likewise, *The Man of Today*, a short-lived quarterly review of fashion, sport and drama published in the summer of 1913, charged £20 for full-page advertisements and attracted only quality retailers in the men's wear market.[19] Its editor was H. Dennis Bradley of Pope & Bradley, Bond Street, whose goal was to emulate Savile Row in order 'not to tailor working London but wealthy London', and he used the magazine to feature a full-colour advertisement for his own company's upmarket 'Le Style c'est l'Homme' campaign, which represented a debonair dandy receiving the admiring looks of fashionable ladies as he saunters by them and which is discussed more fully in Chapter 2 (Figure 5).

None of this is to argue, however, that professional males earning less than £800, whether single or married, would not have been drawn to the type of clothing that retailers like Pope & Bradley or Austin Reed were promoting, nor that working-class men were entirely uninterested in matters of dress. In this regard, Christopher Breward's exemplary research into patterns of consumption among urban males has been instrumental in reassessing the plurality of the market for men's dress in Britain before the First World War. His study includes ample evidence that the diaries and recollections of men, who were employed in white-collar professions at this time, reveal considerable variation in the earnings of different types of middle-class workers and how much they would devote to buying clothes (Breward 1999: 84–8). Thus he cites the example of a married middle class male working as a clerk and earning £150 per annum, who could still typically spend £15 on 'clothes, boots, cigars, gloves, papers &c.', while another, earning £80 per annum, could typically devote £12 to 'Her and my clothes' (Breward 1999: 85). The suits provided by Catesby & Sons, retailing in the region of 35 shillings, for instance, would have been within the pocket of these middle-class clients. In effect, however, the differential in income between these middle-class professionals was capsized by a sense of social decorum and the appropriateness and quality of dress. As West End silk hatter Frederick Willis insisted:

> Bank and similar clerks wore silk hats. People were expected to dress in clothes suitable to their calling . . . Stiff white shirts and collars . . . were indispensable . . . He who could not afford the dignity of the white shirt, carefully built up the illusion of one by covering his chest with a dicky and pinning stiff white cuffs to the wrist bands of his plebeian Oxford shirt. (Breward 1999: 87)

Notwithstanding the exigencies of wearing appropriate dress, the price of clothing was clearly paramount for potential customers, and retailers of suits costing less than 35 shillings were seriously admonished not to overlook this in their promotions: 'With the lower priced suits, prices should of course always be given, as price with this class of buyer is of real consideration' (F.N. Dyer 1914: 216).[20] At the same time, however, men's wear retailers of better quality clothing were advised that: 'It would scarcely be unwise to give prices even with comparatively expensive clothing. In fact, many men are satisfied if they pay a long price, and they need this hall mark of quality to give them confidence in goods' (ibid.). Indeed, without exception, the price of the items being promoted by various retailers was cited in the sample of representative press advertisements reviewed in the *Advertising World* and *Advertiser's Weekly* between 1902 and 1913. At the top end of the market, for example, in 1912 J. & H. Ellis publicised a silk-lined dress suit for 84 shillings and an overcoat for 58 shillings respectively, and Pope & Bradley advertised a lounge suit costing £3 13s 6d (*Advertising World* 1912a:38 and 44).[21] At the lower end of the market, blue serge suits costing 30 shillings were advertised by H.L. Thompson Bros. of Oxford Street in 1902 (*Advertising World*, July 1902:104) and Clayton's of Fenchurch Street in 1913 (Herrick 1913:42).[22] In the same year Catesby & Sons promoted their Burlington suit for 35 shillings, and Hope Brothers a spring suit for 45 shillings (ibid.).[23] Furthermore, as an advertisement in the summer of 1904 for a Catesby suit costing 34 shillings reveals (Figure 3), not only had the price of their garments remained almost unchanged for ten years but also they could be purchased on easy terms (*Advertising World* 1904c:91).[24]

Thus, during the early part of the twentieth century, there was considerable diversity in the men's wear market, in which bespoke garments and ready-made items were widely available and competition between different manufacturers could result in similar garments being sold for different prices, and, sometimes, on easy terms through weekly or monthly instalments without the payment of any interest. This situation not only enabled retailers to attract middle-class males of all incomes through their advertisements but also led to considerable class mobility in terms of dress, with many middle-class men not averse to shopping for bargains.

As early as April 1880, for instance, *Tailor and Cutter* had reported on the fluidity of the clothing market: 'it is well known that while many, moving in the higher circles of society, have their coats and vests from West End houses, they patronise without compunction those firms who advertise trousers made to measure for 13s. 6d.' (Breward 1999:28).[25] Regional shopping could clearly be of benefit in this respect and not infrequently, then, some men's wear retailers resorted to local advertising to make an address to the 'right' audience. H.J. Searle & Son of Old Kent Road, for instance, advertised their suits, trousers and shoes, which were available by weekly or monthly instalments to customers in the London area, in the *Morning Leader* on 4 November 1902 (Figure 4). Likewise in June 1913, the Carlton Advertising Service took five columns in the suburban weekly the *Norwood Press* to publicise shoes by Edward Cook (a footwear specialist in Tulse Hill, south-east London), which cost 10s 9d – a full 6 shillings less than the Saxone shoes advertised on the front page of the *Mail* in 1907 (*Advertiser's Weekly* 1913: 44–5).[26]

Indeed, the expansion of the men's wear market and the availability of ready made clothing and purchase on easy terms led also to social mobility of another kind, in which working-class men could be seen to participate in shopping for garments more usually associated with middle-class lifestyles. In 1906, for instance, A. Goodall remarked that, 'For many years the desire to be well, even ostentatiously, dressed has been on the increase. Nor is it only the artisan or mechanic who spend more on clothes than formerly, but the labourer and unskilled workman'. And in particular, he argued that it was the growth of smart, ready-made clothing, such as the 21 shillings suits promoted by Pettigrew & Stephens Ltd of Glasgow (Figure 1), which had made this demotic situation possible (Goodall 1906:314).[27] This perspective was compounded by Alexander Paterson, who in *Across the Bridges* (1911) remarked that, 'It requires but a showy tailor's window, with offers of cheap ready made suits, to tickle a young man's fancy into wild extravagance. A boy earning twelve or fifteen shillings a week is always saving with an eye for a new suit on Sunday' (quoted in Breward 1999:202). While impugning this type of purchase as inappropriate on the grounds of quality and social etiquette (ibid.), comments such as Paterson's demonstrate nonetheless that working-class youth was willing to emulate precedent in middle-class clothing– even if only for Sunday best.

However, the codes of the tailoring advertisements from the early twentieth century rarely, if ever at all, interpellated working-class males as such. In fact, campaigns for retailers at the lower end of the market such as H.J. Searle and H.L. Thompson of London or Pettigrew & Stephens promoted their wares in verbal and visual rhetoric that was similar to those in the middle market. Thus images of straight-backed, be-hatted and besuited men – the proverbial 'tailor's dummy' ridiculed by many advertising critics of the period – combined with phrases expressing good taste abounded, and connoted a sense of middle-class rectitude (Figures 1 and 4). Moreover, as Breward argues, the predilection among working-class youth was to bricolage together alternative styles of clothing, so that various subcultures manifested their identities through distinct codes of dress and patterns of behaviour. Although the few who were more solvent by dint of petty crime, such as the Titanic Mob, resorted to buying their suits from tailor's shops, for the majority of East End gangs the second-hand markets of Brick Lane were a more usual fecund hunting ground for clothing of all kinds (Breward 1999:213–15). Hence, advertising by any company for any garment at all would have made little or no appeal to such subcultural groups at this time, a point that is sustained by the lack of any promotions that break with the conventional codes of besuited gentleman.

Notes

1. See Walsh (2000), pp. 79–95, and Donald (2002), pp. 14–16 and p. 57.
2. See Breward (1999), Chapters 4 and 6, for a discussion of promotional flyers and showcards in the context of shopping and subcultural style respectively.
3. The 2001 equivalents of these prices are £63.01 and £75.02 respectively. These figures and others for 2001 cited in subsequent footnotes are from McCusker (2003).
4. The 2001 equivalent of £2,000 is £121,439.79.
5. Both of the American agencies are discussed by Laird (1998), pp. 156–65 and 168–71. Mather & Crowther's, advertisement is in the *Advertising World* (May 1902: 181); Smith's advertisement in the *Advertising World* (August 1902: 179), claims nearly 25 years' experience of business.
6. See Smith's Advertising Agency, *Successful Advertising: Its Secrets Explained*, published from the 1880s, and Mather & Crowther, *Practical Advertising: A Handy Guide for Practical Men*, published annually or biennially from the 1890s onwards.
7. Presbrey (1929), pp. 525–6, argues a similar agency structure in the United States between 1900 and 1905.
8. The 2001 equivalents are £30,967.96 and £216,775.96 respectively.
9. See the Sphinx Club of London (1904), *Supplement to The Advertising World*, June. The remaining members were J. Morgan Richards; J.E. Garratt; R.E. Bridge (Quaker Oats); R. Balch (Scott & Browne); R.V. Somerville (Butterick Publishing Co.); H.E. Morgan (Spottiswode & Co.); E.D. Gibbs (National Cash Register Co.); H. Pulman (Pulman & Sons).

10. 2001 equivalent is £4,602.18.
11. The 2001 equivalents are £7,164.48 and £5,970.40 respectively.
12. The 2001 equivalent is £6,376.63.
13. The 2001 equivalent is £43.40.
14. The 2001 equivalent is £20,896.40.
15. The 2001 equivalents are £115.50 and £47.47 respectively.
16. Respective 2001 equivalents as follows: £386.58, £128.86, £257.72 and £122.72.
17. The 2001 equivalents are £49,089.95 and £2,454.50 respectively.
18. The 2001 equivalent is £264.37.
19. The 2001 equivalent is £1,194.08.
20. The 2001 equivalent is £92.99.
21. Respective 2001 equivalents are £256.37, £177.01 and £224.32.
22. The 2001 equivalent is £94.93.
23. Respective 2001 equivalents are £104.48 and £134.33.
24. The 2001 equivalent is £105.15.
25. The 2001 equivalent is £35.07.
26. Respective 2001 equivalents are £32.09 and £49.49.
27. The 2001 equivalent is £63.01.

–2–

'The Habit of Reading Advertisements'
The Interdependence of Eye and Mind in Decoding
Men's Wear Publicity before 1914

There is, in fact, no class of consumers which cannot be affected through the medium of some section or other of the Press.

Clarence Moran, *The Business of Advertising*, 1905

A very large number of magazine readers see each advertisement, but only a few of them will stop to read it through. The advertiser must learn to make the best possible use of this casual glance of the multitude.

Walter Dill Scott, *Advertising World*, June 1904

As Scott's comment indicates, to argue whether or not men of different classes had the wherewithal to buy their clothes from tailors and other men's wear retailers as we did in Chapter 1, is not the same thing as saying that they were persuaded to do so initially by advertising, or that they even perused the advertisements that vied for their attention alongside the other reading matter in the daily and periodical press. This chapter concentrates, therefore, on the aesthetic and psychological appeal of men's wear promotions, and how they deployed words and images on either a reason-why or symbolic level. As we shall see, these issues were as keenly analysed as economic and social factors when it came to considering how well any garment had been represented and in determining what made the male consumer tick.

The Psychology of Ads and the Male Reader

Walter Dill Scott, a professor of psychology at Northwestern University, Illinois, was one of the first to apply psychological precepts to advertising. In 1902 he contributed a series of articles to *Mahin's Magazine*, which were also published in Britain in *Advertising World* between January 1904 and January 1905 and formed the basis of his seminal book, *The Psychology of Advertising* (1908). In the 1890s Scott had studied for a doctorate in Leipzig under the psychologist Wilhelm Wundt and, encouraged by him, he became intensely interested in theories of perceptual and mental association, or apperception, and how these could be of relevance to advertising. At the heart of such theories was the fundamental belief – inherited from the empirical philosopher John Locke – that the human mind was susceptible to emotional motivation, that the way in which we experience the everyday world and encounter words and images could conjure up intense feelings – what Wundt called the *associations of ideas*. According to Locke, these were not necessarily logical associations, but based on similarity or aroused by a particular sense of time and place; thus feelings of terror could be dredged up by revisiting a place in which unhappy events occurred (Mazur Thomson 1996:258). Scott likewise argued that apperception implied 'the comparison, recognition and other processes which are dependent upon former experience and which are not caused directly by the sensations received from the sense organs' (Scott 1904c: 246), and he advised advertisers to 'awaken in the reader as many different kinds of images as the object itself can excite'.

Between 1900 and 1920 the role of this kind of psychological theory in advertising was particularly debated in the United States and several different approaches were propounded by various authors including Harry Hollingworth, a lecturer in business psychology at New York University and Henry Forster Adams, a professor of psychology at the University of Michigan (Mazur Thomson 1996). In line with Scott, Adams emphasised in his work *Advertising and its Mental Laws* (1916) that 'all knowledge is received through the senses . . . in other words, the mind develops in terms of the environment' (Adams 1916: 21 and 23). This was paramount to advertising since, he argued:

> A knowledge of these laws, if applied intelligently, ought to enable the advertiser to construct his copy and plan his campaign so that it will secure better attention, be remembered longer, and induce action in a greater per centage of persons, who will, on the average, act more promptly and energetically than they would in response to less scientific copy. (Adams 1916: 17)

It is interesting to note that Adams invoked a sense of the scientific in speaking about the relationship of psychology to advertising, since its critics thought it was anything but, regarding it more as a pseudo-science. Writing in *Layout in Advertising* (1928), for example, advertising designer W.A. Dwiggins expressed his doubts about the universal application of psychological laws of apperception and whether the disposition of certain shapes and forms led to pleasurable feelings or otherwise, insisting that each assignment necessitated its own unique design solutions (Mazur Thomson 1996: 270). However, Scott's own research was scientifically grounded and not without some relevance concerning the male consumer and how the men's wear advertiser could appeal to him.

In 'The Habit of Reading Advertisements', the sixth of his eight articles that appeared in *Advertising World* in 1904, Scott asserted, 'Thousands of magazine readers read advertisements more than they are aware' (Scott 1904f:17). To test out this hypothesis, he observed the reading habits of 600 men who attended the reading room of the Chicago Public Library and noted that: 'Some of the men who read there have but a few minutes to stay, while others are there to spend the day. As I looked over the room to see how many were reading advertisements it seemed to me that a very large part of them were thus engaged.' After visiting the library six times in all, however, 'going on different days of the week, different seasons of the year, and different hours of the day' and collecting data on each occasion, he extrapolated that 'of the six hundred magazine readers, I found sixty-five reading advertisements and four hundred and thirty five reading from the body of the magazine; that is to say, 10.5 per cent of all the men observed were reading advertisements' (Scott 1904f: 18). Moreover, Scott also conceded the point that this did not mean the 10+ per cent of the men whom he recorded as looking at the advertisements necessarily engaged with the content of the ads and 'were reading in a hasty and indifferent manner' (ibid.: 19). Thus he was forced to conclude that: 'It would not be fair to assume from the data at hand that the average magazine reader spends ten times as much on the advertisements, but it is quite certain that he spends a comparatively short time on the advertisements' (ibid.: 19).

And yet, for Scott, this did not make his study a failure and nor was he arguing for a diminution in the quantity of press advertisements. Rather he was at pains to point out that any publicity – even if glanced at cursorily – could have an insidious subconscious effect on people, and advertisers should not lose sight of the fact that, although few people would ever admit they had been influenced by advertising the opposite was the case when it came to making a purchase. In other words, they had simply forgotten they had originally encountered the product through publicity. To illustrate this idea, he included quite a lengthy description of how he himself had been subject to such a subconscious drive in buying a suit, which is worth including here in full since it crystallises how familiarity with and repeated exposure to advertising can foment a form of selective amnesia for any product:

> For years I have seen the advertisements of a certain tailor. Recently I entered his shop and ordered a suit of clothes. It so happened that the proprietor, who was conducting a vigorous advertising campaign, waited on me himself. As he took my order he asked me whether he had been recommended to me. I promptly replied that he had. I then began to try and recall who had recommended him, but found that I could not recall any such recommendation. I had seen his advertisement so often that I had forgotten the particular advertisements, but had retained the information which they had imparted. (ibid.: 21)

By extension, that we do or do not remember specific advertisements was for Scott related to issues concerning the creative quality of their design and copywriting. Accordingly, he thought the behaviour that he observed concerning the reading patterns of the men in his experiment should be taken by advertisers as a sobering admonition as to how they could improve the appearance of their advertising to attract wider readerships and markets. In this regard he was keen to point out the respective functions of text and image in making an impact on the subconscious mind, arguing that neither should be deployed meretriciously: 'The display type and the picture which merely attract and do not instruct are in many cases worth-less, for in attracting attention to themselves they divert the attention from the thing advertised' (ibid.: 20).

Text and Image – the Design Debate on Men's Wear Advertising

Certainly, the way that advertising could work on the minds of readers was also realised in Britain during the early twentieth century. One year before Scott's articles appeared in *Advertising World*, F.W. Pettit (1903) had explored with its readers the power of psychological persuasion in advertising, while a few years later H. Leslie Underwood, writing about the male consumer and the promotion of neckties in this vein, proceeded to comment that, 'The advertiser's mission is not to reform human nature but to adapt himself to its weaknesses and frailties' (Underwood 1906:504). But so too was the need for well-designed advertising realised, in which the balance and harmony between word and image was properly thought out, and this point was reiterated frequently in the weekly and monthly reviews of men's wear advertisements that appeared in the trade press. Reviewing a press campaign for Samuel Brothers promoting woollen overcoats, for example, *Advertising World* (1906c:542) admired its attractive Art Nouveau-inspired organic motif and found the letterpress 'distinctly good', but it took issue with the inclusion of a small-scale, lifeless drawing of a man dressed in an overcoat and top hat in the top-right corner of the advertisement, which was deemed to detract from the overall effect.

While the lobby for type reform and relative values of using serif and sans serif typefaces did not begin to gain momentum until the 1920s and will, therefore, be assessed more fully in the following chapters, many advertisements for men's wear before the First World War could still demonstrate a clear understanding of how to use different type forms expressively. A promotion for H.J. Searle that appeared in the London daily the *Morning Leader* (4 November 1902:6) is a good example of the way that free style, serif and sans serif typeforms could be combined in order to give a sense of different verbal emphasis to distinct pieces of text (Figure 4). Thus the main body of copy that deals with cut, fit and style of clothing and payment details is set in Della Robbia, a classically understated serif type designed by Thomas Maitland Cleland for Lanston Monotype in 1902; the slogan 'Pay Weekly Or Monthly!' and the firm's name are set in sans serif Standard capitals (underlined and in bold type respectively), originated by the Berthold typefoundry in 1896; the eye-catching words 'Dress Smartly' and 'Overcoats' are similar in style to the organic blackletter or calligraphic faces Boutique, devised by Haas *c*. 1900, and Peter Behrens' Roman, designed in 1900; finally, 'Easy Terms' has been set in an elegant uppercase Morland type, which was originated in 1900.[1] In its entirety, the advertisement appears to deploy the different types in such a way that one's attention is drawn immediately to the most important points, yet it also manages to harness them into a holistic and harmonious designed entity. As is the case with the promotion for Samuel Brothers, however, the sketchy drawing of the male figure is the weakest component of the advertisement. Indeed, standing with cane in hand, stiffly wearing his overcoat and top hat, he bears a marked resemblance to the kind of stock figures or generic 'cuts' that cropped up repeatedly in campaigns for many different men's wear retailers during the first quarter of the twentieth century.[2]

This hackneyed stylistic tendency did not go unheeded by advertising critics. Writing in *Advertiser's Weekly* John Herrick commented that the use of a 'fashion plate of a man' along with some trite copy remarking on the idea that 'clothes make the man' had become formulaic (Herrick 1913:41), while A.H. Williams advised advertisers that:

> the illustrations, which purport to represent the clothes advertised as they would look when worn, must wear just such an appearance as the possible purchaser would wish to show to the world. No one wants to look like a tailor's dummy . . . The few tailoring houses that have been advertising at once most consistently and intelligently are those which have achieved the most outstanding successes of recent times. (A.H. Williams 1912:674)

There were, in fact, several firms who met these criteria in their men's wear promotions and they were singled out as exemplars of good practice for doing so. Thus in 1912 Horne Brothers were congratulated by *Advertising World* for the full-page advertising campaign they had initially launched in the *Daily Mail* in1908 to promote the Cotuna Coat Shirt (from 1910, the brand name became Cutuna), an informal garment to wear while relaxing indoors. The anonymous author thought that the Art Nouveau-inspired publicity was 'characterised by a high level of craftsmanship. It has been uniformly good looking and entirely business-like' (*Advertising World* 1912b:722). In 1911 Graves of Sheffield advertised their 35 shilling 'Ludgate' suit with resort to a drawing of a seated man wearing the garment, smoking in a relaxed manner about which the *Advertising World* (1911c:

704) remarked, 'in treatment [it] could hardly have been bettered for its purpose'. A similar pose was struck in an earlier half-page press promotion for Samuel Brothers, in which we observe a seated man wearing a lounge suit and reading a newspaper, but on this occasion the illustration was a photograph, not a pen and ink drawing. *Advertising World* (1906b:668) regarded this advertisement as ground-breaking in its naturalistic effect, stating that: 'The use of the photograph is something unusual in this kind of advertising it marks a welcome development in tailoring advertisements. No one, we think, will doubt that it is immeasurably superior to the general run of clothing advertising, and for that reason we are glad to see it'.

The use of photographs in newspapers and periodicals had become possible with the evolution in the 1880s of the half-tone process, which involved breaking the image into a matrix of dots by photographing the subject through a screen of intersecting diagonal lines. It was not until 1900, however, after photogravure workshops began to proliferate that half-tones also started to supplant more traditional forms of line reproduction in news reports and magazine features (Jobling and Crowley 1996: 28). Judging from company publicity in the *Advertising World*, a handful of specialist printers and photographers also existed to prepare half-tone images for advertisers before the First World War, including Parkinson and Roy in Leeds (*Advertising World*, July 1902:123), the Press Etching Company and Elliott and Fry in London (ibid., April 1905: 374 and 381) and the Arthur Cox Illustrating Co. Ltd (ibid., February 1911:217). But the advertising agencies appear to have been resistant to the use of half-tone reproduction, and in fashion advertising particularly photographs did not start to make a substantial impact until the 1930s, with hand-drawn illustrations still common between 1950 and 1970 in promotions for retailers such as Austin Reed.

There are a number of technical and aesthetic reasons as to why this should have been the case and these are addressed more fully in the context of promotions for tailoring in Chapter 5. It suffices to say that at this stage in the development of fashion advertising illustrations remained the preferred medium because not only could they be reproduced more easily (especially when it came to colour) but also, given that the visual quality of half-tones on newsprint could be somewhat soft-edged, as Figure 2 demonstrates, they were crisper and cleaner in recording the details of garments. Moreover, as Walter Kudwell lamented, on the infrequent occasions that certain (unspecified) advertisers resorted to using photographs they did so in too literal a manner and the end result was indifferent and lacking in atmosphere: 'Here and there an advertiser uses a photograph – sometimes, alas! his own – to illustrate an advertisement, but they are very poor things as a rule and his imagination rarely soars beyond employing photographs of the actual goods he wishes to sell' (Kudwell 1906:684).

From Reason Why to Atmospheric Advertising

The issue of facticity, however, was not merely the concern of photographic advertising but was evident in those including hand-drawn illustrations as well. For the majority of men's wear promotions what seemed to matter most was to make a direct address to the purchaser through the inclusion of specific details relating any or all of the following points: the price of the article and where and how to buy it, cut and fit, the materials used in its construction, and ideas concerning its overall look and quality. Dyer's advice to prospective advertisers of tailoring, for example, was to keep things 'simple and direct' and to avoid excessive ornamentation:

> It is better to confine the copy to one particular point in each advertisement . . . For example, one day style might be discussed, another day cutting, and again quality, or the special features of some particular cloth and so on – Let each little essay conclude with some definite particulars about a special kind of suit – with the price . . . a fair margin of white space around the type matter looks well and gives an appearance of taste. A border can be used with beneficial effect. (F.W. Dyer 1914:217)

This type of promotion is what was called 'reason-why' advertising, since it emphasised the logical reasons – or actual benefits – to be had from purchasing the garment in question (*Advertising World* 1907a:631).

The roundup of advertisements in John Herrick's (1913) review of men's wear publicity in *Advertiser's Weekly* were all examined from this perspective, with some being better received than others. Thus he dissected two advertisements associated with Pope & Bradley, which had appeared in the *Observer* on 13 April 1913, according to their respective merits: 'Both advertisements were very creditable efforts, each being superior to the other in certain respects'. The one that announced the imminent opening on 14 April of the Pope salon in Kingsway, named after a former co-owner of the company, for instance, included an illustration by William Houghton that was 'a model of an excellent fashion drawing', but was let down by not including a price list of the salon's charges. By contrast the other, which also included illustrations by Houghton, advertised Pope & Bradley's stores in Old Bond Street and Southampton Row and was commended for giving full details of prices but criticised for its copy, which contained too much 'padding' (Herrick 1913:41). A press campaign for the shirt maker Douglas Gordon, meanwhile, was cited as the avatar of excellence in men's wear advertising since it not only 'gives practically all the information required by the prospective buyer, and the copy is particularly well written', but it also 'succeeds in conveying the restrained personality that characterises the good-class tailor' (ibid.: 44).

Reason-why advertising, therefore, was not simply, if ever, a question of hard sell, and, as Herrick's comments indicate, any exhortation to buy should be plied with tasteful restraint. It was, however, related to – yet at the same time distinct from – atmospheric advertising, which tended to be more 'soft sell' and symbolic, a kind of 'restrained message in which the product's consumer was as important as images of the products themselves' (Turbin 2002:474). Herrick himself seemed to be indifferent to this form of advertising, taking to task the 'Don' Tailors of Holborn Viaduct for relying on sporting tropes to promote their leisurewear. Criticising an illustration of a young man swinging a golf club, for instance, he once more adopted a literal point of view, overlooking to assess whether the symbolic association would be a relevant or cogent one for the prospective consumer in terms of its class and age connotations: 'It is a standing wonder to me why, when an advertiser takes the trouble to have a drawing made showing a man in some athletic pursuit, he does not take the trouble to have it drawn correctly' (Herrick 1913:42). Moreover, two of the retailers whose work he liked, the lower-to-middle market tailors Catesby & Sons and the upmarket tailors Pope & Bradley, relied as much on atmospheric messages as they did on reason why advertising.

Indeed, the anonymous reviewer of an atmospheric press advertisement for Catesby's in 1904 (Figure 3) described it as 'one of the best the Tottenham Court Road people have ever put out' (*Advertising World* July 1904d). This promotion was orchestrated by the company's advertising manager J.P. Hunt (who had been in charge of their publicity since 1901) and it contains all the factual signifiers that were expected of a reason-why advertisement, such as the dimension and price of the Gladstone bag, the cost of the man's boots and summer suit, the choice of materials for the latter, and how and where to buy them. Simultaneously, however, the atmospheric illustration by Remy signifies more 'The road to summer pleasure' enunciated by the first line of copy. Here a dandy, wearing a Catesby summer suit and hat and smoking a cigar, jauntily rests his elbow on the top of a framed panoramic view of Scarborough bay, which takes on the aspect of a picture postcard. What is connoted by the image, then, is the register of pleasure on two fronts; the first actualised through the buying and wearing of the stylish garment itself (literally, 'the road to summer pleasure' that leads to Catesby's), and the second, a yet to be realised 'road to summer pleasure', symbolised by the man's contiguity to Scarborough rather than his actual presence in the scene depicted.

At the top end of the market, likewise, promotions for Pope & Bradley had symbolised men's wear in the context of pleasure. This business started on a small scale, catering for an exclusive clientele, or as Maxwell Tregurtha put it, 'wealthy London – the London which considered dress an important item in its career' (*Advertising World* 1912a:43). By royal warrant they were also tailors to King Alfonso XIII of Spain but, as we have seen, following the rise of Class B white-collar workers in the City and Civil Service, their advertisements also promoted suits and other apparel in the region of three and four guineas, which these professional males could also afford.[3] By 1910, they were promoting themselves through various media – posters and the press, principally papers like *The Times*, *Daily Mail* and *Evening Standard*, and a lavishly illustrated mail order brochure issued in spring and autumn entitled 'Clothes – and the Man'. In 1911 the company embarked on a full-colour poster campaign on the London underground called 'Le Style c'est l'Homme' ('Style is the Man') that was to seal its reputation both for quality advertising and clothing. The first poster was in sixteen-sheet format (120 × 80 ins) and advertised morning suits from four guineas.[4] This was followed in 1912 by an eight-sheet poster (60 × 40 ins) promoting the Newbury slip coat, retailing at between three and five guineas (Figure 5). The latter, illustrated by William Houghton, and designed and printed by the Berkeley Press of Holborn, won first prize in the commercial class poster category at the 1912 Advertising Exhibition, held at Wembley, London, which was awarded on the basis of 'Selling Power, Artistic Effect, and Excellence in Printing' (*Advertising World* 1913a:43–4).[5]

In each instance, the 'selling power' and 'artistic effect' of the poster campaign for Pope & Bradley was organised around a central image of a stylish young dandy sauntering past a group of admiring female spectators. The very antithesis of the 'tailor's dummy' or 'waxen puppet' of so much men's wear advertising, Tregurtha called him a '"live man" – *debonnair*, complacent, nonchalant, whose clothes hung as we have always believed they really will hang if correctly cut and shaped' (*Advertising World* 1912a:46). In his self-contained air of confidence and the way that he turns heads as he ambles casually along, then, the male figure in the advertisements seems to fulfil a sense of sartorial good taste that trades on one of the maxims of Henry Pelham, the eponymous dandy hero of Sir Edward Bulwer Lytton's 1828 cult novel: 'Always remember that you dress to fascinate others, not yourself' (Bulwer Lytton 1849:94).[6] In common with the urban culture of dandyism, the type of clothing he and the women in the poster are wearing also implies that this is fashion for display on the street. Yet any actual environmental context has been suppressed since they are represented against a flat grey-coloured background, and this artistic effect serves rather to symbolise a heightened sense of fantasmic or utopian desire in which the male body takes both centre stage and pleasure in being admired.

Moreover, in the way that the women look at him but he stares straight ahead out of the scene knowingly at the spectator of the poster, the image invokes the ambivalent erotic charge and vanity of the dandy as someone who could be represented not only for the admiring look of both the women in the poster and the women who saw it on the hoardings, but also for the male spectators of it. Pelham, for example, has his breath taken away by the sight of the buck Reginald Glanville when he visits him at home:

> When his blue eye lighted up, in answer to the merriment of his lips, and his noble and
> glorious cast of countenance shone out, as if it had never been clouded by grief or

passion, I thought, as I looked at him, that I had never seen so perfect a specimen of masculine beauty, at once physical and intellectual. (ibid.: 96)

The tropes of spectatorial pleasure that are connoted by the 'Le Style c'est l'Homme' campaign and its double address to men and women alike trouble, therefore, any formulaic psychoanalytical attempt to reduce the gaze to something that the active male 'does' to the passive female in order to resolve his castration anxiety and attain phallic mastery by keeping himself out of representation.[7] As such, it set the tone for a new form of men's wear advertising and display of the male body that adumbrates the scenes of men and women socialising in advertisements for Austin Reed and The Fifty Shilling Tailors during the 1930s, or the more sexualised catwalk swagger and dynamic of the gaze evident in contemporary campaigns for the likes of Versace, Dolce & Gabbana and Yves Saint Laurent. At the same time, the way it connotes a modern 'man about town' wearing clothes in a life-like manner, its use of vibrant colour, and uncluttered treatment of form and space, also prefigure the style and content of much men's wear advertising in interwar Britain by the likes of these retailers and others such as Simpson of Piccadilly, which are the subject of analysis in Chapter 5.

Notes

1. I have relied on the following sourcebook to identify the typeforms mentioned in this chapter: W. Pincus Jaspert, W. Turner Berry and A.F. Johnson (2001), *Encyclopaedia of Typefaces*, London: Cassell.
2. *Printers' Ink* (28 July 1938), pp. 83–4, wrote of the practice for buying in cheap stock drawings or 'cuts' in newspaper advertisements, which started in the 1890s, commenting on the 'widely held belief that "any cut was better than no cut at all"'.
3. Respective 2001 equivalents are £192.27 and £256.37.
4. The 2001 equivalent is £196.
5. The 1912 Advertising Exhibition was one of three important large-scale exhibitions before the outbreak of the First World War that focused on the state of play in poster and press advertisements. In April 1914, the First International Advertising Exhibition was held at Holland Park Hall, London with representation from Great Britain, United States, Germany, Italy, Scandinavia, China, Russia and France, and in May 1914 the Toronto Convention was held at which British advertising, including campaigns by the Paul E. Derrick agency for

Dexter Weatherproofs, was on display. See *Advertising World* (1914a), special issue devoted to Holland Park, and *Advertising World* (1914c) for Toronto.

6. Bulwer Lytton's novel, *Pelham, or, Adventures of a Gentleman* was originally published in1828, and a second edition appeared in 1849. This idea of dispassionate display was at the core of the dandy's identity and is also manifest in Beau Brummell's maxim, 'In society, stop until you have made your impression, then go' (cited in J. Barbey D'Aurevilly 1988 [1897], p. 49).

7. See Lacan (1977: 288) on the idea of feminising the phallus through the display of the male body. Thus he writes, 'That is why the demon of . . . shame arises at the very moment when, in the ancient mysteries, the phallus is unveiled'. Laura Mulvey's (1989) essay 'Visual Pleasure and Narrative Cinema' has become the *locus classicus* of this kind of psychoanalytic interpretation of gaze theory for analysing classic Hollywood film. Mulvey argues, 'In a world ordered by sexual imbalance, pleasure in looking has been split between active/male and passive/female. The determining male gaze projects its fantasy onto the female figure which is stylised accordingly' (Mulvey 1989: 19). In analysing the Pope & Bradley poster I am deliberately using the idea of the look, expressed by Lacan in the *Four Fundamental Concepts* (1978) as something that remains within the realm of desire, rather than the gaze (which is outside of it and implies domination) since the male flâneur in the advertisement in no way seems subjugated by the admiring glances that the surrounding females direct his way.

–3–

From A to E

Men's Wear Advertising and Market Research between 1914 and 1939

Ask me to review the last decade and I could fill a book with a story of how a small and distrusted and inexpert industry called advertising rose to the power and position and proud promise it holds today.

William Crawford, Modern Publicity, 1930

As we have seen, the formative period before the First World War was instrumental in raising many of the crucial issues relating to the production and consumption of men's wear publicity such as the buying of advertising space in the daily and periodical press, the need to address consumer behaviour, and how best to target different sections of the market in terms of class and income. Along with the rise of quantitative and qualitative surveys, all of these socio-economic factors were to be consolidated with vigour between 1919 and 1939, which period was one of the highpoints in men's wear publicity and forms the central focus of this chapter. It would be erroneous, however, to believe that the outbreak of war in 1914 put an end to such considerations tout court. Before moving on to assess how the promotion of clothing was debated in the interwar years, then, it is instructive to evaluate the way that men's wear advertisers sought to maintain both sales and their reputations at a time of national crisis and acute shortages in raw materials.

Advertising and Men's Wear During the First World War

In its front-page editorial on 6 November 1914, the *Advertiser's Weekly* actively set out to encourage manufacturers that publicity should not be discontinued in unusual and adverse circumstances, but rather exploited as a way of keeping business ticking over: 'Advertising stands to trade in such a relationship that it is not an expense to be dropped with the coming of war and taken up again in the piping times of peace. Advertising is the one cheap method of making sales, and if you are in a position to sell you must advertise to get your fair share of the trade.' Indeed, this point of view was amplified by various retailers and advertising agents themselves, including Richard Burbidge, the managing director of Harrods, who put it this way: 'If I were asked, then, whether business in war time offered less reason for advertising, I should reply that, on the contrary, it offered more' (*Advertiser's Weekly*, 11 September 1914: 184).

Of course, this is not to suggest that things simply remained as they were before 1914 either. Both the press and advertisers were seriously hampered by the material conditions of warfare, notably restrictions on the use of paper and display of posters, which took effect from 10 March 1917. Thus Board of Trade Order (no. 203) initially prohibited the production and circulation of any poster larger than 600 square inches, and restricted their display to the windows of newspaper offices and retailers. Shortly afterwards, however, the Royal Commission on Paper relaxed the restrictions on the use of paper with paragraph six of its Paper Restriction Order of 1917, stating that the size of posters could be larger, provided that advertisers kept to one-third of the paper capacity they had been using during the period 1 August 1916 and 31 January 1917. Neither Order had placed any restrictions on press advertising, which before and after the war accounted for the lion's share of expenditure on publicity.[1] But, given that the daily newspapers had already been reduced to fewer – and smaller – pages, the press was already hard pushed to meet the existing demand from advertisers, let alone pick up any supplementary advertising from new customers or those disillusioned by the restrictions on posters. To this end, an advertisement for the *Daily Express* in *Advertiser's Weekly* (14 April 1917:13) pronounced: 'We cannot accommodate all advertisers at present, owing to paper restrictions; we will, however, endeavour to insert advertisements in rotation as they are received'. In fact, according to figures in *Advertising World* (December 1915), display advertising in most London penny dailies had dropped by 28 per cent between August 1914 and November 1915. Some other advertising companies, meanwhile, devised more imaginative solutions to overcome the shortage of paper; Sydney Presbury & Co. of Brixton, for example, promoted the manufacture of lantern slide advertisements for use in music halls and cinemas, advising retailers that for an average outlay of £25, about 1 million people would see their advertisements (*Advertiser's Weekly*, 19 May 1917:95).[2]

With regard to men's wear, raw materials such as wool, cotton and leather were also requisitioned for the war effort, and the manpower in textile and clothing factories diminished by those who volunteered for active service, so that civilian garments often increased in cost. Nonetheless in the early days of the war, hosiery manufacturers were still able to meet the needs of the army and navy while supplying the demands of home and export markets (Firm 1917).[3] Yet the shortage of high-grade materials, particularly all wool cloths, made life difficult for most tailors save those who may have stockpiled before the outbreak of war (A. Knight 1917), and drove retail prices upwards. A front-page report in the *Daily Telegraph* on 12 September 1917 cited a rise of nearly 100 per cent in the cost per yard of silk linings from 4s 6d to 8s 6d and an almost concomitant rise in the cost of reliable tweeds, which 'for morning and afternoon wear are not now to be obtained under 19s. a yard'.[4] The article concluded:

> There was, in fact . . . a better profit to be made on the tweed suit at 6 guineas . . . of three years ago than there is today on the corresponding suit at 8 guineas, which is the very lowest price at which it can be turned out. Even in the far less exclusive shops the rise is not less marked, and the erstwhile suit of 55s. will now be 90s., and probably a poorer material at that.[5]

This meant that advertisers had to encourage the public to buy garments, which not only cost more than they expected but also were made from inferior materials than they were used to. As one critic commented in *Advertiser's Weekly*, 'The effect of the war and the increased prices will be to encourage the public to exercise more care in buying' (F.W. Dyer 1915: 280). Yet the high price of clothing during the First World War meant the working classes were excluded from making the most rudimentary purchases and this was the cause of considerable civil unrest. Accordingly, in the winter of 1918 the government introduced the 'Standard Goods Scheme' to address shortages in clothing, although this was restricted mostly to hosiery and underwear and a quantity of suits for demobilised servicemen. In fact, it wasn't until the war was over that companies like Pontings of Kensington found they could pass on to the public high quality army and navy surplus underwear and trench coats at 50 per cent discount. In an advertisement in the *Daily Mail* on 13 April 1925, for instance, lightweight woollen officers' vests were offered at 5s 6d rather than 10s 9d, and triple-proof trench coats for 30 shillings.[6]

While the dearth of advertising space and demand on clothing materials made the First World War a lean period in promotions for civilian clothing, at the same time these conditions seem to have concentrated the minds of advertising artists and copywriters both to be more concise when it came to 'reasons why' and to conceive their men's wear campaigns as part of a wider, 'atmospheric' propaganda machine. This led manufacturers to promote clothing with resort to patriotic verbal and visual rhetoric, and the use of various garments by the armed forces was taken as a recommendation for men who stayed on to work at home. Hence, Austin Reed began to advertise their Summit collars with this kind of double address and campaigns like 'With the Fleet' and 'On Active Service' in *Punch* in 1916 foregrounded the same qualities for servicemen and civilians alike: 'Active men who knew the comfort and "dressiness" of Summit Soft Collars in more peaceful times are writing home for Summits for field wear. They wear a special Khaki Summit, but the famous White Summit Soft Collars are still most favoured by the active man who must stay at home' (*Punch*, 26 July 1916). The 'Two Worlds' press advertisements for trench coats stocked by Thresher & Glenny of the Strand and originated by Carlton Studios made a similar kind of appeal throughout 1916 and

1917, stating that the garment was practical wear for men in cold, wet weather, wherever they were and whatever they were doing.

By contrast, Rameses underwear adopted a more adversarial tone in one of their campaigns for long johns, which was designed by Lawson Wood in 1915. This consisted of an illustration of a boxing match, in which a British man wearing the Rameses brand has just floored a corpulent German with ill-fitting underwear and a Kaiser moustache, and the caption (lest anyone failed to get the chauvinistic connotation of the somewhat hackneyed picture), 'Another Knock-out for Germany'. In fact, this type of war propaganda was deemed to be superior to government-sponsored and official advertising by Pope & Bradley, which produced a series of 'spoof' advertisements called 'Progress and Advertising: A Critical Survey' that appeared in *Land and Water* and *Town Topics* in 1916. In these wordy promotions, which looked more like newspaper articles, Dennis Bradley deconstructed the normative format of advertising itself while taking the opportunity to praise his own men's wear promotions and to criticise the unadventurous typographical army recruitment posters, often produced by jobbing printers on behalf of the government, which looked more like straightforward announcements than pieces of poster design (Warrington 1916).

According to Sidney Garland (1919), the former advertising manager of Selfridge & Co., probably the most salutary lesson to be learnt by men's wear manufacturers and advertisers in the period immediately after the First World War was the need to deal with quality and individuality. As he appositely argued shortly after the cessation of hostilities, not only had the high standard and comfort of garments made for servicemen, such as underwear and trench coats, made men more demanding of good quality civilian clothing but so also were they more aware of style and more willing to pay for it: 'Generally speaking the average man to-day is paying much more attention to the question of clothing . . . our returning warriors . . . have a greater appreciation of the many things which make for comfort; and evidence shows that the "new man" is a keener buyer than he was before the war' (S.T. Garland 1919:5). To this end, Garland singled out Austin Reed as the exemplar of how to build up a good reputation and appreciative clientele for modern men's wear through advertising, arguing that *'the supplying of merchandising which proves the wisdom of their propaganda*, gain for them a foremost place in the minds of thoughtful and discriminating men' (ibid.: 6, original emphasis).

Garland does not refer to any specific advertisements by Austin Reed in this context, but the so-called 'wisdom of their propaganda' will be addressed in the discussion about markets and media in this chapter. At the same time, as we shall see in Chapter 5, the company was but one of a new generation of tailors who demonstrated a clear commitment to quality merchandise and to quality advertising as well. Furthermore, such activity was the outcome of an intense professionalisation of both the men's wear and advertising industries during the interwar period that coalesced with the rise of market research by the press and advertising agencies, and a burgeoning arena for debate in book and periodical publishing concerning the social and cultural impact of advertising.

The Role of the Media in Promoting Men's Wear after 1919

One of the first post-war initiatives to regenerate public and professional interest in all forms of advertising came with the International Advertising Exhibition that was held at White City between 29 November and 4 December 1920. Although it was billed as an international forum, in effect the list of 220 exhibitors reveals that the event was more a showcase of national talent. The Department of Overseas Trade and the International Trade Intelligence both had stands, but apart from a handful of overseas representatives, namely the French printing house Deberny and Peignot, the German electrical company Siemens, the *Irish Times*, *Baltic Review* and *Swiss Exporter*, every other space was occupied by British companies and organisations (*Advertiser's Weekly*, 26 November 1920:269). Thus it featured representation from every national daily, trade literature such as *Advertising World*, *Advertiser's Weekly* and *Draper's Record*, and popular periodicals like *Illustrated London News*, *The Sketch* and *Punch*. At the same time a multitude of printers and publishers had stands, including the Curwen Press, the Hulton Group and Odhams, as did advertising agencies, including Carlton Studios, W.S. Crawford, Highams, Dorland and London Press Exchange, and posters from the London Underground were also on special display.[7] While it was open to the public for only one week, White City drew massive crowds – fifty thousand people attended the first day of the exhibition alone (*Advertiser's Weekly*, 30 November 1920: 324) – and the event heralded the start of one of the most productive and creative periods in the history of British advertising.

The intensification of interest in advertising was also manifest in other exhibitions and conventions throughout the 1920s and 1930s, principally the International Advertising Convention at the British Empire Exhibition at Wembley in 1924 at which Charles Higham delivered a speech on the future of advertising, the Advertising and Marketing Exhibition at Olympia, Earl's Court in 1933, and a series of British Advertising Conventions, the first of which was held in Harrogate in July 1925.[8] But it can also be witnessed in the founding of the Advertising Association on 28 January 1926 as well as the unprecedented number of books and periodicals that were published dealing with various aspects of publicity and the professionalisation of the industry. Between 1900 and 1924, thirty-seven titles had been published, such as E.A. Spiers' *The Art of Publicity* (1910), Cyril Sheldon's *Billposting* (1916), Charles Higham's *Scientific Distribution* (1916) and *Advertising*

– *Looking Forward* (1920); seventeen of these titles, however, had appeared in the five years from 1919 to 1924 (Morison 1924). In 1927 alone, thirty-nine new books were published in which 'every subject of research, marketing and publicity of all kinds are written upon with a lucidity which cannot help but be for the betterment of advertising as a whole' (Morison 1928:92). These titles included seminal works such as Cyril Sheldon's *Poster Advertising* (1927), Geoffrey Holme's *Posters and Publicity* (1926), and Maxwell Tregurtha's *Types and Type-faces* (1927).

In addition to these works, we have to take into account the growth of trade literature, which also became a fertile ground for current debates concerning all aspects of advertising. Alongside *Advertising World* (which folded in 1940) and *Advertiser's Weekly*, therefore, periodicals such as *Commercial Art* (1922–31), *Advertising Display* (1926–35), *Advertising Monthly* (1937–40), *Art and Industry* (1936–58) and the *Penrose Annual* (f. 1895) dealt with poster and press publicity on a regular basis. While none of these periodicals restricted its assessment of advertising to men's wear promotions, none the less they did deal with it from time to time, and in conjunction with the intermittent editorials in the international trade monthly *MAN and his Clothes*, they provide us with an interesting insight into contemporaneous perspectives about the scope and nature of modern fashion promotion.

MAN and his Clothes was published between September 1926 and May 1959 in London and Paris. Affiliated to the textile and clothing monthly Fairchild's International Magazine until February 1932, and thereafter published by Textiles Journals Ltd, it offered all manner of advice to British retailers and concerned itself with addressing, and even identifying, the fashionable male, at home and overseas. It accrued a respectable average circulation of 10,000 copies during the 1930s among retailers, but judging from the correspondence it sometimes published, its readership was by no means restricted exclusively to those in the rag trade, and its editorial remit to provide 'an open forum for discussion on the subject of clothes' has to be interpreted in broad terms. An article that appeared in its issue of February 1928 entitled 'Making a Collar Known among Men' is paradigmatic of the kind of double address or appeal that the magazine sought to make to retailers and consumers alike. For on one level, the piece is of interest to both the shop-owner and potential customer in the way that it describes how Rowans Ltd promoted a particular brand – the Arkit shirt collar – in its Birmingham store. But on another level, it pinpoints how *MAN and his Clothes* envisaged a complementary relationship between merchandising and advertising; the collar had been publicised in several teaser campaigns in Birmingham newspapers in the winter of 1927, prior to its window and shop-floor display in Rowans.

The intertextual nexus between visual and verbal forms of publicity was also dealt with in other ways in articles in *MAN and his Clothes*. In June 1928, for instance, Mackenzie Brown commended as good business sense how a Midlands retailer had attached hand-written cards, with messages of thirty words on them, to garments in his windows in order to arrest the attention of the passer-by. And in March 1927, the idea of using publicity showcards with rhyming couplets as a form of indirect advertising was exemplified thus: 'For yachting in the bay or channel, Blue serge goes well with snow-white flannel'. While the magazine was singular in the way that it dealt with debates about advertising with specific reference to men's clothing, in common with *Advertiser's Weekly* it also gave emphasis to the form and content of press campaigns. In comparison to other forms of publicity, press advertising for the Adquisitor (the nom-de-plume of one of *MAN and his Clothes* regular columnists) had the virtue of being studied at home or in the office and could, therefore, 'exert much more influence in getting the man – or woman – inside the shop' (Adquisitor 1932b:24). If for this reason and no other, then, men's wear retailers were advised to spend an average of 2.5 per cent of their annual turnover on advertising in 1928, and by 1931 anything in the region of 7 to 10 per cent (Mackenzie Brown 1928: 13; Aquisitor 1931b: 31).

This idea, concerning the persuasive power of the media, was not infrequently rehearsed during the 1920s and 1930s by the press itself. In 1927, for instance, a promotion for the *Daily Mirror* claimed that its 'Men readers . . . are no less interested in pictures and advertisements that show the latest vogues for *them*' (*Advertiser's Weekly*, 15 April 1927: 74), while the advertising manager of *The Times* asserted that:

> Men, generally speaking, are far better dressed since the advertising of clothes. The continued advertising of men's wear in The Times proves how mistaken is the supposition that [it] appeals only to more exclusive sections of society. The influence of its advertisement columns extends throughout the country, wherever men of taste and education gather. (*Advertiser's Weekly*, 15 April 1927: 74)

Notwithstanding these claims, of course, the social class and income of male consumers and whether they took any notice of advertising at all were just as pivotal to men's wear retailers as they had been before the First World War. Only now, with the proliferation of advertising agencies, the rivalry between newspapers with respect to sales figures and advertising space rates, the impact of popular photo-weeklies such as *Picture Post* and other mass circulation periodicals like the *Radio Times*, the design debates on typography and period style, and the rise of market classifications, the choices facing them concerning where and how to advertise were more varied and complex than they had ever been before.

How Men's Wear Advertising Overlapped with Market Research and New Ways of Classifying Consumers' Reading Preferences

Generally speaking, the interwar period witnessed an intensification in the quantity of men's wear advertising that appeared in the press. In the autumn of 1927, for instance, *Punch*'s advertising manager Marion Jean Lyon boasted of a stratospheric compound increase in men's wear advertising in the magazine of 7,867 per cent between 1899 and 1926, while in the same year the *Daily Express* yielded a global advertising revenue of nearly £1.25 million against an average daily net sale of just over 1 million copies (*Advertiser's Weekly*, 25 November 1927:313, 12 July 1951: 90).[9] We can get a more representative indication of just how much the market for male clothing had grown, however, from the comparative figures concerning expenditure on men's wear advertising that were first collated during the 1930s. Thus 'The Space Market', conducted by Media Records Ltd between November 1933 and December 1934, revealed an interesting paradigmatic pattern for men's wear, tailoring and underwear press advertising both in terms of the amounts spent and where it was spent (Tables 1–3).

As these figures demonstrate, in all three cases the lion's share of space buying generally took place in the national dailies. But there were exceptions with regard to how and when the amounts were spent across the four different media cate-

Table 1 'The Space Market', November 1933 to December 1934 – data supplied by Media Records Ltd

Advertising Expenditure for Men's Wear

Date	No. of advertisers	£ Total expenditure	£ per four chief media categories			
			I	II	III	IV
Nov. 1933	11	15,803	4,012	4,048	4,043	2,679
Dec. 1933	11	10,738	2,875	3,308	2,098	845
Jan. 1934	8	3,748	994	1,361	1,177	56
Feb. 1934	5	1,226	317	260	221	428
March 1934	9	12,313	3,271	3,571	2,510	1,773
April 1934	9	13,168	3,584	3,184	2,570	2,585
May 1934	9	20,258	7,446	4,519	4,481	2,372
June 1934	7	11,251	3,511	2,455	2,226	1,981
July 1934	9	9,750	2,598	3,707	2,409	870
Aug. 1934	6	2,517	615	539	1,041	322
Sept. 1934	9	8,672	2,043	2,012	2,037	852
Oct. 1934	9	21,374	7,389	5,270	4,527	2,995
Nov. 1934	9	13,955	3,904	3,992	3,138	2,482
Dec. 1934	9	11,247	3,051	2,963	2,839	1,297

Source: Advertiser's Weekly, 13 January 1934 to 21 January 1935 (table collated by the author)

Note: I National Dailies; II London Evening Papers; III Provincial Dailies; IV Magazines

Table 2 'The Space Market', November 1933 to December 1934 – data supplied by Media Records Ltd

Advertising Expenditure for Tailors

Date	No. of advertisers	£ Total expenditure	£ per four chief media categories			
			I	II	III	IV
Nov. 1933	5	13,513	5,332	1,200	5,116	70
Dec. 1933	5	10,322	3,972	816	3,523	95
Jan. 1934	4	3,055	1,007	362	1,283	16
Feb. 1934	4	6,139	2,627	932	1,867	15
March 1934	4	17,481	4,812	2,136	5,769	1,618
April 1934	4	11,247	4,629	1,978	2,302	1,316
May 1934	4	10,217	4,586	1,759	2,047	1,030
June 1934	4	13,810	6,631	1,852	3,382	1,061
July 1934	4	6,300	2,557	1,323	1,685	–
Aug. 1934	3	4,848	3,655	905	175	10
Sept. 1934	3	10,010	3,161	945	2,442	11
Oct. 1934	4	16,590	6,823	1,766	4,626	845
Nov. 1934	8	16,263	7,606	1,589	3,899	1,032
Dec. 1934	7	9,357	2,197	533	2,559	520

Source: Advertiser's Weekly, 13 January1934 to 21 January 1935 (table collated by the author)
Note: I National Dailies; II London Evening Papers; III Provincial Dailies; IV Magazines

Table 3 'The Space Market', November 1933 to December 1934 – data supplied by Media Records Ltd

Advertising Expenditure for Underwear (men's, women's and children's)

Date	No. of advertisers	£ Total expenditure	£ per four chief media categories			
			I	II	III	IV
Nov. 1933	29	22,985	12,348	1,686	2,650	5,004
Dec. 1933	30	4,822	1,766	517	192	2,221
Jan. 1934	13	2,335	796	32	485	575
Feb. 1934	14	4,459	2,121	403	587	944
March 1934	15	6,423	4,161	–	–	920
April 1934	13	7,114	5,334	75	686	814
May 1934	18	11,519	8,925	88	579	1,612
June 1934	14	3,361	1,496	–	63	1,417
July 1934	11	3,219	1,863	41	–	992
August 1934	11	3,669	2,602	–	–	546
Sept. 1934	16	10,619	7,458	281	108	1,438
Oct. 1934	20	38,708	21,845	878	6,972	7,324
Nov. 1934	19	28,799	14,992	572	5,434	6,447
Dec. 1934	15	12,229	5,955	32	1,235	4,544

Source: *Advertiser's Weekly*, 13 January1934 to 21 January 1935 (table collated by the author)
Note: National Dailies; II London Evening Papers; III Provincial Dailies; IV Magazines

gories. Thus the second largest expenditure for men's wear advertising was generally the London evening papers, while for tailors it was the provincial dailies, and for underwear it was magazines. The figures also reveal that men's wear advertisements appeared in all four media categories, as they did in the case of tailors with one notable exception – no advertising for them appeared in magazines during July 1934. When we turn to underwear, we can see that no advertising was placed in the London and provincial papers in March and August 1934, none appeared in the London press in June 1934 and none in the provincial dailies in July 1934.

The prioritising of different second-choice media by different sections of the clothing market expressed by these figures can partly be put down to nothing more than the personal preference of the retailers involved, but there are also some specific socio-economic reasons for such discrepancies. As there was a higher concentration of retailing outlets in the capital than any other town, for instance, it is hardly surprising to find more publicity for men's wear in general in the London dailies. By comparison, the predilection by tailors for provincial dailies has to be explained by the fact that multiple retailing of suits had also become a common feature by the 1930s. Thus by 1936 there were 199 chief men's wear organisations with 1,695 separate branches between them; Montague Burton, for example, owned 450 shops nation-wide at this time, and The Fifty Shilling Tailors and Hepworths had between 200 and 300 shops apiece (Chisholm 1936). And the dedication of larger amounts of money to advertising in the national dailies and magazines by underwear manufacturers is due to the fact that these garments were not retailed independently or in certain regions only but were more generally stocked by men's outfitters and department stores across the land. Hence, it would have been both more convenient and viable to target potential customers by blanket advertising in nationally circulated media.

'The Space Market' figures also portray some seasonal variation in the placing of advertising for each type of retailer. Accordingly, the peak months for men's wear were November 1933, May 1934 and October 1934, when more than £15,000 was spent on each occasion; while for tailoring, they were November 1933 and March, June, October and November 1934, when more than £13,000 was spent each month; and for underwear they were November 1933 and October and November 1934, when more than £20,000 was spent in each instance, and May, September and December 1934, when more than £10,000 was spent per month.[10] These peaks generally coincide with the seasonal demand for cooler or warmer garments in spring and autumn, with a slight variation for tailoring due to the notice required to manufacture made-to-measure suits in time for the new season (something which is borne out by the total absence of advertising for tailors in July 1934).

Although 'The Space Market' did not mention newspapers and magazines by name, we can glean a clear understanding of why men's wear advertisers would have preferred some titles more than others from the comparative figures of net sales and advertising space of several newspapers for 1921 and 1930 respectively that appeared in *Advertiser's Weekly*. Thus in 1921 the average net sales of the *Daily Mail* were 1,245,267 copies and its rate per column inch of advertising was £6, while sales of the *Daily Express* were 587,779 and its column rate stood at £3 5s.[11] By 1930, the daily net sales of the *Mail* had increased to 1,872,418 copies but its advertising rates had remained the same, whereas net sales of the *Express* had risen exponentially to 1,701,000 copies with a concomitant increase in advertising rates to £5 10s (*Advertiser's Weekly*, 15 August 1930:182).[12] However, in each of these years the ratio of readers to the cost per standard column inch of advertising space meant that both papers offered the same value for money to advertisers, and that they were slightly cheaper for advertising than the *Daily Herald*. By contrast, the ratio of readers to the cost of advertising in *The Times* meant each standard column inch was four times more expensive to buy.[13]

Among periodicals, *Punch* had a circulation of 200,000 copies in 1930 and charged £200 for a full-page advertisement in monochrome (the equivalent of £1 for every 2,000 readers), whereas the *Radio Times*, with an average weekly sale of 2 million copies, had a full-page rate of £600 (the equivalent of £1 for every 3,333 readers, and consequently more economical for advertisers to exploit on a per capita basis).[14] These periodical full-page rates stand comparison with the *Daily Mail*, which charged £1,400 for its front page in 1927 on an average daily circulation of 1,800,000 copies (the equivalent of £1 for every 1,285 readers).[15] But, the relationship of circulation to space rates affords us only a partial impression concerning the preferences of men's wear advertisers during the interwar period for certain media over others. In addition to economic considerations such as these, therefore, advertisers were also interested in the actual class profile of readers and it was on this basis that several market research organisations conducted surveys to determine who was reading what and why. As one advertising manager argued at the time, what mattered was not the net sales of newspapers and magazines per se, rather the relationship of sales to potential customers (*Advertiser's Weekly*, 29 October 1936).

To this end, independent research was carried out in 1932 by Repford Ltd, one of several market research companies, which also included Gallup, established after the First World War; in 1934 and 1939 by the advertising agency J. Walter Thompson (JWT); and in 1936 by the Incorporated Society of British Advertisers (ISBA). Conducted by Thomas D. Morison, Repford's survey analysed the reading habits of nearly 54,000 adults in the upper class and middle class, or A, B and C, income range in 181 towns in England, Wales and Scotland. Their findings revealed that 66 per cent of those in Class A and B, and approximately 16 per cent from Class C read the *Daily Mail*, whereas approximately 34 per cent from all three groups read the *Daily Herald*. In many ways these figures were unsurprising and served to reveal nothing but stasis in the class profile of newspaper readers. *Advertiser's Weekly* (1932a), while commending the report as a 'milestone in space-buying practice', took issue with the more or less even distribution of readers by Repford across the three categories, which it felt distorted the findings by ignoring the fact that there were approximately ten Class C readers for every one in Class A.

J. Walter Thompson's survey in 1939 was also class based but took the novel step of asking 17,000 individuals (instead of households) in thirty towns 'Did you read a newspaper yesterday?' rather than the usual question 'What newspapers do you always read?' Their results broke the mould of some usual readership assumptions by revealing that only one person in ten read a national daily, whereas 98 per cent of people read a local newspaper, and more people earning £250 per annum (Class C) tended to read a national daily than those earning £500 per annum (Class B).[16] However, as *Advertiser's Weekly* pointed out, the survey would need to have been conducted on a daily basis to be of any conclusive value (30 March 1939: 444). By contrast, the 1934 JWT survey took its cue from advertising psychologist Walter Dill Scott in so far as it was more concerned with analysing how many people read the editorial and how many the advertisements in the newspapers they consulted (*Advertiser's Weekly* 1934b). Based on a sample of 8,296 correspondents and four daily newspapers – the *Mail*, the *Express*, the *Herald* and the *News Chronicle* – the findings of this report would have been a sobering reminder to advertisers not to take their readers for granted. Only 17 per cent of the sample admitted to reading the advertisements, which meant taking in all the headlines and copy, while more people from the 'poorer classes' read them than their 'well-to-do' counterparts (nineteen per cent as against 14 per cent), and more women (19 per cent) than men (16 per cent).

The ISBA survey of 1936 was probably the most sustained – but also the most widely debated – of such interwar consumer behaviour surveys. This investigation analysed the reading habits of some 82,613 households in England, Wales and Scotland, which is to say one household was taken proportionally to represent one hundred and sixteen homes in the same socio-economic category.[17] In common with the Repford survey, therefore, the ISBA study was not based on the tastes of individuals. But in comparison to Repford, which had dealt exclusively with the preferences of upper- and middle-class readers, its results were based on the categorisation of five different household annual incomes, namely Class A (£1,000 gross and over per annum), Class B (£500–999), Class C (£250–499), Class D (£125–249) and Class E (less than £125).[18] Moreover, income was to be the sine qua non for quantifying consumer behaviour as far as the ISBA was concerned. Accepting that 'some controversy, may . . . arise from the I.S.B.A.'s . . . innovation related to class-grading' the report argued nevertheless that: 'Differences of social habit and outlook are not capable of statistical measurement, however easily they may be recognised subjectively . . . What is fundamental to a family's position in the social scale is its income, and the income is decided by the occupation followed' (*Advertiser's Weekly* 1936c:276). In fact, this type of audience classification is still in use by the National Readership Survey. Since it determines social class on the basis of the major wage-earner (usually male) in any family, however, nowadays it is also supplemented by qualitative or lifestyle surveys – the very subjective data rejected by the ISBA – such as the Values and Lifestyles System (VALS), initiated by the Stanford Research Institute, California in 1978, and Outlook, pioneered in Britain in 1987.[19]

As much as the other consumer behaviour surveys from the period did, the specific findings of the ISBA Survey compounded the class profiles of various newspapers and magazines, but it also illuminated a few anomalies. Accordingly, both the *Daily Mail* and *Daily Express* had large Class C readerships, but the *Mail* was equally as popular with Class A. The *Daily Herald* was most popular with Class D and E, and *The Times* was the most popular daily among Class A readers, while, remarkably, the *Daily Mirror* had the fourth largest circulation among Class A readers. The survey also revealed how social class could be related to geography, so that the *Evening Standard* was the most popular daily paper of any description in the south-east with people earning £500 and over, of whom nearly 29 per cent were among Class A and B. With regard to periodical publishing, the *Radio Times*, which by this time had accrued a weekly circulation of 2 million copies, had by far the largest proportion of readers with incomes of £500 and over, and the majority of *Punch's* readers came from the same income bracket; while *Vogue* appealed equally as much to Class A, B and C, and *Weekly Illustrated*, newly launched in 1934, had rapidly found favour with all social grades, but most of all with Class D, which constituted just over 58 per cent of its circulation (*Advertiser's Weekly* 1936b).

Several publications, however, took exception to the ISBA's findings. Will Davenport, the advertising manager of *Vogue*, found it hard to believe that 'all doctors, or directors, or widows, have the same identical income', and even harder to justify how nobody with an income of £1,000 and over in South Wales, the East and West Midlands or East Anglia read it at all (*Advertiser's Weekly*, 17 December 1936:387). And the tabloids felt particularly aggrieved that readerships had been determined in terms of households rather than individuals (*Advertiser's Weekly*, 1936e). Alan Whitworth, general secretary of the ISBA, retaliated by stating that the ISBA survey had allocated *Vogue* with 13,020 readers among Class A and B in comparison to the 1,513 represented in the 1932 survey by Repford. He also reiterated that the aim of the survey was not to determine total circulations, rather to represent a random sampling of class categories, and that in any case the distribution of incomes across the different class groups used by the ISBA coincided with those compiled by Repford and the London Press Exchange (*Advertiser's Weekly* 1936d: 57–8).

The myriad data provided by these market research surveys certainly make for a perplexing situation for anyone researching the relationship of advertising to the class and income-based circulations of mass media newspapers and periodicals. Nonetheless, they do bear some correlation to how men's wear advertising was distributed in the interwar years. Moreover, this kind of quantitative analysis found general acceptance among advertising agencies as a basis for targeting the most appropriate consumers, especially if taken into consideration alongside the advertising rates of particular titles.

Consequently, it comes as no surprise to find that Austin Reed (whose agents were Winter Thomas Company in 1928 and F.C. Pritchard Wood & Partners between 1932 and 1954) did not ever advertise in the *Daily Herald* or *Daily Mirror*, but continued to cater to the same white-collar market and to buy space in the *Daily Mail*, *Daily Express*, *The Times*, *Guardian*, *Evening News*, *Evening Standard* and *Punch*, as it had done before 1914 (Currington 1921: 37), as well as advertising in the *Radio Times* between 1932 and 1939. Indeed, Herbert Dennett, the records manager of Austin Reed during the 1930s, concurred that it was company policy to trade with a higher class of people, namely the A and B markets who could afford to pay between five and eight guineas for one of their suits or overcoats, and that the preferred media were those press and periodical titles listed above as well as extensive poster advertising (*Advertiser's Weekly* 1937).[20] Aquascutum (represented by Elliott Advertising), likewise, favoured upmarket media like *Punch* and the *Daily Telegraph*, and Stephens Advertising Service Ltd., the agents for '232' Flannels, spent nearly 95 per cent of the retailer's advertising appropriation on space in the *Daily Mail* (Selby 1930: 416). The initial campaign for '232', to the tune of £3,800, appeared in the *Mail* in 1923 and helped to multiply their sales twenty-fold (*Advertiser's Weekly*, 9 June 1932:334–5).[21] On a regional basis, Stephensons advertising agency promoted London tailors Hector Powe every Tuesday throughout the autumn of 1923 in the *Evening News* (Nemo 1923:241), while The Rego Clothiers, Ltd, which began trading in 1875 and had one hundred branches across the London and the Home Counties by 1935, promoted their 45 shillings suits and overcoats every Friday in the *Evening News* and the *Star* between September 1935 and June 1936 (Figure 26).[22] The multiple tailors Colletts of London also began to advertise their shirts and overcoats for the first time after thirty-four years of trading in the *Evening Standard* in 1932 (*Advertiser's Weekly*, 1932c), and in the North of England, Weaver to Wearer Ltd, which had been established in 1930, was spending £6,000 pounds per annum on advertising by 1936 in the *Manchester Evening News*, *Newcastle Evening Chronicle*, *Yorkshire Evening Post* and *Liverpool Echo* (*Advertiser's Weekly*, December 1936f).[23]

This strict stereotyping is vexed, however, by the fact that some manufacturers and retailers advertised themselves across the board and thus worked on the basis that everyone desired good quality clothing and garments at affordable prices, irrespective of their social class. In the *Daily Mail* (24 April 1925:2), for instance, Rego had advertised the same 45 shillings tweed and indigo serge suit that it proceeded to promote ten years later in the *Evening News*,[24] and Barratt Shoes (represented by W.S. Crawford) and Viyella (represented by London Press Exchange) both advertised in the *Daily Mirror* and *Daily Mail* (*Advertiser's Weekly*, 20 May 1927:269). Rumble, Crowther & Nicholas Ltd promoted The Fifty Shilling Tailors on the front page of the *Daily Mail* (6 August 1937), as well as in the *Daily Express* and *Daily Herald* in 1932, and the *Radio Times* between 1934 and 1938 (Figures 33–36); indeed, their agents had spent £16,171 on buying advertising space during October and December 1937 alone (*Advertiser's Weekly*, 21 August 1938:170).[25] Several underwear manufacturers also tended to advertise their products to a wide class spectrum of readers; in 1936, for example, Courtaulds bought space in fifty-eight different newspapers and magazines with a combined circulation of over 17 million copies, including the *Daily Mirror*, *Daily Mail*, *Daily Telegraph*, *Vogue*, *Radio Times* and *Leisure* (*MAN and his Clothes*, May 1936:11).

It is interesting to observe that market and media research was not only advanced but also took on added urgency at a time when retailers were trying to gage the economic impact of the Great Depression on consumption patterns. During the 1930s, therefore, advertising came very much to be regarded as a motor that could galvanise the economy. The majority of those living in the suburban white-collar communities of London such as Uxbridge or Hendon, and in towns like Leicester and Coventry, where the automobile, electrical and textile industries continued to thrive, remained relatively unscathed by the economic slump of the 1930s and were still an affluent target for advertisers. But even unemployed people living in the industrial regions of Britain that had been so badly decimated by the Depression were regarded as potential customers by the advertising industry. George Orwell, for instance, commented in *The Road to Wigan Pier* (1937) on the material acquisitiveness of the British working classes and the unemployed notwithstanding the financial hardship of the 1930s, claiming that 'the consumption of all cheap luxuries has increased' (Orwell 1962:79).

Indeed, even the Board of Trade mobilised advertising at this time in order to protect and bolster the production of Harris Tweed among poor communities in the Outer Hebrides. This economy had been gradually undermined since the First World War by the manufacture of imitation tweeds for sport's wear in Yorkshire, the United States and Japan, and was faced with complete ruin at the outset of the Depression. To help overcome such a dire situation, the Board established the Harris Tweed Association in August 1935 to hallmark the Hebridean origins of the brand, and appointed Dorland Advertising to promote the cloths that the islanders produced. In conjunction with the Association and crofters, Dorland raised funds for advertising by levying a stamp duty of one penny on every yard of genuine tweed spun, and used this revenue to promote the product in media with affluent readers, such as *The Times* and *Punch* (*Advertiser's Weekly* 1935).[26]

In the socio-economic climate of the Depression, then, the function of advertising did not decline in importance and nor did advertising expenditure diminish significantly: in the twelve months between July 1929 and July 1930 the ratio of advertisements to total page space in the *Daily Mail* had decreased by only 1 per cent, while it had increased by 1 per cent in the *Daily Mirror* for the same period (*Advertiser's Weekly* 1930b). Moreover, as we have just witnessed, advertisers exploited any information they could about the class breakdown of newspaper and periodical readerships in order to decide whether it was good value for money to buy advertising space in them.

More specific details of advertising expenditure by named retailers – though not of the newspapers or magazines in which their promotions appeared – were tabulated in the *Advertiser's Weekly*'s 'Quarterly Analysis of Press Advertising', which covered the period from July 1932 to September 1933. According to these, Austin Reed's monthly press advertising budget was consistently between £5,000 and £10,000 (with peak periods in October, November, April and May) save for August 1932 and August 1933, when it dropped to around £3,000, and February 1933, when it dipped to a relatively meagre £60.[27] By extension, the annual press advertising budget for the company averaged £65,638 in the early 1930s, an increase of more than one-third on the annual average of £41,021 of ten years before.[28] As we have already seen, Austin Reed advertised widely on a national basis, but these figures also demonstrate that they repeatedly spent the largest sums of any men's outfitters on buying press advertising space, while the London tailor Collett's, which advertised exclusively in the *Evening Standard*, spent the least. Between July and December 1932, for instance, Austin Reed spent £41,228 on press promotions and Collett's £866 of the total £57,243 cited for the eight men's outfitters in the survey.[29] Between January and September 1933, the outlay for the former was £40,820 and the latter £1,143 of a total £55,804 spent by nine outfitters.[30] The press advertising budget for Hope Bros. was the second largest for the period July–December 1932, standing at £4,272, but between January and September 1933 Hope Bros. was eclipsed by Horne Bros., with an outlay of £8,255.[31] Furthermore, the seasonal pattern of expenditure of these retailers during the 1930s not only overlaps with that for Austin Reed but also is replicated in the placement of advertisements in the *Radio Times*, which provides us with an instructive paradigm for interrogating the nexus of men's wear promotions to class markets.

Men's Wear Advertising and the *Radio Times*

The first weekly issue of the *Radio Times* was published on 28 September 1923 and the first men's wear promotion, which was for a trench coat costing £2 sold by

Curzon Bros. of New Bridge Street, London EC4, appeared just two months later on 30 November. This was followed by a handful of advertisements between 1924 and 1932 for various retailers and outfitters such as H.J. Nicholl and Co. Ltd, which had branches in London's Regent Street and Dalton Street, Manchester.[32] It was not until the autumn of 1932, however, that a more consistent pattern of men's wear advertising emerged, from which time campaigns for Austin Reed's two-guinea raincoat (Figure 17) and Barratt Shoes (Figures 8 and 9) began to appear on a regular basis until the outbreak of the Second World War in September 1939. Advertisements for The Fifty Shilling Tailors, '232' Flannels, Horne Bros., Simpson DAKS trousers, Guinea Guards slacks, Radiac shirts, and underwear by Courtauld's, Aertex, Meridian and Morley were also promoted on a regular basis between March 1933 and September 1939 (Figures 27–9 and 37). As the *Radio Times* was produced with newsprint quality paper, in common with the dailies the advertisements that appeared in its pages – whether they featured illustrations or photographs – were exclusively monochromatic.

By far the most frequent advertisers were Austin Reed, Barratt and The Fifty Shilling Tailors, and these accounts are discussed in more detail below. The majority of all the men's wear campaigns in the magazine were promoted in the spring and autumn months (Austin Reed, Horne Bros., '232' Flannels, The Fifty Shilling Tailors, Simpson DAKS), but Barratt's advertising was more concentrated during the winter period, and promotions for underwear tended to appear in summer as well as spring and autumn to tie in with sporting events such as the Davis Cup and Wimbledon tennis championships.[33] Indeed, even Austin Reed took advantage of unsettled weather in July 1937 by advertising its two-guinea raincoat out of season.[34]

Yet it is instructive to note not just the seasonal pattern of men's wear advertising in the *Radio Times* but the range of companies and garments that were promoted between 1923 and 1939 as well. Clearly, campaigns for the likes of Austin Reed, Horne Bros. and Simpson DAKS would have made an appeal to their solid base of Class A, B and upper to middle Class C readers, while these and advertisements such as those for Hope Bros. and Barratt's would also have been targeted at upper and middle Class C. But promotions for other companies seem to have been aimed at lower Class C and Class D readers. The tailors Willerby's and Kenyon Clarke, for example, offered their garments on easy term monthly instalments, and the latter even offered £500 of free personal insurance with every suit purchased (*Radio Times*, 1 March 1929:521).[35] This trend is substantiated by George Orwell, who testified in *The Road to Wigan Pier* that hire-purchase of garments like these was also the province of low income and unemployed males in the interwar period: 'The youth who leaves school at fourteen and gets a blind-alley job is out of work at twenty, probably for life; but for two pounds ten on the hire-purchase he can buy himself a suit which, for a little while and at a distance, looks as though it had been tailored in Savile Row' (Orwell 1962: 79).

It is probable that the company to which Orwell was alluding in this context was The Fifty Shilling Tailors, and he was right to contend that garments such as theirs would have been within the pocket of both classes. But we also have to take into account the fact that, shortly after his book was published in 1937, purchase of a suit for 50 shillings was the equivalent of nearly one week's wages for working class males, who earned on average £3 10s, and cost 2 shillings more than the average weekly unemployment benefit (*Picture Post*, 11 March 1939).[36] In either case, then, it is unlikely that this class of customer would have been disposed to buy more than one or two such suits every year, and male consumers in the North of England could anyway take avail of bespoke tailoring for as little as 30 shillings from Weaver to Wearer, which had sixty branches across the region in 1936 (*Advertiser's Weekly* 1936f).[37] Furthermore, as two articles on unemployment in *Picture Post* (1939a, 1939b) also reveal, shopping for new and second-hand clothes from market stalls was a common feature of everyday life for the wives and mothers of unemployed males.

It is precisely because suits by The Fifty Shilling Tailors were within the reach of working-class and unemployed males that the company has traditionally been regarded as infra dig in comparison to their upmarket competitors, Austin Reed and Simpson. Yet their advertisements appeared alongside those of their rivals in the *Radio Times*, on average once every three to four weeks between 1935 and 1938, and also stressed the fact that The Fifty Shilling Tailors could offer the same quality materials and number of different suit styles as more expensive outfitters did for half the price. The fact that campaigns for all three of these companies appeared in the *Radio Times*, therefore, is a clear indication of inclusiveness in the marketing and promotion of men's wear and provides a particular test case when it comes to determining the class of readers and clients. Hence, the magazine featured advertisements that would appeal to the broadest category of male readers, while at the same time companies such as The Fifty Shilling Tailors realised that they could prosper only by attracting upper- and middle-class men as well as working-class and unemployed males, and by emphasising not just price but quality in their campaigns (Figures 27–9). In this sense, then, the fluidity of the clothing market remarked on by the *Tailor and Cutter* as early as 1880 through which middle-class men were not averse to seeking out clothing bargains still seemed to persist during the interwar period (Breward 1999:28). But, as both Orwell and men's wear magnate Montague Burton insisted, so too had the sartorial expectations of working-class males in Britain resulted in the democratisation and levelling of clothing styles during the 1920s and 1930s: 'now the young miner dresses exactly like the bank clerk, and the same refined designs and styles which sell freely in a fashionable south coast town are also popular in the industrial areas' (Burton, quoted in *Men's Wear*, 30 July 1932).

In fact, the *Radio Times* drew a correlation between the amount of advertising it carried and the proportion of clothing that was purchased, claiming in a self-promotion in 1934 that 'one fifth of all clothing sold in Great Britain is bought by readers of the Radio Times' (*Advertiser's Weekly*, 3 May 1934:107). This statistic clearly includes women's as well as men's dress but, by dint of the total lack of any other evidence, it would also be difficult to corroborate in precise terms. Nonetheless, it does convey a sort of general truth, pinpointing two interrelated factors about the *Radio Times*: the broad scope of its circulation across the A–E class spectrum and the popularity of the magazine with a diverse set of clothing retailers. In the same year that it staked its claim, advertisements for the following principal men's outfitters appeared in its pages: Austin Reed, The Fifty Shilling Tailors, Courtauld's underwear and Barratt Shoes.

When it came to propounding a straightforward one-to-one relationship between advertising and sales of any product, however, most manufacturers, retailers and advertising agents tended to tread cautiously, and nor did they conduct market research to prove the point. For example, H. Lewis Selby, the publicity and merchandising director of '232' Flannels, collaborated with the agency Stephens Advertising Service Ltd in order to promote the brand on a national basis in the *Daily Mail* and *John Bull*, and after increasing his advertising appropriation between 1922 and 1930 found that sales had soared from 3,000 to 500,000 garments. But he realised that advertising was only one factor contributing to this success, arguing: 'advertising, in the case of a product like ours at any rate, is not a magic wand which brings results at a wave . . . Advertising is simply part of the mechanics of selling . . . I sold the idea of a branded garment to the retailers during the first year. Newspaper advertising acted simply as an extension of my dealer-aids' (Selby 1930:416).

Rather than treating publicity as an exactly quantifiable science, whose inevitable and sole purpose was increased sales, Selby seemed to settle for press advertising as a blunt economic instrument, a means of keeping a brand name in the public eye. If it was not to be regarded exactly as a fiscal 'magic wand', then, advertising at least should aim to grab the attention of newspaper and magazine readers by making them inquisitive not just about the immediate use value of the things that were promoted but of the cultural and symbolic value of them in their lives as well. And instrumental to this dyadic psychological process of recognition and persuasion was the role of design and copywriting, or the creation of an apposite advertising atmosphere in text and image.

Notes

1. See Dunbar 1977. Dunbar estimates that in 1912 press advertising totalled £13 million while poster and transport advertising was worth £2 million; in 1920, press advertising totalled £28 million and poster and transport advertising £3 million.
2. The 2001 equivalent is £775.75. This figure and others cited in subsequent footnotes are from McCusker (2003).
3. Cotton hosiery to the value of £1,336,690 and woollen hosiery totalling £3,445,508 were exported between 1914 and 1915.
4. Respective 2001 equivalents are £6.98, £13.19 and £29.48.
5. Respective 2001 equivalents for six and eight guineas are £334.77 and £260.65, and for 55s and 90s are £85.33 and £139.64.
6. Respective 2001 equivalents are £9.81, £19.18 and £53.53.
7. Some notable exhibitors at White City, who are discussed later in this chapter, were Greenly's, the *Daily Express*, *Daily Mail*, *Daily Mirror* and *Daily Herald*. The Design and Industries Association, which had been founded in 1915 to promote the quality of craftsmanship in industrial production, also had a stall.
8. The Convention at Wembley ran between 14 and 19 July 1924. Higham's speech had been adumbrated in *Advertiser's Weekly* on 16 July 1924, pp. 182 and 186. See special issues of *Advertiser's Weekly*, 13 and 18 July 1933, for full details of the Olympia show, and the special issues of 10 and 17 July 1925 and 8 June 1928, which are representative of how it covered the British Advertising Conventions.
9. The 2001 equivalent is £5,091,088.67. Between 1920 and 1938, advertising expenditure rose from £13 million to £59 million, with press advertising accounting for 87 per cent of the latter total. See Nevett (1982: 146).
10. Respective equivalents for 2001 are: £826,425.18 and £833,353.29 (£15,000 in 1933 and 1934); £716,235.15 and £722,239.52 (£13,000 in 1933 and 1934); £1,101,900.24 and £1,111,137.72 (£20,000 in 1933 and 1934); and £555,568.86 (£10,000 in 1934).
11. Respective equivalents for 2001 are £178.54 and £96.71.
12. Respective 2001 equivalents for £6 and £5 10s are £286.95 and £263.04.
13. The net sales and advertising column rates of the *Daily Herald* were 285,000 and £1 5s respectively in 1921, and 1,078,000 and £3 5s respectively in 1930 (2001 equivalents are £37.20 and £89.27), while figures for *The Times* were 113,231 and £3 in 1921, and 193,681 and £3 in 1930 (2001 equivalents are £155.43 and £143.47).
14. The 2001 equivalents for £200 and £600 are £9,564.95 and £28,694.85, while the equivalent of £1 is £47.82.

15. The 2001 equivalents are £570,201.93 and £40.73.
16. The 2001 equivalents are £12,605.98 and £25,211.96.
17. The total number of households in mid-1934 stood at 9,466,296. By consulting the sample it did, the ISBA Survey claimed to have covered 80.73 per cent of private family households in Great Britain, arguing:

> For the first time a media research has covered not merely the great centres of dense population, but the small towns and even villages. It has penetrated to 75 places with more than 100,000 inhabitants, 83 with more than 50,000, and less than 100,000, 144 with more than 25,000 and less than 50,000, 542 with between 5,000 and 25,000, and 388 with fewer than 5,000. (*Advertiser's Weekly* 1936b: 276)

18. The 2001 equivalents are £50,314.53 (£1,000), £25,157.27 (£500), £12,578.63 (£250) and £6,289.32 (£125).
19. The current economic classifications for the National Readership Survey and Joint Industry Commission on National Audience and Readership Surveys are as follows:

Class	Professional type	% of population
A	Higher managerial, administrative and professional (company directors, bank managers, doctors, lawyers, social workers, teachers, librarians, clergy, police inspectors, corporate managers)	3.0
B	Intermediate managerial, administrative and professional (journalists, actors and musicians, police, nurses, midwives)	19.3
C1	Supervisory or clerical and junior managerial, administrative and professional (secretaries, clerks, driving instructors, computer operators, telephone fitters, farmers, publicans)	27.1
C2	Skilled manual (printers, plumbers, butchers, train drivers, bus inspectors, TV engineers)	22.5
D	Semi-skilled and unskilled manual (shop assistants, traffic wardens, cooks, bus drivers, hairdressers, postal workers)	16.4
E	Casual labourers (waiters, road sweepers, cleaners, couriers, refuse collectors), state pensioners, students and unemployed people	11.7

VALS consists of the following chief types: Actualisers (successful, well-off; emerging leaders in business and politics; people with the ability to 'take charge'), Fulfilleds (mature, retired people with a disposable income), Believers (conventional, patriotic, safe), Achievers (work-oriented people who value stability; conspicuous consumers who seek out products to demonstrate their success to others), Strivers (want the approval of others; who they want to be or what they want to buy is usually out of reach), Experiencers (young, impulsive, rebellious, seek variety), Makers (practical and self-sufficient; only interested in function and utility, and unimpressed by material possessions), and Strugglers (cautious consumers who are poor, badly-educated, despairing and passive). Outlook is based on following six lifestyle groups: Trendies (15%), Pleasure seekers (15%), The indifferent (18%), Working-class puritans (15%), Sociable spenders (14%) and Moralists (16%).

20. Respective 2001 equivalents are £251.08 and £401.73.

21. The 2001 equivalent is £134,156.77.

22. The 2001 equivalent is £119.43.

23. The 2001 equivalent is £301,887.

24. Respective 2001 equivalents for 45 shillings in 1925 and 1935 are £80.29 and £119.43.

25. The 2001 equivalent is £773,373.91.

26. The 2001 equivalent of one penny is 22 pence.

27. The 2001 equivalents of £5,000 and £10,000 for 1932 are £286,004.93, £572,009.86 and for 1933 are £275,475.06 and £550,950.12; the equivalent of £3000 for 1932 is £171,602.96 and for 1933 is £165,285.04, while the equivalent of £60 is £3305.70.

28. Respective 2001 equivalents are £3,139,120.43 and £96,499.98.

29. Respective 2001 figures are £2,358,282.27, £49,536.05 and £3,274,356.07.

30. Respective 2001 figures are £2,248,978.38, £62,973.60 and £3,074,522.04.

31. Respective 2001 figures are £244,362.61 and £454,809.32. For the period July 1932 to March 1933, the other men's wear retailers were Colletts, Forsyth, Harrod's men's shop, Hope Bros., Horne Bros., Meaker's and Nicoll's; between April and September 1933 they were joined by Moss Bros.

32. In the early days of the *Radio Times*, thirteen specific men's wear advertisements appeared in its pages, as follows: Curzon Bros. (30 November 1923, p. 264 (trench coat), 5 November 1926, p. 359 (winter overcoat), Catesby's new suit (7 March 1924, p. 450), Willerby's lounge suit (1 April 1926, p. 186), Blanford tailor's (12 October 1928, p. 133), Kenyon Clarke, Manchester, made-to-measure suits (1 March 1929, p. 521), H.J. Nicholl, lounge suits (3 May 1929, p. 261, and 11 April 1930, p. 99), John Temple Ltd, general clothing (30 May 1930, p. 522), Courtauld's, rayon underwear (10 April 1931, p. 90, 24 April 1931, p. 211, and 22 May 1931, p. 453), Aertex, underwear (31 July 1931, p. 239. At the same time, two advertisements per year promoted trench coats for men and women in Burberry's winter sale.

33. Both Meridian underwear (24 May 1935, p. 75) and Courtaulds underwear (14 June 1935, p. 63), for example, were advertised with resort to sporting paradigms; the Meridian ad actually featured a man playing tennis. These underwear promotions are discussed more fully in Chapter 7 of this book.
34. The weather forecast in *The Times* on 1 July 1937 (p. 37), for instance, had predicted a period of unsettled weather across the British Isles with occasional local outbreaks of rain.
35. The 2001 equivalent is £20,169.57.
36. The 2001 equivalent of 50 shillings is £119.56 and £3 10s is £167.39.
37. The 2001 equivalent is £75.47.

−4−

'Selling with Wit, Style and Sincerity'

Modernism, Class and Gender in Men's Wear Publicity during the Interwar Period

An advertising designer is nearer in spirit to the dress designer than he is to the architect.

Howard Wadman, *Penrose Annual*, 1936

We live in wonderful times when advertising is just awakening to the startling discovery that it is not the picture which counts but the WORD. This is typography's coming of age.

Maximilen Vox, *Commercial Art*, August 1928

As much as the economic considerations we have just explored, the aesthetic and psychological issues that affected the popularity of advertising among men were just as hotly debated in the interwar period as they had been before the outbreak of the First World War. The anonymous reviewer of an exhibition of press and poster publicity since 1900 organised by *Punch*, for example, expatiated that between 1924 and 1928 British advertisements 'led the world, selling with wit, style and sincerity; the shyness wore off and the national genius for good taste asserted itself' (*Advertising Display* October 1932b). In dealing with such issues as style and taste it is not surprising to find, therefore, that the tension between reason-why and atmospheric advertising continued to be evaluated by various writers in the trade literature for both the clothing and publicity industries. Allied to such concerns, this chapter analyses design issues such as the choice of photo-graphic or hand-drawn forms of illustration, the use and evolution of different typefaces, and the balance between text and image, as well as the rhetorical form and content of advertising campaigns for Barratt Shoes.

'Do Men Read Ads?' Reason-why, Atmosphere and the Psychology of the Male Consumer

On the side of reason-why promotions A.J. Aitken argued in 1923 that copy should appeal to men by being concise, stating 'concrete facts', and espousing an impersonal and detached tone in addressing male customers (Aitken 1923:269). To this end, he singled out a recent campaign for Lincoln Bennett hats, which eschewed any symbolic effects and hint of individuality ('the word "you" is conspicuously absent'), and relied instead on relating the actual qualities of the product in an understated fashion. Thus the copy commented on the fact that the hat was hand-made from felt that would never appear shabby but would 'always look just new enough' and that it cost 27 shillings, while the five accompanying illustrations represented a series of sober heads wearing the hat from different angles.[1] He insisted that brevity in advertising copy was preferable since men, unlike women, have not been trained to read advertisements: 'You can't make a man discard a perfectly good overcoat and buy one of yours by telling him that yours is the latest fashion'. And, in any case, he concluded that 'Only a limited number of men – those of an artistic nature – are really fascinated by pleasing pictures of what might happen in the future if they use your good' (Aitken 1923: 269).

The paternalistic view expressed by Aitken that men were resistant to changes in fashion styles was still being upheld by some manufacturers in the 1930s. An advertising campaign for a new garment produced by Shepherd's Shirts Ltd in 1932, for example, was conceived on the basis that 'Men are known to be die-hard conservatives in the matter of wearing apparel; they are suspicious of new inven-tions' (*Advertising Display* 1933:12). The invention in question was a shirt that required no back stud to keep its collar in place, which instead was attached to a small rim around the neckband of the shirt. And, although Shepherd's had usually made bespoke shirts for an upper-class clientele, the press campaign for the new product was orchestrated to make a wide class appeal by the advertising agency Greenly's (f. 1914), who bought space across the board to the value of £4,000 on the first day of promotion.[2] Thus, on 2 December 1932, quad-column advertise-ments appeared in the *Daily Express*, *Daily Telegraph* and *Daily Herald*, while a whole front-page advertisement was taken in the *Daily Mail*. In its entirety, however, the campaign was framed in such a way as to reassure the men who wore it that the shirt was no mere gimmick. The copy comprised a frank statement to men by the inventor of the garment, explaining how the invention worked and stressing the factual health benefits of the studless shirt and collar (the medical testimony of several doctors, who believed that the wearing of stud presses on the back of the neck contributed to neural discomfort and round-shoulderedness, was cited in several advertisements). At bottom line, the message the advertising campaign emphasised was that the new Shepherd shirt was more comfortable and healthy to wear but that it did not look any different from other shirt collars – a point that would have been keenly appreciated at the time, given proposals by the Men's Dress Reform Party (f. 1929) which, on the grounds of health, sought to replace men's shirts with blouses, and trousers with shorts.[3]

In contrast to the straightforward rhetoric of reason-why advertising several commentators advocated a more symbolic approach to men's wear promotions, which would rely on the power of suggestion. In this regard, a pivotal article entitled 'Do Men *Read* Men's Wear Advertisements?' appeared in *MAN and his Clothes* in October 1927. Written by Cyril King, at that time the advertising manager of the retailer Hope Bros. Ltd, the article crystallised what came to be an underlying leitmotiv in many other articles as well, namely, a concern for making advertisements for men's clothing more relevant, more visually appealing, more distinctive. King (1927) impugned the haphazard state of most campaigns for men's clothing, but he did realise that men from every class could be enticed to buy garments by advertising that not only contained facts about the merchandise it was promoting, but also struck a symbolic association for any product by enveloping it in atmosphere. According to Marcel Valotaire (1927), therefore, fashion publicity could escape altogether the rational or scientific messages encoded in promotions for washing soap, which set out to prove the efficacy of a particular brand in removing stains, and could rely instead on atmosphere or suggestion, or what he preferred to call *notorieté*, by which means 'the great modistes form and hold together their clientele' (Valotaire 1927:254–5). As Aldous Huxley (1931) put it in more humanly direct terms, this kind of advertising would be Machiavellian in the way it played on the individual's weaknesses and feelings: 'It makes its appeal, not to reason or the subconscious, but to emotions and prejudices, to instinct and socially organised sentiment' (Huxley 1931: 68). Hence, a familiar catchword, first debated during the early twentieth century, continued to be used to describe those advertisements that put the product into a situational context and, in contrast to the impersonal address of reason-why advertisements such as those for the Lincoln Bennett hat, spoke to the potential customer from his own perspective rather than merely the retailer's (Adquisitor 1932a:18). A good example of this kind of advertising was the 'Walk the Barratt Way' campaign, to which I shall return in due course. However, in common with reason-why advertising, atmosphere could be achieved by dint of humour, which according to Aitken (1923: 269 had 'a powerful appeal to men'.

This was precisely the tack taken in a promotion by men's outfitter Edgar Barrow of Morecombe for the 'Deversum' collar stud in 1924. In contrast to the earnest rhetoric of the later Shepherd Shirt campaign, it featured a cartoon satirising the abortive daily struggle to attach a shirt collar single-handedly, which apparently attracted a large male clientele to buy the product (Hallowell 1924). During the 1920s Tootal Broadhurst Lee Co. Ltd also relied on humour, although of a more highbrow nature, in a campaign for their 'Pyramid' brand handkerchiefs for men. This was masterminded by the advertising agency Paul E. Derrick, which employed the cartoonist Fougasse (the alias of Cyril Bird) to produce a series of narrative cartoons in the style of a picture story in *Punch*. In 1926–7, one of them represented in twelve pictures the train of thought of a man reading a newspaper advertisement that prompts him to ruminate on the meaning of progress in human civilisation and its relationship to the brand name. Starting with the invention of electricity and electric light, he proceeds to think backwards in time to what would happen if the light went out. This reminds him in turn of Moses' period in darkness – presumably a reference to his concealment for three months as a baby before he is sent to salvation in a basket down the Nile (Exodus 2:1–22) – which then evokes images of the Egyptian Pyramids that, as the punch line of the last picture proclaims, 'inevitably remind us of handkerchiefs!'

Modernism and the style debate

Fougasse also went on to produce cartoon advertisements for Austin Reed between 1937 and 1948, many of which appeared in London underground trains (Figure 6), and was one of a number of commercial artists during the interwar period who transformed the style and aesthetics of modern publicity for men's wear. Indeed, as Earnest Elmo Calkins of the Calkins & Holden Advertising Agency in New York remarked, advertising was a pioneering profession that had 'seized upon the power of the artist to say things which could not be said in words alone' (Calkins 1927: 145). One of his chief acolytes was Joseph Christian Leyendecker, who produced a series of advertisements in the United States of America for Arrow Collars between 1905 and 1935, organised around the trope of a heroic and idealised – and not infrequently homoerotic – masculinity.[4] Yet it was British advertising design that was more frequently invoked during the 1920s and 1930s to evaluate the strengths and weaknesses of modern publicity. Editorial in *Poster and Publicity* contended in 1927, for instance, that 'England is now considered quite generally on the Continent and in America to have the best travel posters'. At the same time, however, developments in press and poster advertising for various men's wear retailers should not be overlooked.

Several important agencies began to get involved with the promotion of men's dress in the interwar period. Publicity Arts Ltd had been founded in 1914 with the express intention of tackling 'every conceivable kind of advertisement'; in 1926, for example, one of their affiliates, C.V. Strangeman, executed showcard designs for Lissu handkerchiefs (*Commercial Art*, March 1926b: 66). Carlton Studios, which had been established in 1900 by Canadian artist Archie Martin, employed designers on a freelance basis and opened their own fashion illustration department in 1925 to offer 'catalogue illustration . . . from one guinea upwards, or a really important fashion painting from ten to thirty guineas, or something between these extremes' (*Advertiser's Weekly*, 3 July 1925: 55).[5] According to graphic designer James Gardner, a typical Carlton tyro earned in the region of £3 per week in the early 1930s (Gardner 1993:60).[6] Among the artists who specialised in fashion there were Francis Marshall (drawings for Jaeger women's wear between 1937 and 1941 and men's wear between 1951 and 1952), Pearl Falconer (illustrations for the Hulton Press and advertising campaigns for Clarks women's shoes and Celanese women's underwear), C.B. Bowmar (illustrations for Moss Bros. in the early 1930s and The Fifty Shilling Tailors between 1932 and 1940), Traus (advertisements for British Celanese in 1932 – see front cover illustration), Fred Furnivall, and Rex Osborne, who was involved with Aertex advertising until 1955.

Osborne was also registered with the Brockhurst Studios, which ran a series of advertisements in *Commercial Art* and *Advertiser's Weekly* between 1923 and 1928 to celebrate the fact that they employed artists such as Osborne, Fyffe and Harold Lisle, all of whom specialised in depicting men's wear and who represented 'Real people – naturally posed – perfectly drawn standing out vividly from the printed page' (*Advertiser's Weekly*, 30 March 1928:580).[7] By the mid-1930s these two organisations had been joined by the JKM Advertising Studios, which also promoted themselves as specialists in tailor's advertising (*MAN and his Clothes*, November 1936:50).

In the footsteps of these commercial studios came a handful of small craft-based organisations: the Curwen Press, which had been run by Harold Curwen since 1914 and was dedicated to fine book printing, collaborated in the design and production of promotional literature for the Rational Underwear Company in 1928 and a brochure for Austin Reed entitled 'Clothes Instead of Cloth' with a cover motif by Paul Nash, in the mid-1930s (Wadman 1936:43); the Bassett Gray Studio, which started life in 1921, took its name after its founders Charles Bassett and Milner Gray and was a collaborative workshop of freelance artists. The majority of its members had studied painting and printmaking at Goldsmith's College and they fed this artistic approach into the commercial commissions they received for companies such as Hanan and Sons, the boot makers (*Commercial Art* 1927e); and the Clement Dane Studio, founded in 1927. This also sprung from an art school base and its members included Constance Castle, who trained at Chelsea School of Art and did illustrations for Austin Reed booklets in 1928 (Thorp 1927: 220–23).

A large number of advertising agencies also handled the accounts of well-known manufacturers and retailers of men's clothing during the interwar years. Accordingly, London Press Exchange promoted Viyella shirts between 1932 and 1939; Rumble, Crowther & Nicholas publicised The Fifty Shilling Tailors between 1937 and 1954; W.S. Crawford ran accounts for Simpson, Jaeger, Wolsey socks and Barratt Shoes during the 1930s; while F.C. Pritchard, Wood & Partners were involved with promoting underwear, hosiery and knitwear by I&R Morley (1935–40), Wolsey Underwear (1930–1) and, principally, Austin Reed (1932–54). Although many of the training manuals of the period, including William Crawford's influential *How to Succeed in Advertising* (1931: 6–9), implied that the evolution of a sound advertising account could be attributed to anyone with the right measure of common sense and intelligence, the most successful agencies did employ a wide array of artistic talent in the production of their clients' advertising campaigns. Thus under the aegis of Pritchard and Wood, press and poster campaigns for Austin Reed were designed by the likes of Tom Purvis, Eckersley-Lombers, Fran Sutton and Austin Cooper. (Their work is analysed in closer detail in Chapter 5 concerning promotions for tailoring.) Cooper also designed posters to advertise gloves by I&R Morley in 1930, and Aldo Cosomati, who had trained as an artist in Germany and Switzerland and was associated with the Baynard Press, produced cover illustrations for the company's booklets in 1924 (*Commercial Art* June 1924b). Ashley Havinden, who was art director at Crawford's, meanwhile, was appointed head of publicity design for Simpson between 1933 and 1948 and garnered a reputation for sponsoring avant-garde work by Lázsló Moholy-Nagy and Zéró (Hans Schleger) alongside more figurative representations of masculine dress by Max Hof. (These are discussed in more detail in Chapter 5.)

In the hands of these practitioners atmosphere or suggestion in advertising was closely allied to debates on modernism, which during the interwar period openly engaged with the role of art in the mass media. Der Ring 'Neue Werbegestalter' (The Circle of 'New Advertising Designers'), for instance, an international professional alliance of artists and designers formed in 1927 and including the likes of Moholy-Nagy, Jan Tschichold, Piet Zwart and Kurt Schwitters, promoted the idea that graphic design would be 'part of the foundation on which the *new world* will be built' (Moholy-Nagy 1969:38). In particular, The Circle argued that the style of both illustrations or photographs and typeforms, and how they could be integrated to compose harmony in layouts, was paramount. This point was echoed in Britain by Godfrey Hope Saxon Mills, copywriter at Crawford's advertising agency and nephew of the famous copywriter William Haslam Mills. As he put it in his article 'The New Idea in Advertising' in *Commercial Art*, 'The full use of the suggestion idea demands a specialised understanding of the three aspects of an advertisement – Illustration, Typography, and Copy' (Mills 1923). And design critics were unanimous in agreeing that by no means should any of these aspects be left solely in the hands of the advertiser, who had 'no business with styles' and for whom good design was purely a matter of using any pictures that increased sales. Rather, the manufacturer or retailer must work out his ideas in consultation with the designer and vice versa:

> A nice picture is not enough. The artist becomes a professional designer from the advertising point of view only when he has realised the scientific aspect of his task. That is to say when he has realised that his design must embody an idea and this idea must be expressive of the goods advertised. (*Commercial Art* 1927c:193)

According to Ashley Havinden of Crawford's, usual practice during the interwar period meant that the copywriter, the artist and the account planner would agree a campaign solution before any actual work was carried out. Afterwards, it was left to the art department in the advertising agency to take responsibility for the overall appearance of the advertisement and pull it together in terms of text and image (Havinden 1935–6:15). But both the practical design solutions and the aesthetic debates of the period reveal considerable latitude in what constituted the meaning of graphic modernism, indeed of the advertisement as a designed entity. Thus Sir William Crawford opposed the idea that modernism in advertising was necessarily easy to pin down in stylistic terms since it was more a matter of using ideas that had long been known in 'a new and better way' (Crawford 1930:18).

However, one of the key attributes of the new advertising as far as Crawford was concerned was the idea of simplified form and, taking his cue from Le Corbusier, he likened the simplicity and the use of clean lines in modern graphic design to the 'dynamic virility' of aviation and automobile design, and architecture (Crawford 1930:18).[8] The idea of simplicity and 'dynamic virility' to which he was referring take on added impetus in the context of men's wear publicity. As we shall see here and in subsequent chapters, they were frequently deployed to entice the male consumer to take notice of advertisements and could be identified by several chief factors – the use of white space, austere geometric or abstracted forms, and a tendency to sans serif typeforms. On this level, Crawford's thinking was quite heavily influenced by graphic design in Germany, where he had opened a branch of his agency in Krausenstrasse, Berlin in 1926. Havinden, who had been associated with Crawford's since 1922, also admitted a debt to Germany and, in particular, the example of the Bauhaus school of design and Jan Tschichold's writing on graphic design and the new typography. After a special issue of *Commercial Art* was devoted to his ideas in July 1930, the phrase, 'the new typography' became widely accepted in British graphic design circles as a synonym for modernist practice since it considered not just typeforms but the overall sense of balance and rhythm in press and poster advertisements. This kind of practice embraced the use of an underlying grid and the construction of asymmetrical layouts, sans serif typefaces in different weights and sizes as the expression of the age, and photographs in preference to hand-drawn illustrations (Jobling and Crowley 1996:145).[9]

Certainly, several of the advertisements designed by Havinden for Simpson during the 1930s can be seen to overlap with Tschichold's formal criteria. The national press campaign for their branded DAKS trousers, for example, which began in 1932 but continued in a slightly modified stylistic vein until the 1950s (Figure 31), incorporated cropped photographs of the product laid out with sans serif titles and asymmetric blocks of copy set in Grotesque light. Promotions for several other retailers also conformed à la lettre to the new typographic deal. Thus not only did press publicity for Jaeger men's and women's wear, masterminded by

W.S. Crawford, mobilise the modernist tropes of sans serif type and photographic illustrations, but also they were one of the few fashion houses to exploit the singularly expressive geometrical Bifur alphabet in some of their advertisements as well. This faceted, jewel-like typeface, which combined solid forms and parallel lines in each letter, had been devised by A.M. Cassandre in 1930 specifically for use in advertisement headlines rather than for entire blocks or pages of copy, and consequently he likened its effect to 'the clash of cymbals' (Cassandre 1930:32).

Although the impact of graphic modernism on advertising was widely addressed in the professional and trade literature of the period, *MAN and his Clothes* was pre-eminent among them in framing these issues with respect to promotions for men's wear. On several occasions, for example, Adquisitor found much to praise in the press and poster campaigns for Austin Reed, although he/she omitted to credit such designs to Tom Purvis (Adquisitor 1931c, 1931d). Generally speaking, the identity and artistic status of the designer of any advertisement were not the overriding issues for the magazine's writers. The names of designers are rarely, if ever, cited in its editorial, as evidenced in an article in February 1937 comparing British, French and American advertisements for suits, where an archetypal campaign designed by Ashley Havinden and Max Hof for Simpson is praised for its sense of rhythm and efficient art work, while the names of the artists are overlooked. Exceptionally, Whitby Cox, who was responsible for several of its covers in 1939 and executed advertisements for C&M Sumrie Ltd, Leeds-based makers of ready-to-wear suits and coats, was cited as a 'well-known fashion illustrator' (*MAN and his Clothes* June 1939; February 1937).

What mattered more in the debates on men's wear advertising that the magazine waged were questions of originality, style and taste. In this regard, the reviews of contemporaneous campaigns that *MAN and his Clothes* contained were predominantly didactic in tone, and the magazine set itself up as an arbiter of good taste in men's wear promotions. Invoking once more advertising copy for Austin Reed in May 1928, for instance, an anonymous correspondent contested that, 'Men's shops realise, too, that advertising is often more effective if style is given the primary place and price the secondary position' (*MAN and his Clothes* 1928b:35). In the context of the magazine, style was usually equated with originality, which was another key word in its reviews of advertising. Thus in its issue for September 1930, Adquisitor (1930a) rounded up a series of recent press promotions by the likes of Barkers of Kensington, Pope & Bradley, and Moss Brothers for comparison, and scathingly concluded that men's wear was not being promoted with the same sense of élan and distinction as furniture and cars. (Coincidentally, as if to dispel this idea, the *Daily Express* (8 May 1931: 15) carried advertisements for both the Austin Motor Company and British Car Manufacturers alongside a promotion titled 'Smooth Running . . .' for Courtaulds rayon underwear, representing a man driving a motor car in his vest and shorts.) In October 1931, *Advertiser's*

Weekly likewise condemned the stylistic similarity between promotions for one brand and another – in this case collars by Austin Reed and Meakers, respectively – accusing men's wear advertisers of blatant plagiarism (The Look-Out Man 1931).

For *MAN and his Clothes*, however, plagiarism implied more than mere style raiding; equally as much it led to a levelling of taste that collapsed the distinction between cheap and expensive garments. By extension, the difference in class markets, it argued, was being sacrificed to a kind of universal advertising code that represented men like wooden figures or 'dead-as-mutton dummies', no matter what garments they were wearing or who had manufactured them (Adquisitor 1932a). Certainly, the lifeless mannequins that had already been ridiculed by advertising critics such as Herrick and Williams before the First World War (Figures 1 and 4) lingered on during the interwar period in the press campaigns for several men's wear retailers at both the top and bottom ends of the market. Thus in autumn 1930 Burberry promoted a hunting suit in *Punch* in such a way that, according to Adquisitor, it evinced 'sketches reminiscent of the *Times*, 1900!', while one year later Harry Hall of Oxford Street and Cheapside advertised some riding breeches costing 42 shillings in a similar manner (Adquisitor October 1930b).[10] Accordingly, the critic went on to lament the fact that, 'tailoring advertising has not yet achieved a class-consciousness', arguing: 'If Rolls Royce advertised like Ford the motor trade would laugh. But a firm of good-trade tailors, building bespoke suits at six to twelve guineas, can put out advertising that might pass for a chain of forty-shilling shops, and no one seems to heave a sigh' (Adquisitor 1931a:19). The bespoke tailors to which he/she was alluding in this instance were Austin Reed and Moss Brothers, but the forty-shilling tailors were not identified. As we shall see in Chapter 5 on promotions for tailors, there was something in this argument concerning the similarity in advertising campaigns for retailers from different ends of the market. But, what Adquisitor also omits from his/her argument is any consideration of the way that male consumers from Class A and B were not necessarily adverse to shopping for bargains, not to mention the fact that some advertisers bought space across a broad spectrum of media, or, as the ISBA Survey of 1936 discussed in Chapter 3 went on to reveal, that the socio-economic class of newspaper readers could not always be taken for granted.

If critics like Adquisitor could find much to quibble about men's wear advertising, what did constitute the essence of good or acceptable practice in men's wear publicity for some of the other authors who contributed to *MAN and his Clothes*? In marked contrast to Adquisitor, Cyril King dealt with the new style of promoting male fashion in more positive terms, and nor did he frame his argument in terms of class. Hence, he argued modern advertising should be based on original illustrations or photographs, and not stock or stereotyped imagery, that would be allied in turn to imaginative copy set out by 'good, legible type display' (King 1927:29). At the same time, he argued that a sense of realism was desirable for any advertising campaign, contending: 'well-drawn illustrations – depicting men that look like real individuals, in natural positions and normal surroundings – play an important part' (Marteau 1925: 436). To this end he drew attention to a recent underwear advertisement for his own company Hope Brothers as the avatar of the new style to which other retailers should aspire (Figure 7). This promotion is organised around an imaginative interplay of text and image: the sinuous wave of the headline's type conveys the sense of swaying movement of the man relaxing in the hammock, while the remaining copy is laid out geometrically as a series of expressive counter-composed triangles, the text in the central one laid out in order to pivot on the punch-line, 'Therefore – come to the point', and to carry the eye down to the name of the advertiser, 'Choose *your* Underwear at Hope Brothers'.

While King rightly admired the formal qualities and suggestive atmosphere of this advertisement, it is debatable whether it satisfies his call for 'good, legible type display' and nor does it fit the style of the new typography. The text in the two small triangles, which relays details of the quality and weight of material and the prices of the garments, is cramped in comparison to the central triangle of copy they flank. The copy, along with the various headlines, have been set in various weights of Goudy Modern, which takes it name from its American inventor Frederick Goudy, who originated the face in 1918. This Roman typeface, which relies on serifs and mimics the fluency of handwriting, is traditional in appearance and came second in popularity to Cheltenham (another Roman face, first used in the United States in 1896) in a sample of 1,152 press advertisements analysed by Harold Butler 1928.[11] As such, it predates the popularity of the modernist German sans serif typefaces that began to take over by 1930, but even when fonts like Futura, Kabel and Erbar were in ascendancy, Goudy managed to hold its own in advertising display, and was ranked fourth of all the typefaces used in press advertising in 1932 (Butler 1933:16).

With the changes in mechanical composition facilitated by the Monotype and Intertype systems since the 1890s, there was now a vast array of typeforms for designers and printers to work with. Moreover, the choice of type was no mere fancy on the part of designers but part of the expressive make-up of any advertisement as a holistic entity, and Robert Braun argued this point in somewhat poetic terms at the time: 'Nowadays almost anything can be done with type. There are beautiful "faces" which convey almost any shade of emotion . . . Type is like music in that it can be made to produce an infinite variety of beautiful harmonies. But whereas music is played from A to G, type can be played from A to Z' (April 1927:168–9). The choice of the wrong kind of typeface could, therefore, not only completely spoil the effect of the illustration in any advertising campaign but also inhibit the reading public from taking any notice of it in the first instance. In this respect, the *Daily Express* was singled out by *Modern Publicity* in 1937–8 as the newspaper that had done most to achieve an intelligent application of typography. Much like Tschichold had argued with his idea of the new typography, this did not just mean the use of typefaces per se, but how they were regarded as an integral part of the spatial and rhythmic layout of the news page – or advertisement – alongside the illustrations and photographs: 'A sense of proportion in which size, whether of text or illustration is wittily relevant to meaning, dramatic value or importance of the subject matter ensures that the paper is read' (*Modern Publicity* 1937–8: 8).

Text and Image – 'Walk the Barratt Way': a Case Study

The sense of balance conveyed by the text and image themselves, as well as the relationship of text to image, therefore, were accorded considerable importance in the debates on modern advertising during the interwar period. The articles in *MAN and his Clothes* harped on this kind of intertextuality on many occasions and, as a general rule of thumb, Adquisitor concluded that white space or breathing space in any advertisement was paramount. In 1930, for example, he/she argued, 'the less copy there is in any advertisement, the smarter it looks' (Adquisitor 1930b:23), although Adquisitor did concede that an economical use of text was probably more important in poster advertising where, 'Rarely should more than fifty words be used', in order that 'he who runs, may read' (Adquisitor 1931d:33). Similarly, Ashley Havinden took pains to emphasise the symbiosis of text and image, insisting that: 'The idea of picture and words being complementary to each other is one of the most important developments of contemporary advertising presentation' (*Havinden* 1935–6: 15). At this point in our argument, then, it is worth concentrating in particular on how promotions for Barratt shoes dealt with the nexus of word and image, and the extent to which they managed to convert reason-why into atmospheric advertising in order to compete with other shoe manufacturers.

W. Barratt & Co. originally started life in 1903 as a mail-order business, set up by two brothers, William and Richard Barratt. Their trade soon prospered, but as cheaper and faster rail transport made it easier for people in outlying districts to travel into town centres to buy their own goods, they decided to take advantage of the situation and began to open a chain of shops in 1919, which operated in conjunction with the mail-order business. Owing to the trade depression that ensued in the early years after the First World War, however, they decided to concentrate exclusively on mail-order advertising in the daily papers. Produced by printers rather than an advertising agency, this was unadventurous, reason-why publicity that sought to couple low prices with high quality workmanship. Accordingly, the advertisements for mail-order usually consisted of hand-drawn or photographic illustrations of the shoes and copy describing the quality of materials used in making them and how much they cost (in the early 1930s the average price of a pair of Barratt shoes was between 18 shillings and £1).[12]

As competition with other shoe manufacturers such as Norvic, Lotus and K Shoes began to intensify during the 1920s, however, the Barratt brothers realised the need to take on their rivals by running a more suggestive campaign, which coordinated both their mail-order and retail outlets. In 1924, for example, K Shoes had employed the advertising agency, S.H. Benson, which devised the successful 'Plus Fours for Feet' press and showcard campaign (Nicoll 1929), while photographer E.O. Hoppé had produced photographic posters for Lilley and Skinner in 1925 (Tregurtha 1926:28–9), and the London Press Exchange and the poster designer Horace Taylor had been involved with the promotion of Lotus shoes between 1928 and 1931 (*Penrose's Annual* 1928:42). As Frederick Horn (1935) argued, therefore, with so many manufacturers vying for the public's attention at this time originality in advertising became a sine qua non in the promotion of all items of clothing: 'It is essential, in this age of fierce competition, to give an advertisement such an appearance from the visual and artistic standpoint that the particular community to whom it is intended to appeal must find in it something original, a feeling of freshness and of worth' (Horn 1935:58). Taking a cue from this more inventive approach to publicity, then, Barratt enlisted the services of W.S. Crawford (f. 1914) to run their advertising campaign in 1929.

From the outset, Crawford's broke away from the stereotypical reason-why formula of the earlier advertisements for Barratt, and came up with the idea of promoting their shoes on a more personal level in the 'Walk the Barratt Way' press campaign. To this end, images of the shoes themselves were abolished from the publicity altogether. Instead, Andrew Johnson's drawings represented the figure of William Barratt as the model of moral rectitude and in the guise of an expert salesman, and copy by G.H. Saxon Mills elaborated a series of fictive conversations on foot troubles between him and different kinds of male and female clients (Figures 8 and 9). Given that imports of foreign shoes from central Europe had started to increase by 1930 (the Czech firm Bata was a key player in this respect), the fact that Barratt shoes were manufactured in Northampton was also always mentioned.

Crawford's space-buying policy was to take out large spaces in a few papers and periodicals with large-scale circulations among Class A, B and C readers, principally, the *Daily Mail*, *Punch* and the *Radio Times* (Foster 1934). The 'Walk the Barratt way' campaign became one of the most prolific to appear in the pages of the latter between 1933 and 1939 with full-page advertisements appearing nearly every fortnight between 1936 and 1938, and it was continued in *Picture Post* for the duration of the Second World War. Barratt was also one of the first companies to take advantage of two-colour advertising in the *Daily Mail*, with a half-page promotion appearing on 26 May 1933. In fact, in the 'Quarterly Analysis of Press

Advertising' in *Advertiser's Weekly*, it was consistently the footwear retailer to spend the most on publicity, on average buying monthly advertising space worth £4,236 for the period September through November 1932 (*Advertiser's Weekly* 1932d, 1933a).[13] Moreover, what set the 'Walk the Barratt way' advertisements apart from those of the closest footwear competitors – indeed from most other men's wear advertisers – was the length of the copy they used, with 300 words or so cropping up in each of the dialogues between Barratt and his customers.

While the wordiness of the Barratt campaign ran contrary to Adquisitor's admonition to advertisers to be succinct in order to maximise the amount of white space, nevertheless their advertisements are not cluttered. One of the main reasons why the campaign achieved such a harmonious impression of space and proportion was due to the fact that Crawford's always bought a Solus, or stand alone, position for each of the press promotions. This meant that either the advertisements usually occupied a whole page facing only editorial matter or, if they were half or quarter-page in size, appeared only alongside editorial rather than other advertisements. But probably more important was the way that the advertisements were organised typographically, with arresting captions set in Gill Sans inaugurating the main copy that was arranged into tidy columns of text and set in a contrasting serif typeface called Mono Plantin. Gills Sans, one of the new sans serif typefaces of the interwar period, had been designed by the British typographer Eric Gill and was put into production in 1927 by the Monotype Corporation. It was deployed principally as a display letter for titles and headlines rather than as a book type for close reading and, as in the case of the Barratt advertisements, was usually complemented by a typeface for the main copy that was deemed more legible (Harrison 1930b). As Eliot Hodgkin attested, therefore, the typographical layout of these advertisements created 'a good impression whether you read them or not' (Hodgkin 1935:145). Judging from the longevity of the campaign, however, which ran for some twenty years, the narratives related in the copy of the advertisements must have been studied on more than a superficial basis by quite a sizeable readership, and it is not simply their form that we have to take into account in any consideration of the relationship of text to image but their content as well. Consequently, with this idea in mind I have chosen a paradigmatic sample of advertisements from the campaign aimed at the male consumer that appeared in the *Radio Times* between 1933 and 1938 for a close textual analysis.

The formal structure of all the advertisements has been organised around a set of specific rhetorical devices. Thus each of them consists of an opening proposition adumbrating the narrative theme of the remaining copy that follows, an illustration of Mr Barratt (usually represented standing) in conversation with one of his male clients (represented either standing or sitting), and the slogan 'Walk the **Barratt** way', which appears at the foot of the advertisement and brings the copy to a point of closure (Figures 8 and 9). This exhortation is an interesting pun that works on two interconnected levels: hence, one of its meanings is that you must literally take a walk in the direction of your nearest Barratt store (a point which is reinforced by the printing of the company name in bold type and the tagline beneath stating the number of shops that existed at any given time); and a second meaning conveys the idea that the shoes you purchase there will make you walk better. Each of the opening propositions, meanwhile, is either a complete and self-contained statement of principle such as, 'A man is as young as his feet, Mr Barratt!' (Figure 8), or an incomplete line of thought such as, 'I'm no film star about the feet, Mr Barratt . . .' (Figure 9). And overall, the narrative structure of each of the advertisements has been orchestrated to dispel the popular mythology that foot ailments are a natural and ineluctable fact of life, and that comfort has to be achieved at the expense of appearance.

In this regard, then, many of the Barratt advertisements aimed at men connoted the sense of pleasure that they took in looking good as well as feeling healthy. In one advertisement, for example, a customer relates how the smart appearance of his new shoes led his wife to persuade him to buy a new suit to go with them: 'I can tell you . . . it's an expensive business living up to a pair of Barratts' (*Radio Times*, 4 February 1938:73). And in Figure 8, the idea that as we get older we inevitably gain weight and take less exercise because our feet let us down is countered by both Mr Barratt and his satisfied client, who concur that it is inappropriate footwear that causes us to feel unwell. Mr Barratt argues: 'People don't walk half enough. They let ill-fitting shoes gradually work havoc with their feet – until they don't *want* to walk. And then they wonder why they feel crotchety and old before their time'. Hardly surprisingly, he and his client alike advise us all that is needed to remedy this state of affairs is a pair of Barratt shoes, which the copy reminds us are not expensive, and the taking of more fresh air, which, as Mr Barratt obviously states costs nothing. By contrast, an advertisement entitled 'Mr. Barratt . . . you're my last hope' (*Radio Times*, 12 October 1934) deals with the problem of breaking-in shoes until they become a perfect fit. Mr Barratt remonstrates with this idea, pointing out to the man in the advertisement that the cause of his bad feet is 'due entirely to this preposterous idea that shoes must be broken in', and that he need have no fear of expecting the same from a pair of Barratt shoes which are, 'made to fit your foot "from the word go"'.

In expressing these points, the performative lexis of the advertisements is based on the everyday talk or spoken language of the upper- and middle-class markets for whom they were principally intended, and the copywriter Saxon Mills has liberally sprinkled the dialogue with deictic and phatic phrases such as 'Here's this gentleman' or 'Now listen, I said', which help to convey a sense of real speech enacted between actual people that unfolds in space and time. This sense of milieu is particularly underscored by the illustration in Figure 8, which represents Mr Barratt and one of his customers shaking hands on the corner of Thurloe Square,

South Kensington with the recognisable façade of the Victoria and Albert Museum looming behind them. Other prosodic features relating to the pace and rhythm of actual speech patterns are also evident; hence some words appear in italics to give emphasis: 'he seemed to put down all his health and high spirits *to me*!' and 'they don't *want* to walk' in Figure 8, and 'It's all very well for you to advertise the *comfort* of your shoes, Mr Barratt', he said, with a smile, 'but what about their *appearance*?' in Figure 9. Even the company name Barratt is printed in bold type in the slogan 'Walk the **Barratt** way'. In general terms the campaign has been conceived in terms of soft-sell tactics and, rather than quoting actual prices and delivering a series of commands such as 'You must buy Barratt shoes!', the copy relies more on direct and rhetorical questions like 'How long shall I be breaking them in?' and 'And who has ever found a pleasanter or healthier pursuit?' and persuasive statements such as 'We don't believe that a shoe *can* be smart unless first of all it's a really comfortable fit' and 'If you don't know our nearest branch write to me'.

In several of the advertisements Mr Barratt and his respective clients take turns in unravelling the narrative but, because the dialogue is fictive rather than spoken language between two parties, the copy also interpellates the reader of the advertisement as a proactive agent. Thus an opportunity is offered to him to think about the product that is being promoted and ponder heuristically on his role in the process of consumption through the use of phrases like, 'Walking actually exercises three hundred muscles in your system' and 'Some of our lines are carried in no fewer than fifty alternative fittings!' Furthermore, while the use of the personal pronoun 'I' in the dialogue deals with each of Mr Barratt's customers as individuals, it also opens up a space for collective identification between the subjects in the advertisements and the readers of them. As Barthes argued, this process of interpellation is mythological rather than actual, but it succeeds precisely because it makes us feel as if we are being singled out for attention on a personal level: 'Myth has an imperative buttonholing character . . . It is *I* whom it has come to seek. It is turned towards me, I am subjected to its intentional force, it summons me to receive its expansive ambiguity' (Barthes 1973: 134). Accordingly, the fictive 'I', who tells Mr Barratt he has feet too broad for any shoe, or that he has found a new lease of life by wearing Barratt shoes, could also be somebody like the real 'you' who reads the copy.

And yet there is a continual shift from the personal to the impersonal voice in the copy of the advertisements; thus each one is introduced with a caption that sounds as if it is inaugurating a straightforward dialogue between the two protagonists but, nonetheless, is finally structured as narration. It is Mr Barratt who tells the story and directs its outcome and in effect this tactic converts what seems to be a conversation into something more in the nature of a professional consultation. Many of his comments are what we could expect from an expert salesman – his

advice about avoiding ill-fitting shoes and the availability of shoes in fifty alternative sizes, for instance, or the way he boasts about the good leather and craftsmanship that go into their making. The general performative tone of Mr Barratt's
rhetoric is, therefore, both knowledgeable and persuasive, and he is portrayed as
a kindly – if stereotypical – paternalist. Sometimes, however, the voice of a
powerful industrial patriarch asserts itself, for instance when he adds to his
authority by invoking medical opinion – 'Walking actually exercises three hundred
muscles in your system, so a doctor friend tells me', or when he sounds patronising
and overbearing – 'Really, to hear the way some people talk, you'd think this
question of shoe-buying was one of the most difficult problems on earth'. In fact,
in one of the advertisements in the series Barratt actually assumes the role of
physician as his clients exclaim, 'We ought to call you Doctor Barratt!', after he
has informed them that 80 per cent of women and 20 per cent of men suffer from
foot trouble because of ill-fitting shoes (*Radio Times*, 3 December 1937:77).

In both its form and content, the 'Walk the Barratt Way' campaign is certainly
a masterful realisation of the copywriter Saxon Mills' maxim that, 'The full use of
the suggestion idea demands a specialised understanding of the three aspects of an
advertisement – Illustration, Typography, and Copy' (Mills 1923:298). But it was
only one of several inventive approaches that were taken in dealing with the
interdependence of text and image, and by no means the most adventurous. Some
press advertisements, therefore, deviated from a suggestive association between
the illustration and copy, and relied instead on more disjunctive effects to grab the
reader's attention. A striking example of this kind of promotion was the advertisement for K&P Shirts, which appeared in *MAN and his Clothes* in October 1933.

This consisted of a page of copy, on top of which was pasted a chromolithographic illustration by the renowned American-born poster designer Edward
McKnight Kauffer (Figure 10). His avant-garde drawing represents the silhouette
of a hand, whose finger seems to be pointing to the profile of a man's head wearing
a felt hat superimposed over it but, in effect, is guiding the spectator's eye to the
caption 'Read the announcement underneath'. Set in Gill Sans, this was left visible
from the top of the page of copy, but rather than finding an advertisement for
gloves or hats underneath, as the illustration might lead us to believe, we encounter
a promotion (also set in various weights and sizes of Gill Sans) by Knight and
Petch for their K&P Shirt. Without disclosing how much it cost, the copy boasts
that this brand was the dearest of any ready-to-wear shirt on the market, and it
amplifies the message of two other campaigns for the K&P Shirt, which had
appeared in *Punch* on 29 March and 24 May 1933 respectively. These had both
included the price of the shirt (with two collars, it cost 18s 6d),[14] and extolled the
quality of the garment, which was made from only the best materials, was tailored
in cut, and came in three fittings to a size. Although they sought to emphasise the
exclusivity of the brand, however, these two advertisements did so in quite a

straightforward manner: one including a picture of a smiling man, wearing the shirt and putting on a tie; the other with an illustration of a salesman showing the garment to an inquisitive customer, which was drawn by Andrew Johnson, the designer involved in Barratt's advertising.

By contrast, the promotion that had appeared in *MAN and his Clothes* suggested prestige of a higher level. McKnight Kauffer, who was on the original committee of the Society of Poster Artists (f. 1926), had worked for Crawford's advertising agency between 1927 and 1929 and had already garnered a reputation as one of the most brilliant and influential poster designers of his generation, producing work of outstanding symbolic vision for companies such as the London Underground and Shell. At the opening of the Memorial Exhibition held in the year he died, T.S. Eliot summed up his unique artistic contribution to advertising stating: 'He did something for modern art with the public, as well as doing something for the public with modern art' (A. Havinden 1956). The design he executed to promote K&P shirts, one of a handful he did specifically for men's wear retailers including Austin Reed (1931), would also have been regarded in this light and have given added cachet to a brand that was already being promoted for 'those in the know' at a time when the Depression had forced many advertisers into more hard-sell tactics.[15] While Arnold Jackson (1928) had warned advertisers, therefore, that 'Bizarre illustration should be handled gingerly' so as not to alienate prospective consumers, the copywriter W.D.H. McCullough proceeded to take the opposite tack, arguing: 'There has been a stampede into the cheap market . . . A glamour behind an article makes it more desirable' (McCullough 1936: 39). And probably nowhere is this association with glamour and desire, and the tension between target audiences that these authors refer to more in evidence than in the poster and press publicity for tailors such as Austin Reed, Simpson and The Fifty Shilling Tailors, which are the subject of the following chapter.

Notes

1. The 2001 equivalent is £47.66. This figure and others for 2001 cited in subsequent footnotes are from McCusker (2003).
2. The 2001 equivalent is £228,803.95.
3. For a full assessment of the Men's Dress Reform Party see Burman (1995) and Bourke (1996).
4. See Martin (1992, 1996), Boyce (2000) and Turbin (2002) on Leyendecker and his representation of masculine identities in advertising.

5. Respective 2001 figures are £37.47, £374.69 and £1,124.07.
6. The 2001 figure is £171.60.
7. See *Commercial Art*, April 1923, p. 109, and the following issues of *Advertiser's Weekly*: 6 February 1925, p. 221, 30 March 1928, p. 580 and 14 September 1928, p. 407.
8. Crawford's article for *Modern Publicity* (1930), 'What Gives our Dreams their Daring is that they Can be Realised' was actually a quotation by Le Corbusier. In it he goes on to write about advertising, the aeroplane, the motor-car and architecture that:

> They are the expressions of a new age, an age in which our eyes and ears are filled with sights and sounds to which humanity is yet but little accustomed – an age in which young and adventurous and vigorous minds are challenging long accumulated traditions . . . But it is to advertising I think that the new spirit is especially vital.

(Le Corbusier 1978: 18) The new spirit ('L'Esprit Nouveau') was at the heart of Le Corbusier's writing on architecture and design, as were objects of engineering such as cars and aeroplanes.
9. Tschichold's (1995) seminal book, *Die neue Typographie* (*The New Typography*) was first published in Berlin in 1928. Throughout, he was at pains to stress function that was not a matter of puritanism or utilitarianism, but the rational utilisation of the elements available to the graphic designer.
10. The 2001 equivalent is £100.43.
11. Butler consulted one copy of each of the following newspapers and magazines in his survey (the number of ads is in parentheses): *Daily Mail* (101), *Daily Express* (52), *Daily Chronicle* (34), *Daily News and Westminster Gazette* (39), *The Times* (29), *Daily Telegraph* (16), *Morning Post* (17), *Daily Sketch* (42), *Daily Mirror* (42), *The Star* (20), *Evening Standard* (33), *Punch* (102), *Home Chat* (86), *London Opinion* (34), *Bystander* (174) and *Good Housekeeping* (331).
12. The 2001 equivalents of £1 for 1930 and 1935 are £47.82 and £53.08.
13. The 2001 equivalent is £242,303.38.
14. The 2001 equivalent is £50.96.
15. In the catalogue *EMcKK* of work by McKnight Kauffer exhibited at the Lund Humphries & Co. Ltd Gallery, 12 Bedford Square, London between 13 March and 3 April 1935, no mention is made of the design for K&P Shirts. Several items are simply listed as 'Project for a new poster' (8, 19, 20 and 21) or 'Original design for a poster' (13), but the K&P chromolithograph appeared in the form of a press advertisement. Neither is the work mentioned in the posthumous exhibition of 1955, and nor does Haworth-Booth (1979) include it in the checklist of works by the artist.

Figure 1. Pettigrew & Stephens Ltd, Glasgow, press advertisement for flannel lounge suit, 1906 (private collection).

Figure 2. Mather & Crowther, self-promotion, 'Design is just a detail', August 1909 (private collection).

Figure 3. Catesby & Sons, 'The Road to Summer Pleasure', press advertisement, June 1904 (private collection).

Figure 4. H.J. Searle, 'Dress Smartly', advertisement in the *Morning Leader*, 4 November 1902 (private collection).

Figure 5. Pope & Bradley, 'Le Style c'est l'Homme', poster, 60 × 40 ins., 1912, reproduced in *Advertising World*, January 1913 (courtesy of British Library).

Figure 6. Fougasse, 'I mustn't forget Austin Reed's', cartoon advertisement displayed in London Underground trains, *c.* 1937 (courtesy of Austin Reed).

Figure 7. 'Enjoy a place in the sun in cool comfort', press advertisement for underwear at Hope Brothers, 1927 (private collection).

'A man is as young as his feet, Mr Barratt!'

It quite did me good to meet this customer of mine in the street the other day. There he was, striding along like a youth of eighteen (though I happen to know that he's turned the fifty mark). And the funny thing was that he seemed to put down all his health and high spirits *to me*!

'Hope you're as well as I am, Mr. Barratt,' he said, shaking hands. 'Do you remember when I first came to you for a pair of shoes?'

'I do,' I replied. 'About two years ago. I happened to be in the shop at that time.'

'Remember what I was like then? Full of aches and pains, getting too fat, liverish—everything was wrong with me that could be. And all because my feet had let me down. But I walk miles now—thanks to Barratts. And look at the difference in me! A man is as young as his feet, Mr. Barratt,' he added with a cheery laugh.

'And a jolly good expression,' I agreed.

So it is! People don't walk half enough. They let ill-fitting shoes gradually work havoc with their feet—

until they don't *want* to walk. And then they wonder why they feel crotchety and old before their time.

Walk more! I'd like to see that put up on every hoarding. After all, Barratt shoes are not expensive, and fresh air's free! And who has ever found a pleasanter or healthier pursuit? Walking actually exercises three hundred muscles in your system, so a doctor friend tells me. And it not only keeps

you fit, but it keeps that middle-age spread at bay.

But you won't walk, unless your feet are happy. And how are you to ensure that? I'll let you guess! I'll let this be a Barratt advertisement with nothing in it about Barratt shoes!

(If you don't know your nearest Barratt branch a line to me at Footshape Works, Northampton, will bring you the address and a catalogue.)

Walk the **Barratt** way

Barratts, Northampton—and one hundred and thirty-two branches

Figure 8. Walk the **Barratt** Way, 'A man is as young as his feet, Mr Barratt!', full-page press advertisement, *Radio Times*, 20 December 1935 (private collection).

Figure 9. Walk the **Barratt** Way, 'I'm no film star about the feet, Mr Barratt . . .', full-page press advertisement, *Radio Times*, 3 November 1933 (private collection).

Figure 10. Edward McKnight Kauffer, chromolithographic illustration to promote K&P Shirts, *MAN and his Clothes*, October 1933 (private collection).

Figure 11. Grainger Johnson, poster for Hector Powe, *The Poster*, September 1923 (private collection).

Figure 12. 'The Age of Specialisation', cartoon, *Punch*, 9 August 1911 (private collection).

Figure 13. Chamois Gloves, window display for Austin Reed, Regent Street, spring 1936 (courtesy of Austin Reed).

Figure 14. 'The New Tailoring – You Choose Clothes Instead of Cloth', illustration by Tom Purvis, *Punch*, 19 January 1927 (private collection).

You are *you* and should dress as you — taking care to find the clothes that fit your personality — as well as your figure. The New Tailoring enables you to make this important discovery : you can put on suit after suit before a mirror, trying this or that cloth and cut—choosing always clothes, not cloth. • *We make some lounge suits costing more than six guineas and some costing less.*

● **151 FITTINGS IN THE NEW TAILORING**

Austin Reed
OF REGENT STREET

ELEVEN 'NEW TAILORING' CENTRES
West End : 103-113 Regent Street, W.1. 24 Coventry Street, W.1. City : 13 Fenchurch Street, E.C.3
Glasgow, Birmingham, Liverpool, Manchester, Sheffield, Leeds, Bristol, Belfast

AUSTIN REED LTD. LONDON
P. 3744

Figure 15. '151 Fittings in the New Tailoring', advertisement with illustration by Tom Purvis, *Punch*, 18 April 1934 (private collection).

Figure 16. Tom Purvis, 'Austin Reed's of Regent Street, Evening Clothes', poster displayed on hoarding at Victoria Station, June 1931 (courtesy of Austin Reed).

Figure 17. Advertisement for Austin Reed two-guinea raincoat, illustration by Tom Purvis, *Radio Times*, 23 September 1932 (private collection).

Figure 18. Poster advertisement for Austin Reed's Summit Shirts by Tom Purvis, 1932, displayed on London Underground (courtesy of Austin Reed).

Figure 19. Tom Purvis, poster for Austin Reed's, 1932 (courtesy of Austin Reed).

Figure 20. Tom Purvis, three-stage card underground advertisement for Austin Reed two-guinea raincoat, autumn 1936 (courtesy of Austin Reed).

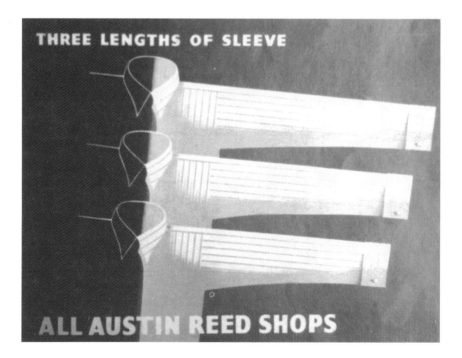

Figure 21. Eckersley-Lombers, poster advertisement for Austin Reed Summit Shirt, late 1930s (courtesy of Austin Reed).

Figure 22. 'The New Tailoring', photographic advertisement, *Punch*, 18 October 1933 (private collection).

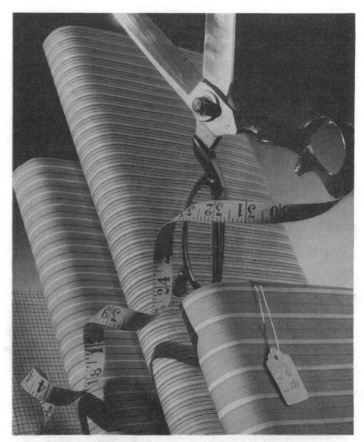

SHIRTS TO MEASURE · There is a great satisfaction in being individual in the matter of shirts and in having them specially made in a pattern and of a material of your own choosing. They can then be cut to your own measure and to include those small personal preferences which make for greater comfort and ease. Nor need this be expensive, for we have a number of patterns, woven for no one but us, in which shirts can be made to measure for as little as 12/6 — or with two collars to match 15/6 May we send these and other patterns to you ?

AUSTIN REED OF REGENT STREET

Twelve City and West End Shops ● Glasgow, Birmingham, Liverpool, Manchester, Sheffield, Leeds, Bristol, Belfast

AUSTIN REED LTD. LONDON   P.463

Figure 23. 'Shirts to Measure', colour photographic advertisement for Austin Reed, *Punch*, 21 June 1933 (private collection).

**Grand weather for an
Austin Reed
2-guinea Raincoat**

Fully proofed gabardine. Proofed gabardine lining,
plain or glencheck pattern. Generously cut. Ample
room. Two styles — with or without belt. Chest
sizes 32' to 50' — five lengths in the principal sizes.

Patterns free on request. When ordering by post, send your height and
chest measurement, taken over your waistcoat, to Austin Reed Ltd.,
103 Regent Street, London, W.1, or any of the addresses below :

AUSTIN REED
OF REGENT STREET

GLASGOW—98 Gordon Street   BELFAST—33 Donegall Place
BIRMINGHAM—41 New Street   BRISTOL—3 Clare Street
COVENTRY & 2 Bond Street   NORWICH—18 London Street
SHEFFIELD—79 Fargate   OXFORD—58 Cornmarket Street
LIVERPOOL—St. George's   MANCHESTER—St. Ann's
Crescent   Square

Figure 24. Advertisement for Austin Reed two-guinea raincoat with scraperboard hatching by Fran Sutton, *Radio Times*, 22 November 1935 (private collection).

Figure 25. Fran Sutton, scraperboard advertisement for Tauttex trouser linings, *MAN and his Clothes*, 1938 (private collection).

Figure 26. 'Tea Freshly Made for Each Customer', advertisement for Rego, *Evening News*, 13 December 1935 (courtesy of British Library).

Figure 27. Advertisement for 'Rational Tailoring', The Fifty Shilling Tailors, *Radio Times*, 6 April 1934 (private collection).

R A T I O N A L   T A I L O R I N G

50/-
NO EXTRAS

Hello! Where did you buy your smart coat?

HE: Glad you like it.

SHE: Very gay! And *it* suits you! But I can't see why you wanted to spend all that money on a Sports coat.

HE: Precisely—that's what I thought!

SHE: Well, then . . . . . .

HE:—why didn't I stick to the Fifty Shilling Tailors? The answer, dear lady, is that I *did!* Twenty-seven and six for the coat, sixteen and six

for the trousers. Total: forty-four shillings. Result: about five pounds less than you expected.

SHE: Alan, I don't believe it !

HE: That's fine. I hope everybody else thinks the same.

SHE: But if it really is true, they must have risen right above themselves this year.

HE: They have ! They've entered into the spirit of the whole thing : their sports gear this season is the

real thing. You know—just the right touch of swagger without being conspicuous-looking—really interesting cloths, and plenty of them, and everything common sense and comfortable in the way they're made.

SHE: And after all that, I think we'd better get into our coach — unless you're too proud now to be seen with poor me, so dowdy !

HE: Fathead !

THE FIFTY SHILLING TAILORS

For Patterns write to :— 110-111 STRAND, W.C.2.   •   42-4 OLDHAM ST., MANCHESTER

84-5 HIGH ST., BIRMINGHAM • 21-7 ARGYLE ST., GLASGOW • 1-3 ROYAL AVENUE, BELFAST

Proprietors : Prices Tailors Ltd.

Figure 28. Advertisement for 'Rational Tailoring', The Fifty Shilling Tailors, *Radio Times*, 15 May 1936 (private collection).

Figure 29. Advertisement for 'Rational Tailoring', The Fifty Shilling Tailors, *Radio Times*, 15 November 1935 (private collection).

Figure 30. Press advertisement for Simpson Piccadilly, 1936, with illustration by Max Hof, logotype and tagline by Ashley Havinden (courtesy of DAKS).

Figure 31. 'You can always tell . . .', advertisement for DAKS flannel trousers, *The Times*, 14 July 1954 (courtesy of DAKS).

Figure 32. Advertisement for The Fifty Shilling Tailors, CC 41 Utility, *Picture Post*, 20 June 1942 (private collection).

Figure 33. 'Let us to the task to the battle and the toil', advertisement for Meridian, *Picture Post* 16 March 1940 (private collection).

Figure 34. Walk the **Barratt** way, 'You've cut down my coal bills, Mr Barratt!', *Picture Post*, 23 December 1939 (private collection).

Figure 35. Morley, Theta Underwear, advertisement in the *Radio Times*, 18 October 1935 (private collection).

Figure 36. 'Celanese', advertisement in the *Daily Mail*, 22 June 1927 (courtesy of British Library).

Figure 37. Courtaulds, 'Confidential – To Wives and Mothers', advertisement in the *Radio Times* 19 March 1937 (private collection).

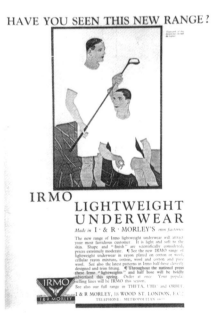

Figure 38. Irmo, 'Have You Seen This New Range?', advertisement with illustration by Tony Castle, *MAN and his Clothes*, March 1930 (private collection).

Figure 39. Meridian, 'The Happy Medium', advertisement in the *Daily Express*, 2 October 1931 (courtesy of British Library).

Figure 40. Chilprufe, advertisement with illustration by Coller, *MAN and his Clothes*, October 1927 (private collection).

–5–

'Dynamic Virility'

Masculine Identities in Advertising for Tailors During the Interwar Period

Once the fashion is established amongst the leisured classes the middle classes will follow under the direction of the small bespoke tailors and the ready-to-wear manufacturers.

Duncan Keith Shaw, *Advertiser's Weekly*, 17 March 1932

Suits are obviously not really inexpressive; they express classical *modernity*, in material design, in politics and in sexuality.

Anne Hollander, *Sex and Suits: The Evolution of Modern Dress*, 1994

As we saw in Chapter 3, the data furnished by 'The Space Market' and 'Quarterly Analysis of Press Advertising', which appeared in *Advertiser's Weekly* between 1932 and 1935, revealed that publicity for tailors constituted one of the largest categories of men's wear promotion in the interwar period. Although most tailors produced and sold quite a wide range of garments such as overcoats, separates and shirts, the two- or three-piece suit was the regular mainstay of such retailers and was available in a variety of styles. By 1930, for instance, both single- and double-breasted jackets were in circulation and could be varied by details like the type of cloth, number of buttons, the shape of shoulders and lapels, and long or short tails (Figures 15 and 28). The most popular and common version of the double-breasted suit, available in plain, plaid or striped wool, came with six buttons, square shoulders and peaked broad lapels, worn with wide, pleat-fronted trousers (either with or without cuffs), all of which were intended to accentuate an athletic V-shaped silhouette (Chenoune 1993: 175–8). From its early manifestation as the bespoke sober garb of the industrial middle classes in the mid-nineteenth century (Kuchta 2002), therefore, the suit had become the ubiquitous form of attire for both work and leisure among men of all classes by the early twentieth century. Consequently Katrina Honeyman has argued that, during the 1920s and 1930s, 'the suit reached a peak of popularity among all social groups at this time and loosened its main association with the world of work' (Honeyman 2002:426).

The changing patterns in the manufacture of the suit, now available ready-to-wear as well as bespoke, were clearly instrumental to this process of social and economic evolution. This is not to argue, however, that class and status no longer mattered in the production and consumption of suits. Writing in *Advertiser's Weekly*, for instance, Leslie Lewis insisted that quality did not – or should not – come cheap: 'There are certain trades in which it is possible to cater both for the general public, combining quality with moderation in price, and for the moneyed class, for whom quality is the one and only consideration. Tailoring is one of many businesses that must appeal to *one* of these classes' (Lewis 1926:201). Yet, as we have also seen, the balance between the quality and quantity of clothing on sale, or the relationship between the class of the customer and the cost of his garment(s), were not necessarily so straightforward. Hence, in this chapter I want to explore in more depth how the visual and verbal codes of the press and poster advertising for retailers like Austin Reed, Simpson, Hector Powe, Rego, and The Fifty Shilling Tailors could either maintain distinctions of class, status and masculine identities or traduce them. Furthermore, the form and style of the campaigns that were devised for these companies lead us to consider the extent to which they did or did not conform to the tenets of modernism that were also introduced in Chapter 4.

The New Tailoring: from Hector Powe to Austin Reed

The first branch of the bespoke outfitter Hector Powe was opened in 1910 in Bishopsgate Street, the City of London, while by 1925 the firm owned six shops in the vicinity and one in Victoria Street, Westminster, as well as employing a special 'Visiting Tailor' to tour the provinces (Marteau 1925).[1] Born in 1890, Hector Powe was himself the son of a tailor and, after training with Fendick and Co. of the Strand, in 1908 he became the manager of Powe and Hancock, a men's outfitters that was co-owned by his father. Aged 20, he began to run the first of his own shops in order 'to give City customers West-end styles at City prices', which he promoted in the London *Evening News* in 1911 (*MAN and his Clothes*, January 1939: 24–6). During the 1920s, for instance, suits could be bought from Hector Powe for anything in the region of four and eight guineas (*Evening News*, 30 October 1923:7), prices that are comparable to those charged by Austin Reed.[2]

From the outset Powe had prided himself on the 'HP Cut', a modus operandi rather than a style of clothing that ensured the perfect fit of any garment as a result of the amount of time and care he could devote to each of his customers individually. This attention to customer service and styling was taken to a new pitch with the concept of 'New Tailoring' that was introduced with the opening of the Cheapside branch in 1923. Designed to function more like a Service Salon rather than a shop, as an advertisement in the *Evening News* on 23 October 1923 reveals, at 54

Cheapside every client was treated on an individual basis in a panelled booth with a divan, where newspapers and cigarettes would be dispensed to him while a page brought a selection of cloths on a noiseless trolley and an expert tailor measured him for a faultless fit. Although he was resistant to advertising during the early years of trading, Powe also came to realise that he would need to resort to publicity in order to consolidate his existing client base and to promote the Service Salon idea. Initially, he employed Stephen's Advertising Service and Watson's Advertising Agency to take charge of the company's press and poster campaigns respectively, but from 1927 until 1932 advertising for Hector Powe was coordinated by A.C.F. Woods (*MAN and his Clothes*, January 1939: 24–6).

Collaborating closely with Powe, Stephens's initial response was a series of tasteful campaigns that ran in illustrated papers and magazines like the *Pall Mall Gazette* and *Punch* and that emphasised the 'something extra' which customers would encounter in having themselves fitted for any garment at Hector Powe. At the same time, punning the surname Powe, the agency coined the idea of 'The Pow-Wow' as the name of a house organ that was edited by Powe and issued on a sporadic basis to existing clients from 1923 onwards (by 1939, he had 100,000 customers on his books). Extracts from Powe's 'Pow-Wows' also formed the basis of a more humorous and light-hearted press campaign with cartoons by Aubrey Hammond that featured as half-columns in the London dailies the *Evening Standard* and *Evening News* for almost ten years. In common with the house journal, the advertisements were conceived as a humorous narrative interface between the manufacturer and his clientele: 'The "Pow Wow" is thus my social link with a man to whom I would offer information of mutual advantage without insulting his intelligence by asking him to believe that I am anything but a well-meaning sort of fellow like himself' (Powe 1929:204). At all costs, then, Powe wanted to eschew a patronising tone in his advertising, and he was certainly against the kind of rhetoric that would either bemuse or confuse his clientele: 'I cannot believe that my potential customer is either a dude or professor of psychology' (ibid.: 203). Consequently, with these guidelines in mind, the 'Pow-Wow' advertising campaign was conceived as a subtle blend of entertainment and edification.

In 'The Man Who Didn't Know How to Dress' (*Evening News*, 9 October 1923), the idea that clothing by Hector Powe can rescue even the most sartorially challenged individual is conveyed entirely in pictorial terms as a vertical cartoon strip, but in most other advertisements meaning was connoted in text and image. The copy of another advertisement in the *Evening News* on 20 November 1923, for instance, takes Powe's initials 'H.P.' to stand for 'Have Pity' in order to elaborate a chatty message concerning the exigencies imposed on tailors during the Christmas rush, while the cartoon of an exhausted tailor being carried away on a stretcher, compounds the idea that, like his clients, he is only human. If the comments of an anonymous layman writing in *MAN and his Clothes* in May 1938 are anything to go by, then Powe had indeed struck exactly the right chord with this type of humorous homosocial appeal since, he argued, it was directed at male consumers without making them feel that, 'if we wear a particular make of suit or shirt or trousers we will be promptly rewarded with promotion in our job, with a beautiful wife, with social success, and with a good dollop of health, wealth and happiness thrown in' (ibid.: 33).

In addition to press and brochure publicity, the Watson Advertising Agency promoted the 'HP Cut' through colour poster advertising on the London Underground. In 1923 a poster designed by Grainger Johnson (Figure 11) was singled out for praise by the *Advertiser's Weekly* correspondent 'Pelican', who commented that, 'Here is a real live, clean open-air man – a rattling good fellow and an obvious sportsman. At once the thought comes to mind: "I should like to appear like that to my friends. I'll get a suit from where he has his clothes made"' ('Pelican' 1923:25). While the male figure in the poster is athletic in build, it isn't entirely clear why 'Pelican' regarded him as an 'obvious sportsman'; he is represented smoking and fully attired in a Powe tailored suit, complete with fedora, cane and kid gloves. Rather than participating in any particular sports activity, then, the character appears effortlessly sporting (much as Hollywood stars like Gary Cooper were to look in the 1930s dressed in their plaid sports jackets and slacks), his athletic prowess connoted by the fit of his suit and the raising of his arms as if in a rowing position, both of which show off his classically v-shaped torso.

As such, Johnson's design transcended the somewhat banal association drawn between sport and men's wear that had been common since the early twentieth century. John Herrick's opposition to this kind of atmospheric advertising by the 'Don' tailors has already been cited in Chapter 1 (Herrick 1913: 42), but he was not alone in voicing such an opinion. In 1911, for example, *Advertising World* (1911d: 281–2) had commented, 'It is safe to say that there is not a sportsman of any description who has not at times been amused or disgusted, according to his habit of mind, with advertisement illustrations supposed specially to appeal to him'; similarly *Punch* had satirised this tendency in its cartoon 'The Age of Specialisation' on 9 August 1911 (Figure 12). But stylistically, Johnson's depiction of a youthful and masculine individual, heroically occupying his own ground, also broke the mould of the tailor's dummy that had proliferated in many men's wear promotions of the period. And, in particular, it adumbrated the debonair and *soigné* male bodies that were to become the promotional stock-in-trade after 1925 for one its main competitors in tailoring – Austin Reed (Figures 14–16).

The first branch of Austin Reed was opened at 167 Fenchurch Street on 7 July 1900 to consolidate the millinery and hosiery business that William Bilkey Reed had been running in Broad Street, Reading since 1881. From the start, as we have seen, his son Austin Reed's express intention was to make an appeal to 'young men of taste and discrimination; men with a new outlook on life, and men to whom new ideas appealed strongly' (Ritchie 1990: 19), and he reoriented the shop pre-eminently to market shirts and collars to middle-class males working in the city. Exploiting the retail experience he had accrued between 1893 and 1896 in the United States, where he had been working for Wanamaker's department store in Philadelphia among others, Reed began to promote his goods in enticing shop window displays, with shirts and ties clearly mounted on stands along with their price tags. In effect, shop windows were regarded as an initial form of publicity for the company, organised from 1907 by 'Willie' Williams and Robert Shorter:

> With a constantly crowded pavement we take the fullest advantage of the advertising facilities offered by our windows, which are made as bright as we know how, fresh dressing in one or the other going on every day, and we use only the most attractive showcards and price-tickets we can devise, all of which are hand written or printed by our own men on our own premises. (*Advertising World* 1909b: 162)

By 1902, the annual turnover of the first Austin Reed store was almost £7,000 and in the same year the firm started to advertise in earnest, publicising their central product, the Stanaust shirt, which was available in three different sleeve lengths, in *Punch* and the *Daily Mail*. Eventually the Stanaust brand was supplanted by the Summit shirt and collar, which formed the staple of Austin Reed publicity right up until the First World War, by which time the company owned three shops in the City of London at Fenchurch Street, St Mary Axe and Cheapside, another in Regent Street, and branches in Birmingham and Manchester.

Within the space of a decade, press publicity for Austin Reed had been singled out for the highest praise in terms of its aesthetic appeal and social cachet. In 1909, for instance, *Advertising World* (1909b: 168) argued that, 'Mr. Reed's advertising . . . is uniformly of the best quality – in ideas and in appearance – and is among the "livest", most attractive and thoroughly done advertising we have seen issued by any retailer', while the following year, *Printer's Ink* (1910: 13) opined that: 'There is an individuality, a style running through all that not only leaves a pleasing impression, but stamps the producer as a man of undeniably good taste'. But Reed did not settle on press advertising only and under the aegis of its advertising manager, Percy Epps, publicity for the company appeared in many different forms including circulars, brochures and pamphlets, posters, and, from 1907, cards on London underground trains. The latter, designed and printed by Charles Jones and Co. of Chancery Lane, were posted on the Central, City and Great Northern lines, since they all had termini close to Austin Reed shops in the City of London, and were changed on a monthly basis.

In common with their press advertisements, the underground cards usually consisted of a head and shoulders portrait of a man wearing a particular shape of Summit Collar and a block of copy set in bold Morland type describing the functional qualities of the collar in question ('This is the approved shape for dress wear', for example) along with its price. The Summit collar came in twenty-five distinct shapes and quarter-inch sizes to suit different activities and functions, and the advertising campaigns devised by Higham's Advertising Agency for each model sought, therefore, to emphasise its unique qualities. The Summit 40 was publicised as the most versatile model, since it was available in five different depths, ranging from one and three-quarter inches to two and three-quarter inches, as well as a number of different quarter-inch neck sizes, while in contrast, the Summit 60, with a rounded collar design, was advertised as offering ease of movement when playing golf.

The initial phase of press and poster publicity for Austin Reed, which ran roughly until 1921, was mostly orchestrated, therefore, around the company's keynote brand product and was effectively concerned with reason-why advertising and the need to 'select the class from the mass' (Currington 1921:37). After the First World War, while the idea of class was still important, there was also a discernible shift of emphasis toward atmosphere and quality in the company's promotional policy. Shop windows were sparsely arranged and colour-coded to foreground a limited range of specially selected lines – sometimes only £50 worth of goods would be put on display – while press advertising would also sometimes promote the same garments on show in the store's window. A typical example of this kind of tie-in was a window display for chamois leather gloves in the flagship Regent Street store during spring 1936 that overlapped with a press advertising campaign in the *Evening Standard*, which carried an illustration and banner based on the poster design by Austin Cooper included in the window setting (Figure 13).

Generally, Austin Reed's press advertising during the 1920s and 1930s was broadened both in terms of the number of products it promoted and the form and content of the advertisements themselves. Stylistically, this meant that advertisements would feature plenty of white space and be organised economically around a particular slogan or phrase with a complementary illustration of a man in action. In an advertisement which ran in *Punch*, the *Evening Standard* and *The Times* during the spring of 1921, for instance, a number of garments for use in sport, ranging from golf jackets to tennis shirts, were rounded up under the well-turned line 'Breeze-Blown Skies Call Out of Doors' and a picture of a man walking his dog on the beach. It was this new style of advertising that was eventually espoused for the 'New Tailoring' campaign, which was initiated in 1925 by W.D.H. McCullough, who had taken over from Epps as the company's advertising manager. In 1932 McCullough went on to work as a copywriter for the advertising agency F.C. Pritchard Wood and Partners, which had been established in 1923 by Fleetwood Pritchard and Sinclair Wood, but he also took the Austin Reed account with him (*Advertiser's Weekly*, 10 March 1932: 368). In 1938 Pritchard and Wood went on to open a creative centre in Savile Row with an exhibition space demonstrating how their campaigns were evolved, which was used by their own employees and prospective clients alike (*Advertiser's Weekly*, 15 September 1938: 348).[3]

The 'New Tailoring' was the longest running of the Austin Reed advertising campaigns, continuing for a period of roughly twelve years until 1937, and it overlapped with a period of considerable expansion in the company's activities. By 1925, following a dip in its fortunes during the post-war trade recession, profits had begun to recover and Summit House, a new head office designed by Percy West-wood, was built at Red Lion Square, Holborn. One year later, the company's flagship store in Regent Street was opened on 25 October and promoted by a major press campaign. The addition of the new shop in Regent Street meant that by 1926 there were twelve branches of Austin Reed in London, and one each in Birming-ham, Manchester, Preston, Bristol, Leeds, Liverpool and Sheffield. At the same time, the expansion in the number of stores was matched by an exponential rise in Austin Reed's press advertising expenses account; for the year ended 20 February 1921, just over £23,000 had been spent on promoting all of its stores, whereas for the year ended 20 February 1926, the total had risen more than twofold to almost £57,000.[4] In addition to such sums, however, it has to be borne in mind that Austin Reed were heavily involved with poster promotions as well. During the late 1920s, Cyril Sheldon estimated that the average sixteen-sheet poster campaign would have cost £2,000 to produce and £16,000 to display nationally for a period of three months (Sheldon 1927:5). Given that Austin Reed clothing was usually promoted on a seasonal basis, the company must have also allocated at least four times this amount to their annual poster campaign budget during the interwar period.

Publicity during the interwar years was not just marked by an increase in advertising expenditure but also a more adventurous spirit that was decidedly design-led. It embraced the 'New Tailoring', 'Men about Regent Street' and 'It's Just a part Of The Austin Reed Service' press and poster campaigns, and involved a wide array of artistic talent such as Austin Cooper, Eckersley-Lombers, Fougasse, Robb, Theyre Lee-Elliott, Fran Sutton and Tom Purvis. As McCullough argued: 'it is the Austin Reed policy only to use the best obtainable. The question to put to the artist is, how good and how effective, not how cheap and how quick' (McCullough 1929: 58).

It is Purvis who was the most prolific and celebrated designer of press and poster advertisements for Austin Reed. He had studied painting and figure drawing at Camberwell School of Art in the early twentieth century, and after matriculating found employment with the advertising agency Mather and Crowther, with whom he remained associated as late as 1938. By the early 1920s he had already garnered a reputation as one of the most inventive commercial artists of his generation with the poster work he executed for the London Midland and Scottish Railway, and the press advertisements for Aquascutum. In 1932 he became a member of the com-mittee of the British Society of Poster Designers, which had been founded in 1926, and in 1936 he was the first ever commercial artist to be awarded the title of Royal Designer for Industry by the Royal Society of Arts. John Hewitt, in what still remains the most perceptive and balanced account of Purvis's career as a commercial artist, contends that he does not seem to have begun working for Austin Reed until the early part of 1926 (Hewitt 1996:11). However, judging from the style of some campaigns executed before this time, there is some evidence to suggest that Purvis could have been associated with Austin Reed press advertising during the immediate post-war period (if only on an intermittent basis). For instance, the charcoal illustration in a promotion for the Shape 40 Summit Collar that appeared in *Punch* on 4 February 1920, although unsigned, bears the stylistic hallmarks of his later work in its chiaroscuro effects and depiction of a classically proportioned and strong-jawed masculine head in profile (Figures 14–16). At any rate, what is clear is that Purvis carried out well over five hundred different designs for various Austin Reed poster and press campaigns between 1925 and 1941.

The 'New Tailoring' advertisements were devised to promote the scheme for quasi-bespoke garments that had been launched in 1925 and was directed by Captain C.H. Mills. Capitalising on the way that Summit shirts and collars had been marketed in any number of shapes and sizes in order to cater for different lifestyles, Mills also wanted to offer Austin Reed customers the choice of the best cloths and latest styles for tailored clothing in 150 different fittings. The idea of semi-ready clothing had originated in Canada in 1899 and was a short cut to made-to-measure tailoring insofar as clothes were made up in advance and the nearest fit was then customised to match the individual's requirements. This greatly expedited the production of the finished garment, but initially met with resistance in Britain where bespoke tailoring was still held an unassailable ideal. In 1910, however, Marcus Heber Smith had predicted that if the idea were to take hold, it would do so by appealing mostly to men from Class B, and this is precisely the market that the 'New Tailoring' went on to exploit (Heber Smith 1910:423). That it did succeed must also be due in no small part to the offer for every customer to try on even the finished garment before committing himself to paying for it. As such the concept embraced everything from formal and informal daywear (averaging six guineas in 1933) to evening dress (approximately £11 for a three-piece outfit) and sports clothing to overcoats (in the region of two guineas per item),[5] which were promoted on a seasonal basis (Figures 14–17 and 22): 'Austin Reed's man was comfortable in business suits, plus fours and formal evening wear as the occasion demanded' (Hewitt 1996: 12).

All of the press advertisements in the 'New Tailoring' campaign were conceived initially in terms of their copy, which was written by McCullough, and afterwards Purvis contributed a suitable illustration to complement the text. However, there was also some latitude in this practice since on a number of occasions the same illustration by Purvis was recycled for use with different taglines and copy. A portrait of a man smoking a pipe and wrapped up in the Austin Reed two-guinea gabardine raincoat, for example, first appeared in an advertisement in the *Radio Times* on 23 September 1932 with the caption 'rain or sun – who cares?' and again shortly afterwards on 18 November with the caption 'Wet or fine you won't care' (Figure 17).[6] The copy in both of these advertisements, however, was similar in content, and it focused on the climatic versatility of the gabardine material, which was light enough to carry in fine weather, but sufficiently proofed and amply cut to keep out the cold and the rain. Clearly, this kind of recycling occurred only when stock imagery by Purvis fitted the bill, but it would also have been a useful expedient when he was too committed to come up with a fresh design. In 1933, for example, advertisements for the two-guinea raincoat appeared in the *Radio Times* on a fortnightly basis, while between 1927 and 1932 promotions for the 'New Tailoring' appeared in *Punch* and dailies such as the *Mail* and *Express* almost once a week, the majority of them illustrated by Purvis.

While the text came first, McCullough's objective was not to compete with the artist but to collaborate in achieving an overall effect of atmospheric unity and harmony, and he appreciated that it would probably be the illustration that initially caught the eye of the reader: 'With the exception of a few extremely intellectual appeals, nearly every sort of advertising depends on pictorial art for a large proportion of its effect' (McCullough 1929: 55). Nonetheless, the personal tone he adopted in his copy was approachable and upbeat, and he always managed to express succinctly the main idea of the campaign, which centred on the axiom of choosing clothes rather than cloth. Thus the lexis that he tended to rely on was that of the salesman in the shop, speaking to the potential customer through a form of ad-hominem address. The client is directly interpellated as someone who matters and who is distinct from anyone else: witness the phrase in Figure 15, 'You are *you* and should dress as you – taking care to find the clothes that fit your personality – as well as your figure', or the headline, 'A Sports Suit *intimately* Your Own', and the declaration, 'In the New Tailoring Showroom you can select . . . the sort of suit in which you stride on to the first tee feeling that you will go round well under bogey' in an advertisement for plus fours in the *Daily Mail* (2 April 1925:6).

This rhetoric invests each of the advertisements with an intimately humanist quality, which is compounded by Purvis's atmospheric illustrations of men wearing garments in appropriate situational contexts, reading a newspaper in a lounge suit, for instance, or smoking a cigarette in a dinner jacket. At the same time, the use of typography is highly expressive. Occasionally, therefore, prosodic emphasis is given to certain words in order to mimic the impact of spoken language – 'You are *you*' (Figure 15) or 'After all, you can only discover whether your Dress Clothes *will* be all that you consider they *must* be . . . *before* you decide to buy them' (Figure 14). Whereas at other times, the eye-catching use of different weights and sizes of the Bodoni type itself serves to signify its own expressive personality.

Bodoni Monotype was widely regarded as the serif lettering that was most appropriate for use in both headlines and body text; A.S. Wildman, for example, regarded it as the 'most orderly and precise of types', and one that 'does most jobs so well' (Wildman 1930: 110). This was obviously one of the reasons why Pritchard and Wood favoured it as the most apposite type for Austin Reed advertising and they deployed it without exception in the company's press campaigns. But any risk of monotony was also transcended by the varying italic and bold faces and upper- and lowercase letters in any given advertisement, as Figure 17 reveals.

By comparison, the posters designed by Purvis had to deal with the idea of the 'New Tailoring' in a more oblique way, by incorporating an illustration, the company's name and the address of one or another of its branches, but without the use of copy (Figures 18 and 19). Purvis himself clearly realised that the distinction between effective press advertising and poster design could be attributed to the question of visual impact: 'I always endeavour to get the complete message to the complete comprehension of the spectator in not more than three seconds . . . A good poster should not puzzle people; it should be like a boxer's punch – straight, hard and quick – and should deliver its message in a flash' (Purvis 1930: 306). Thus his posters were conceived according to the premise, 'he who runs may read' (Adquisitor 1931d: 33), such that we can detect a sparing but powerful representation of form and space in his work. One of the earliest known posters by him, promoting Dewar's Whiskey, can be traced back to 1907 and in its depiction of an idealised male figure wearing full evening dress, John Hewitt has rightly argued that it prefigures many of the stylistic conventions that were to become the hallmark of his later poster and press campaigns for Austin Reed – see, for example, his 1931 poster 'Evening Clothes' (Figure 16). But in the main the Austin Reed posters are closer in style to turn of the century graphic work by the likes of the Beggarstaff Brothers and the German designers Ludwig Hohlwein and Andreas Karl Hemberger, whose economic – and occasionally abstracted – treatment of form, tendency to flatten out space, and reliance on unmodulated colour owes much, in turn, to the pictorial aesthetics of Japanese woodblock prints.

In Purvis's work a similar modernist tendency is clearly discernible (Figures 18 and 19), one that his contemporary Ashley Havinden (1959) summed up as the pinnacle of artistic achievement in poster design in an obituary in the *Journal of the Royal Society of Arts*. But so too is a sympathetic understanding of the poster's commercial function as an arresting piece of publicity rather than a work of art to be hung in a gallery, something that Purvis was keen to emphasise in his own writing and lectures: 'The whole essential point in designing a poster is that it should sincerely radiate the story of the commodity it has to sell' (Purvis 1930: 306). Thus the stylistic conventions of simplifying form and space, the stark contrast between light and shade, and the predilection for strong, vibrant colours and various forms of uppercase sans serif lettering evident in the Austin Reed posters have also to be explained with regard to practical environmental factors; which is to say that the majority of posters were designed for display under conditions of artificial lighting on the London Underground, such as the promotion for Summit Shirts in 1932, printed in black, ochre and red (Figure 18), or to take account of the way they could be skied high up on the hoardings in other public spaces like railway stations, such as the advertisement for evening clothes in 1931, which was printed in dramatic shades of red and black (Figure 16). In any case, with the enactment of the Town and Country Planning Bill in 1932 (after which point in time Purvis executed the majority of his posters for Austin Reed), the display of posters outdoors was more strictly policed by local authorities, who were empowered to remove any advertisement hoarding that they thought defaced the public space it occupied (*Advertising Display* 1932a: 246).

Accordingly, arenas such as shop windows, railway stations and the London Underground remained more acceptable and reliable spaces for anyone wishing to promote their product(s) and service(s) in poster format. As we can see in Figure 18, for example, the Austin Reed poster and the two on either side of it, for Jantzen sportswear and Manfield 'Waukenphast' shoes respectively, are all neatly contained within a tiled border (in fact, the Austin Reed poster also has a supplementary ceramic frame of its own).[7] Furthermore, the juxtaposition of promotions for garments and footwear like this suggests that a thematic grouping of posters was also a possibility, something which is borne out by the composite underground site at Waterloo station subsequently taken out by the agency T.B. Browne to display five posters promoting Moss Bros. (which had advertised on the Tube since 1916) in 1951 (*Advertiser's Weekly*, 19 April 1951: 126). In several instances, sequential cards were also designed to catch the attention of passengers as they travelled up and down underground railway escalators. These were usually designed as a set of three separate images, each with its own copy, intended to convey a similar sense of movement and direction as the spectators who encountered them, and to unfold dynamically the atmospheric- and use-value of the product in question. Whereas this was conveyed by the copy and one static image only in the press advertisements, the sequence of cards involved a dialectic unfolding of both text and image to get the point across, as an inventive promotion for the two-guinea raincoat in the autumn of 1936 representing a man putting on the garment in a sudden downpour demonstrates (Figure 20).[8] The critic Eliot Hodgkin, in particular, was struck by this kind of harmonious interplay of text and image in Purvis's posters, which he believed did not detract from the 'strength and virility' of the design (Hodgkin 1935: 146).

Although, on the surface, the poster may have been conceived as a form of telegrammatic publicity whose appeal was to the person on the go, as McKnight Kauffer also professed, posters which appeared on the Underground would also have the potential to 'make a fast moving public leisured for a moment' (McKnight

Kauffer 1924: 43). And this would especially be the case if, like those by Purvis, they combined atmosphere and suggestion that worked on the subconscious mind (J.F. Braun 1933: 112). Indeed, the designer Ashley Havinden argued that all poster advertising worked on the level of 'graphic imagery as a thought form', since the illustration was no longer necessarily an adjunct to the copy (Havinden 1935–6: 15). But, of course, if the visual symbolism of any company's advertising was to hit the mark, then it had to make an appeal to a certain class of consumers and, as W.G. Raffé systematically put it, to encode 'an item of interest to a possible user' (Raffé 1929: 23). In dealing with such a point of symbolic association between the clothes and wearer for Austin Reed, and in common with the imagery in their press advertising, therefore, Purvis himself spoke about how the poster should embody the 'personality of the commodity' (Hewitt 1995: 297) and to this end his posters mobilised the central trope of the upper-middle-class gentleman.[9] According to Hewitt's trenchant observation, the way that the men wear their clothes in the advertisements with an air of relaxed and confident gracefulness evinces the idea of a body 'hexis', which Pierre Bourdieu discusses in the *Outline of a Theory of Practice* (1977) and through which one unconsciously performs class membership by the way one moves or deports oneself socially. But, as he also argues, the advertisements transform this notion of the body 'hexis' into something discursive, something about which we are made to feel more conscious and knowing; in other words, they imply that class and taste are marketable commodities and not just inbred or intuitive qualities (Hewitt 1996: 13). As we shall see, this idea of buying into a lifestyle, is also evident in promotions for men's wear retailers at the other end of the market, such as The Fifty Shilling Tailors discussed below, or to the underwear advertising addressed in Chapter 7.

At the same time, it is interesting to see how Purvis frequently rendered the male figures in his Austin Reed posters without any discernible facial features or expressions (Figure 19). Indeed, in the underground advertisement for Summit Shirts (Figure 18) even the heads of the two men have been truncated by the picture's edge. These pictorial devices were common in Japanese woodblock prints and we also find them occasionally in work by the Beggarstaff Brothers, both of which he openly admired. As a point of comparison it is also worth noting that a showcard by Andreas Karl Hemberger promoting men's evening wear for Bamberger and Hertz in 1928 contains an almost identical motif of two headless individuals to Purvis's 1932 poster, although there is no documentary evidence to suggest that he was aware of this design.[10] On a pragmatic level, Purvis claimed that in certain instances the total lack of or blanking out of facial features was intended to portray the effect of subjects bathed in bright sunlight (*Journal of the Royal Society of Arts*, May 1929: 652, cited by Hewitt 1996: 4 and 24 n. 7). This certainly was the case in a poster called 'Girls in Boats' for LNER in 1926, and could equally apply to two Austin Reed posters from 1927–8 that represent men in the shadow of the sun's glare. In the context of the class and gender connotations of Austin Reed advertising, however, the obliteration of eyes, nose and mouth seems both to compound and complement the commodification of the body 'hexis' suggested by the male figures. Rather than being portraits of recognisable types, then, these inscrutable masculine stereotypes function on the level of the anonymous everyman, and while the spectator is denied the opportunity of looking at their features or to discern precisely what kind of people they are, nevertheless he is afforded a form of fantasmatic identification with the men in the posters and the opportunity to envisage his own face in the place of their blank physiognomy; in other words to *be* the man in the poster rather than just be *like* him.

Thus the 'virility in design' of these posters, about which Hodgkin commented, seems also to arouse curiosity about recognition and identity, and the relationship of representation to reality. Although Purvis clearly realised that he was working as an artist in a commercial sphere and likened the immediate effect of the poster to a 'boxer's punch', by the same token it is interesting to hear him acknowledge the symbolic impact of advertising and the need to connote 'the personality of the commodity' as well. It is for this reason, therefore, that I want to suggest his images can be productively framed in terms of Lacanian gaze theory, yet in such a way that inverts the normative specular economy involving the ego, which Lacan posits in *Seminar I* is always an imaginary construct that stands in relation to the corporeal subject, who he argues regards the ego as an object of desire (Lacan 1988: 141). For, as he also contends in the *Four Fundamental Concepts* (1978), it is in the process of 'becoming a picture' or a screen that the identity of the subject – who or what he desires to become – is established. But what the screen represents and how it does so can also be prone to negotiation by the subject, since Lacan defines the screen as a form of mask or a double, through which 'the being gives of himself, or receives from the other' (Lacan 1978: 107). It is with this kind of reciprocal identification and transference between the imaginary ego and the living subject, which the trope of the screen enables, that I would argue the depiction of 'faceless' males in many of Purvis's posters operates; the subject, therefore, not only completes or sees himself mirrored in the other who is represented in the image, but completes the very same image by envisaging that it looks like or is reflected in him as well.

The inversion or conflation between the ego and the subject suggested by this kind of imagery is further amplified by the motif of the two men, ostensibly involved in conversation, with 'cut-off' heads in the Summit Shirt poster.[11] For Lacan also speaks of the real subject, which he calls the *je*, as a metaphorically acephalic or headless being that is 'devoid of the self' in comparison to the illusory plenitude of the ego, which he refers to as the *moi* (Lacan 1988: 170). However, it is precisely the two imaginary egos represented in poster form by Purvis that are incomplete or lacking in this sense. Apparently faceless and not infrequently depicted against a blank background, as if it belongs nowhere, the imaginary ego in many of Purvis's poster designs relies, therefore, on the look or gaze of the putative acephalic spectator/subject for its identificatory fulfilment as much as the subject fulfils his own fantasies or lack of identity in it.

John Hewitt has contended that, 'It was by his poster designs that Purvis achieved his eminence in the 1920s and 1930s, and not by his press work' (Hewitt 1996: 9), and in regard to both their artistic form and symbolic content it is easy to understand why this should be the case. But editorials in both *Advertiser's Weekly* and *MAN and his Clothes* focused their attention on his press advertisements as well as his posters, insisting that, irrespective of format: 'Austin Reed Ltd, certainly put distinction into their tailoring advertising' (Marteau 1925:436). What is more, in lionising Purvis we should not overlook the fact that he was not single-handedly responsible for all the illustrations in Austin Reed press and poster advertising. Tom Eckersley and Eric Lombers, who met as students at Salford School of Art and collaborated professionally under the joint name Eckersley-Lombers from 1935, and Austin Cooper were also involved with the design of many posters in a modernist vein similar to Purvis (Figure 21). Norman Howard provided illustrations for the series of advertisements promoting their Tropical Kit Department, which had been introduced in 1927 to cater for tourists and expatriate workers alike. And Fougasse was involved principally with the provision of droll cartoons from *c*.1933 for the 'Men about Regent Street' and 'Just a Part of the Austin Reed Service' press campaigns, which appeared in the *Evening Standard*, *Daily Mail* and *Daily Express*, and posters and showcards for London Underground platforms and trains (Figure 6). In contrast to other advertising for Austin Reed, the tone of these campaigns was lighter and humorous. The posters in particular were hailed by art and design historian Nikolaus Pevsner as a unique definition of the British sense of wit in their depiction of 'plump little men, near relations of seals and sea-lions' (Pevsner 1936: 36). In the press advertisements, meanwhile, these zoomorphic figures were incorporated alongside copy by McCullough that interwove facts and figures about the range of styles and sizes available at Austin Reed with light-hearted skit, relating how men of all different sizes could find anything to suit their particular needs: 'When rain is falling the height of an umbrella is unimportant, but between showers tall men like tall umbrellas and less tall men like short ones. That is why we have three lengths of umbrellas to lean on'.

By the late 1920s, photographs were also occasionally used in the company's press and Underground showcard advertisements. Most often these were straight-forward shots of men wearing a particular kind of clothing in different social contexts (Figure 22), but sometimes more adventurous forms of photographic imagery were deployed. In 1929, for example, a photomontage representing the various grooming and ticket-booking services available on the lower ground floor of the Regent Street flagship store appeared on Underground trains. During the interwar period, photomontage was almost exclusively used by the likes of John Heartfield in Germany and Gustav Klutsis in the Soviet Union as a form of political propaganda (Teitelbaum 1992), but in 1930 Anton Breuhl had also executed an experimental photomontage, superimposing solarised images of tailors' hands with the torso of a man wearing a suit, which was included in advertisements for the New York men's wear outfitters, Weber and Heilbronner (*Advertising Display*, August 1930:91). Owing to its predominantly politicised nature in the revolutionary milieu of Germany and Russia, however, photomontage in advertising was perceived in the United States and Britain at this time as something which was 'directed to an intellectual body' (*Advertising Display*, August 1930: 91) and both Bruehl's design and the showcard for Austin Reed are rare examples, therefore, of its use in a commercial context.[12]

Less problematic was the reception of photography itself. By the mid-1920s many critics were united in conceding that it 'has a definite place in publicity' (Tregurtha 1926: 27), and by the early 1930s the *Advertiser's Weekly* commented, 'The more one sees of modern photography the better' (17 March 1932: 409). In 1926 George Mewes established Photographic Advertising Limited for the provision of stock photographic imagery to advertisers as well as publishing advisory booklets containing sample advertisements (Wilkinson 1997). At the same time, many photographers had begun to carve out a career for themselves in advertising – in 1938 there were 800 commercial photographers working in Britain (Searle Austin 1938) – including E.O. Hoppé, who was involved with promotions for Lilley and Skinner shoes, and Howard Coster, who produced imagery for Forsyth golfing clothes, Diemel shirt fabrics and Dexter overcoats (Tregurtha 1926; Coster 1934). During the interwar period, photographs had consequently become common currency in the advertisements of several men's wear outfitters. In addition to Austin Reed, for example, Barratt Shoes, K Shoes, Simpson, Weaver to Wearer and The Fifty Shilling Tailors all used photographic imagery in their publicity.[13]

It was the United States that took the lead, however, in pioneering the evolution of photographic advertising during the early 1920s, with Clarence White, who had founded a school of photography in New York in his own name in 1914 and the Art Center in 1921, becoming one of the first apologists for its application. In the catalogue for the first exhibition at the Art Center in 1921 he wrote that: 'The visitors will be interested in the recent developments in artistic photography as applied to modern advertising shown in these galleries . . . and the American advertiser is becoming more and more aware of this fact' (Yochelson 1983: 33). The modern style alluded to here was manifested in many of the photographs executed by two of the White School's most well known graduates Edward Steichen and Paul Outerbridge. The latter promoted the idea of straight photography in advertising campaigns such as that for the Ide Shirt Collar, which appeared in

Vanity Fair in November 1922. With its sharp focus, simple geometry and oblique perspective the photograph, which represented the collar in isolation against a chequer board background, was the archetype of the modernist, straight style of photography advocated by Paul Strand, who had argued in *Camerawork* (June 1917) that 'Objectivity is the very essence of photography'.[14]

In Europe also the idea of objective photography had taken root during the 1920s with the advent of the *Neue Sachlichkeit* (New Objectivity), a term coined in May 1923 by Gustav Hartlaub, curator of the Kunsthalle in Mannheim, to describe a cool sense of detachment in art based on the observation of things from everyday life.[15] László Moholy-Nagy, who had promoted the machine aesthetic as a teacher at the German design school the Bauhaus between 1923 and 1928, was one of the first to champion this new vision in photography and to ally its use to publicity, arguing in his 1927 essay 'Photography in Advertising' that: 'The appeal of what is new and still unused is one of the most effective factors in *advertising*; therefore it is appropriate, even from the most superficial point of view, to include *photography* in advertising' (Moholy-Nagy 1927, quoted in Phillips 1989: 87, original emphases). In this manifesto and subsequent writings such as 'A New Instrument of Vision', Moholy-Nagy (1936) espoused a battery of different techniques, including photomontage and the photogram, and a range of different stylistic approaches to the object, such as the introduction of the greatest contrasts, the use of texture and structure, and the use of different or unfamiliar perspectives – achieved by 'positioning the camera obliquely, or pointing it up or down', which offered 'new experiences of space' (Moholy-Nagy 1936: 36).[16] We can discern all of these formal concerns in an advertisement for Austin Reed shirts featuring a colour photograph, which appeared in *Punch* on 21 June 1933 and which invites us to contemplate everyday objects from a fresh vantage point (Figure 23). Thus the bales of different striped and checked materials have been photographed from an aerial perspective and on the diagonal, giving the impression of skyscrapers toppling over on top of each other; this sense of direction is reinforced by one of the blades of the scissors, which gleams in the light, yet is countered by the other, which stands vertically proud. And, in marked contrast to the hard texture both of the scissors and the falling towers of shirting, a sinuous tape measure meanders its way from the bottom left of the image, emerging half-way up on a horizontal line that seems to harness the conflicting spaces and directions in the composition.

While Harold Haliday Costain could argue in the light of colour advertisements such as this one that, 'today's photography, so brilliant in texture, form and feeling of colour values, has definitely replaced in our advertising pages the flat, weak and hazy reproductions formerly used', nonetheless he did concede that 'there are many instances where the clear-cut mechanical use of the camera must give place to the more gentle treatment of the free hand illustrative artist' (Costain 1935–6: 20–1). One of the main technical problems with the photographic illustrations in some magazines and all daily newspapers being referred to here was the loss of definition and tone caused by reproducing them on poor quality newsprint. This was not so much a problem for magazines like *MAN and his Clothes* or *Punch*, which used better quality paper. Many of Austin Reed's photographic advertisements appeared in *Punch*, for instance, very occasionally in colour (Figure 23) but the majority in monochrome. Otherwise, a common technique used by both newspapers and the *Radio Times* during the 1930s in order to offset any diminution of quality and detail was scraperboard, which involved the drawing and cutting of lines onto a surface covered with a black ink ground. Appealing to craftsmen and artists alike, this process afforded solid blacks and clear whites as well as an unlimited range of textural effects, achieved by way of lines, broken lines, interlacing lines or stipples. Sometimes it was used to translate a photograph into a line drawing and to overcome the bland uniformity of the half-tone process (see Chapter 1), and at others to produce original work that mimicked the sense of light, shade and detail found in photographs.

Fran Sutton, who was represented by the artist's agency J.S. Goodman (f. 1931), was responsible for Austin Reed scraperboard advertising during the interwar period and he deployed both methods to equally good effect. In 1934, for example, he converted the colour photograph in the *Punch* shirt advertisement we have just discussed into a monochrome scraperboard design for reproduction in the 'Six-Point Summit Shirt' campaign in the dailies (*MAN and his Clothes*, June 1934: 22), and one year later he used the technique to achieve the effect of falling rain, by cross-hatching white lines over a photograph in the 'Two-Guinea Raincoat' series of advertisements that appeared in the *Radio Times* (Figure 24). Sutton was also involved with the original design of dextrous scraperboard illustrations for other advertisers, including promotions in *MAN and his Clothes* in 1938 for Tauttex, a lining of raised mohair fabric manufactured by Drey Simpson & Co. that was sewn inside the waistband of trousers to prevent them from slipping down (Figure 25).

In a review of current advertising in *Penrose Annual* in 1940 John Betjeman thought the scraperboard technique 'a most hideous medium', and he lampooned many of the other formal devices that had become popular in modern advertising such as the setting of copy at an angle and the vogue for Gill Sans, concluding: 'True artists who are employed in advertising and designing for commercial sales should not escape into mental Cotswolds' (Betjeman 1940: 20). Nor was he alone in voicing such opposition to the impact of modernism on British advertising. Reginald Wilson, for example, impugned what he called the 'Germanic touch' and the 'craze for wavy headlines', decrying the need 'to be modern for the sake of being different' (Wilson 1930:360). And yet, as work by the likes of Purvis, Sutton and other commercial artists working for Austin Reed amply demonstrates, there was considerable variation in the pictorial styles they deployed across different media, as well as a clear understanding of how to ally the aesthetics of modernism to a commercial understanding of the men's wear market.

Stealing the Emperor's New Clothes: Rego and The Fifty Shillings Tailors

Moreover, the modernist style of many Austin Reed promotions was but one way of appealing to the male consumer and other men's outfitters at both ends of the market eschewed avant-garde aesthetics, tending to a more naturalistic form of representation. This was certainly the case in poster promotions for three retailers at the top end of the spectrum: Harry Hall, the breeches, habit and costume specialist founded in 1891, Moss Brothers & Co. (f. 1880) and Bernard Weatherill, for example, all resorted to the straightforward depiction of men modelling their garments, although with varying degrees of success. In 1931, Adquisitor complained that in comparison to the male figures in Austin Reed's posters, the men in Harry Hall's were '"dead" fashion plates' and that Weatherill's suffered from a drab and conservative use of colours. And while he found the type in a recent poster for Moss Brothers 'runs to small sizes', nonetheless he conceded that they did manage to combine prestige with an air of verisimilitude in the way that the male figures were depicted (Adquisitor 1931d). At the cheaper end of the market retailers such as Rego and The Fifty Shilling Tailors likewise deployed naturalistic forms of representation and, much like Barratt Shoes, adopted demotic forms of rhetoric in their copy, while, in addition to press advertising, Burton's deployed inventive window displays, such as their Ashton store's tie up with the film *The Front Page* in 1932 (*Advertiser's Weekly*, 11 February 1932: 186). As Katrina Honeyman has argued, this new impetus in marketing and advertising by multiple tailors coincided with a peak in demand for men's suits during the 1920s and 1930s (Honeyman 2002: 434), and accordingly they were promoted as the item of clothing that could be worn at work and at leisure by all kinds of men.

The Rego Clothiers, which began trading in 1875, claimed to be the original multiple tailors and were involved with popularising 'wholesale bespoke', a form of mass production and consumption in clothing first developed in Leeds at the turn of the century (Honeyman 2002). By 1925 Rego had sixty branches across the London area, but their advertising policy was rather hit and miss. Initially, the company's press advertising campaigns had depended on hard-sell tactics, promoting a range of garments in composite advertisements with stereotypical illustrations and copy that foregrounded the idea of 'staggering values' and 'amazing offers'. According to A.G. Rossiter, the managing director, these had done little to stimulate sales, however, and he gradually cut out press advertising altogether in favour of circularising the 500,000 existing customers that Rego had on their books.

While this strategy helped to maintain sales it did not augment them and Rossiter came to realise that the early press advertising had failed not because the medium itself was at fault but because the company's hard-sell approach was unimaginative and unappealing. Consequently, in the mid-1930s, when Rego had one hundred branches across London and the home counties, he decided to resort to advertising once again and to promote their 45 shillings suits and overcoats every Friday in a solus position on the sports pages of two London dailies, the *Evening News* and the *Star*, between September 1935 and June 1936.[17]

In comparison to their first press campaign, the new one neither displayed nor described the garments per se. Rather, Rossiter hit upon the idea of demystifying how multiple tailoring was run as a business and explaining how Rego was able to offer bespoke tailoring for a mere 45 shillings. Each of the advertisements included a photograph of Rossiter, though not necessarily as he appeared in 1935, nor in recognisable terms. Thus one advertisement featuring a portrait of him as a child proclaimed, 'I used to look like this, but nowadays I shouldn't dream of showing my face in an advertisement', while another focused only on his hands holding a pipe (*Evening News*, 27 September 1935:13, 18 October 1935: 17). Most frequently, however, his image was montaged into a situational context and his facial features would appear *sous rature* with a sign that read, 'It's my business I'm proud of – not my face' posted over them, along with captivating headlines such as 'Tea freshly made for each customer' or 'Come up and see me sometime' (Figure 26). This kind of statement was used to elaborate a similar message about Rego tailoring in the copy that followed, which was organised as a personal talk by Rossiter to the average man where he stressed the fact that the low price of their clothing was due to the mass buying of materials rather than the machine production of garments. The copy generally maintained, then, that a 45 shillings suit by Rego was just as good as one that would cost you a great deal more elsewhere. Indeed, in one promotion he also took a back-handed swipe at the concept of Austin Reed's more expensive 'New Tailoring' by stating: 'There are no stocks of half-finished suits in my workrooms waiting to be "adjusted" to "fit" unsuspecting customers who are paying for "made-to-measure"' (*Evening News*, 29 November 1935). And just in case this made him sound a little too pious, occasionally the ingenuous copy also admitted that Rego had received customer complaints about their own products – although these would be 'always promptly and courteously dealt with under the famous Rego guarantee'. While Rego customers were mainly white-collar clerical workers from Class C, who had to be well dressed on a limited income, nonetheless professional men from Class A and B were addressed from time to time in the advertisements. One of them captioned 'There's no class war in *my* business', for example, represented a barrister waiting to see Rossiter and claimed that lawyers, doctors, bank officials and stockbrokers had also 'found out that more money doesn't necessarily mean better clothes' (*Evening News*, 29 November 1935).

Consequently, the candid ad-hominem rhetoric deployed in the copy made a universal appeal to all kinds of male customers and had a profound impact on how the public viewed the company, with sales of the 45 shilling suits alone increasing by 63 per cent after the first advertisements had appeared and 2,000 fresh customers visiting Rego's shops every week during the first few months of the campaign (*Advertiser's Weekly* 1936a: 354).

Promotions for Rego, therefore, were keen to emphasise that they were just as interested in producing bespoke quality clothing as their upmarket competitors and equally ingenuous in the game of one-upmanship that they seemed to play with the likes of Austin Reed. But, as a London-based company, they were also small bait in comparison to national multiple tailors like Burton's and The Fifty Shilling Tailors, which managed to provide 'wholesale bespoke' on a much grander scale. Burton's, 'the tailor of taste', was the largest manufacturer and retailer of men's wear during the interwar period, owning 450 branches nationwide by the mid-1930s, which were promoted by Montague Burton on a democratic basis by 'putting good clothes within the reach of all' (Honeyman 2002: 429). As Frank Mort has demonstrated, from the 1930s to the mid-1950s the promotional rhetoric for the company 'centred on one clearly identifiable icon of masculinity . . . the gentleman'. And, whether he was depicted at work or leisure, in isolation or alongside other men, he embodied 'a decidedly English world-view' and 'always appeared correctly dressed' (Mort 1996: 137). He claims that it was exactly Burton's market position as 'the tailor of taste' that differentiated Burton's from the likes of The Fifty Shilling Tailors, which he argues by contrast, placed the emphasis in their publicity 'almost exclusively on price' (ibid.) Yet, as we shall see in our analysis of the company's advertising, this kind of sweeping comparison is misleading and instead the rhetoric and styling of their press campaigns played down cost and underscored quality.

The Fifty Shilling Tailors, which was run by Price's Tailors Ltd, had more than two hundred branches during the 1930s. Their publicity was handled by Rumble, Crowther & Nicholas until the spring of 1954, by which time they had been taken over by United Drapery Stores, rechristened John Collier, and the Greenly's agency invited to run the new company's advertising account (*Advertiser's Weekly*, 6 May 1954: 288–9). Around 1932 a press advertising campaign was launched to promote the idea of 'Rational Tailoring' (a large-scale counterpart to Austin Reed's 'New Tailoring') in the *Daily Mail*, *Daily Express*, *Daily Herald* and the *Radio Times*, and space to the value of £16,171 was bought between October and December 1937 alone (*Advertiser's Weekly*, 21 August 1938: 170).[18] In the first of the company's full-page advertisements in the *Radio Times* (2 March 1934: 652) Henry Price, the managing director of the company, took the opportunity to answer the question 'What is Rational Tailoring?' Accordingly, the copy was written as if it were a diegetic letter or monologue from him to potential customers and to reassure them that quantity was not achieved at the expense of quality. In common with Rego, we are told that the reason he can put his clothing on the market for so little is due to bulk-buying 'fine All-British cloths' rather than skimping on standards in tailoring. At bottom line he testifies that: 'Rational Tailoring is not mass production. Such methods, obviously, cannot be used in tailoring with any satisfaction, and that is why The Fifty Shilling tailors have been so careful in preserving a COMPLETELY INDIVIDUAL SERVICE'. Unlike the figure of Rossiter in the Rego press campaign, however, Price went a step further in accounting for the manufacture of his company's garments, relating the fact that the efficiency of production in 'wholesale bespoke' was achieved through the employment of skilled labour.

Of course, much wholesale tailoring during the interwar period was made possible only through the use of intensive sweatshop labour. For the rapid turnover of garments on a weekly cycle alongside the rationalisation of hand-cutting had encouraged employment of female and juvenile labour at lower wages of pay than male workers at a time when salaries for tailors and garment workers were anyway caught in a downward spiral; by the end of the 1920s, week-time rates had stagnated at their 1922 level of £1 8s. for women and £2 8s for men (Kershen 1995: 171–3).[19] However, in a series of testimonial advertisements that ran in 1936, Price invited Major General the Rt Hon. Lord Loch to vouch in one of them that sweated labour was never used by The Fifty Shilling Tailors in the manufacture of their garments (*Radio Times*, 14 August 1936:39). At the same time, the social conscience both of The Fifty Shilling Tailors and their juror was asseverated in the guarantee of a cheque to be paid to the Hedingham Training Scheme, a welfare trust that operated to find work for unemployed skilled males from depressed areas, in exchange for Loch's cooperation.

Testimonial advertising had become a common feature of 1930s publicity for products as polarised as breakfast cereals and cigarettes (Wilkinson 1997: 32–3), and in deploying a similar tactic The Fifty Shilling Tailors also sought to 'prove' the efficacy of their Rational Tailoring scheme. Furthermore, a range of social and professional types, who would not usually have been associated with mass clothing, acted as jurors in their advertisements and argued from different perspectives the fact that its garments were just as good – if not more varied – in terms of cut, fit, style and quality as those which cost 'four or five times the money'.[20] This thought was expressed by John Powell-Jones, 'a typical public schoolboy, now in the City', who attested: 'I don't think I am exaggerating when I say that there is no wider range of materials at any Tailors – patterns of every kind, ranging from the striking to the extremely sober. If you couldn't find your particular taste here, you would have to get your own cloth spun' (*Radio Times*, 25 September 1936: 60). In contrast, the artist Capt. Oswald Birley MC invoked historical precedent, including the example of Beau Brummell, in order to justify his interest in clothing as the signifier of individuality and character: 'From the portrait painter's point of view men's clothes have therefore become a difficult problem, and he is always thankful to find a "subject" who expresses something of his own personality – a character in his clothes and does not merely allow himself to be dressed by his tailor' (*Radio Times*, 23 October 1936: 44).

The roll call of individuals featured in these somewhat sententious testimonial advertisements was a blatant way of denoting that The Fifty Shilling Tailors had indeed transcended barriers of class and that they had penetrated the Class A and B markets more usually associated with the likes of Austin Reed. What is more, they even went so far as to mimic the style of their competitor's publicity in some advertisements for the 'Rational Tailoring'. A clear example of this is a 1935 promotion for evening dress, with an illustration of three dandies in conversation by C.B. Bowmar that is redolent of Tom Purvis's portrayal of the gentleman (Figures 29 and 14). It is not just the picture of confident masculine individuals that signifies a modern approach to advertising in this instance, but the harmonious use of typography as well. Thus the words 'Rational Tailoring' are printed in Erbar Condensed, an elegant sans serif typeface originated in 1922, while Plantin Old Style, named after the famous sixteenth century Antwerp printer, Christophe Plantin, has been used for the headline 'Don't worry . . . they'll give you the *Style*', and Venezia, devised in London in 1928 by Linotype, for the main copy below. At other times, Kabel Light was used to print the slogan 'Rational Tailoring' and Gill Sans in bold to introduce the dialogue of the respective speakers in the advertisement (Figure 27).

In several instances the prosodic dialogue in the copy of the advertisements takes place between men and women, and this tactic seems to operate on two levels. First, to prove that the male purchaser of the garment in question is a man of taste and discernment, someone with a good eye for a bargain but who is also interested in his appearance. In Figure 27, for example, the husband wearing a new suit proudly announces to his wife that, 'You really *must* admit it's a fine suit! I've never had a better one – at *any* price', and this air of self-satisfaction is compounded in the illustration of him admiring the cut and quality of the fitted jacket like a preening peacock. At the same time, his wife is portrayed sitting in an armchair and staring up at him as she devotedly replies, 'Yes, Jack, it looks every bit as good as any suit you ever had – even in your extravagant days'. In a later promotion for a sports coat and trousers, both the adoring look of the female and the idea of the male as an object of desire are more acutely rendered in image and text (Figure 28). Here we can see the gesture of smiling admiration on the woman's face as she stares at the man in the foreground and self-deprecatingly tells him that his new outfit makes her feel dowdy. Thus The Fifty Shilling Tailors incorporated the trope of the admiring female look in their publicity some twenty years earlier than advertising for their nearest competitor in the mass market, Burton's.[21]

But the rhetoric of both advertisements functions on another level, which serves to connote that, even though males were keen shoppers, women's approval of what men purchased nonetheless mattered and thus they had a vital part to play in the way that clothing as well as men's bodies were commodified. In Figure 27, the wife concludes, 'Well, if you're pleased I certainly am, You've convinced *me* that they really do live up to their advertisements!', while in Figure 28 the female subject is pleasantly surprised to discover that a handsome male/outfit doesn't have to cost the earth. The inclusion of female subjects in advertisements for men's dress, therefore, also acknowledges the influence of women on what men buy and how they look. *Advertiser's Weekly*, for example, reported in its issue of 4 August 1932 that women were involved with 80 per cent of suit sales (p. 206), and in a self-promotion in *The Times* (28 June 1937:11), W.S. Crawford stated that 75 per cent of men's shirts were selected by women and that it would foolish to 'under-estimate it in your advertising'. But, if the comments of an anonymous layman in 1938 are anything to go by, the gender balance in advertising had to be just right in order not to alienate male clients and there was no point in going 'all womanish', which he contested also included the representation of women in men's clothing advertisements (*MAN and his Clothes*, May 1938: 33). One way of resolving such tensions, as Austin Reed realised, was to turn the tables and the ironical copy of their Christmas advertising from 1936 onwards suggested instead that women could be led by men to purchase male garments as presents. This is particularly evident in the gender script of one of their press advertisements from November 1936, 'George *was* infuriating', which laid the bait for women to shop at Austin Reed by representing it as the place 'where men buy presents for themselves', while simultaneously portraying women as more adept shoppers; the copy relates how the sulky blonde in the photograph, abandoned by 'George' in her time of need, also managed to purchase a whole range of gifts under one roof and 'in about half an hour'.

The similarity in the form and style of pictures and typography, if not the specific content of the copy, across advertisements for men's wear retailers at opposite ends of the economic spectrum during the interwar period, is clear testimony to the way that the market had coalesced in making an appeal to a core market of male consumers. And yet such developments did not go unopposed. In 'The Well-Dressed Man' column in November 1937, for example, *Men Only* berated what it called the 'fordism in tailoring' that had been a result of the rise in mass markets and idealised in its place the individual styling offered by Savile Row (Greenfield et al. 1999: 188). At the same time the convergence of symbolism in men's wear advertising led some designers and critics to express their fear of plagiarism. Thus Tom Purvis (1932) attacked the '"scroungers" who debase the originality of the hall-marked designer' and called for adequate copyright protec-tion, while Maxwell Tregurtha detected a 'trickle down' in the style of modern advertising by which: 'The public observe the 'art' and wonder. Then the plagiarist arrives on the scene and imitates the "art" *sans* its "soul". The cult spreads' (Tregurtha 1931: 50).

In the light of such comments and the formal correspondences in the publicity for the likes of Austin Reed and The Fifty Shilling Tailors, it is tempting to believe that distinctions in taste and quality had indeed evaporated and that the ubiquity of the suit as a garment for a wide spectrum of men had levelled out any class differences between them. But the idea of the hierarchy of appearances that Daniel Roche uses to analyse how dress was worn to convey and maintain distinctions of class and profession, and social decorum in seventeenth- and eighteenth-century France (Roche 1994: 33–41), still seems to have mattered in interwar Britain. Certain advertisements in Austin Reed's 'New Tailoring' campaign, such as those in which women appeared alongside men at the races or playing post-prandial games of chess, for example, avow and consolidate both the class position of the subjects represented and a concomitant sense of propriety in dress as much as they connote any flirtation or sexual attraction taking place between male(s) and female(s). Thus the opening words of copy in Figure 22, 'Only the rich or famous can afford to dress badly – a thing some men forget', combined with the prices cited for the garments (seven guineas for an evening tail coat, for instance) suggest a tasteful juste milieu in which ostentatious clothes, as much as dress suits costing 50 shillings, may equally be considered infra dig.

Along with Austin Reed, several other men's wear retailers made no concession to inclusiveness in their publicity. Woodright Publicity and Press Service Ltd, which became advertising agents for Aquascutum in 1932, for example, recognised that while the company's raincoat could be made appealing to 'Mr Smith of Upper Tooting', it did so because of its 'snob appeal' (*Advertiser's Weekly* 1932b). Hence, Woodwright mobilised the metaphor of transport to convey the exclusivity of Aquascutum's product, illustrating one advertisement with a Rolls-Royce car and another with an airliner, and promoted the company only in periodicals and newspapers with a predominantly Class A–B readership, including the *Daily Telegraph*, *Punch*, *Tatler* and *Illustrated London News*. The transport metaphor was also mobilised in a 1936 promotion for Hector Powe by Dorland Advertising (which had taken over the account from A.C.F. Woods in 1932), in which Dorland compared the quality of Powe's clothing with that of The Fifty Shilling Tailors by stating 'It is impossible to get a £1000 car for £250' (*Advertising Review*, 28 November 1936).

That considerations of class, status and clothing were still important is compounded by Laura Ugolino in her comparative study of male dress and group identities in Oxford during the interwar period. Consequently she argues that we can detect 'a powerful picture of interplay between status and consumption' in the different dress codes adopted by undergraduates, scholars and workers in the car industry, and contends: 'Boundaries of "correct dress" had not entirely broken down . . . It seems clear that to some extent at least, despite claims of homogeneity, the cost, value and quality of clothes remained visible and important indicators of social status' (Ugolino 2000: 429 and 431). Whereas undergraduates were, therefore, prepared to gravitate toward stores like Austin Reed, which had opened a branch in Oxford in 1935 alongside other independent traders of quality merchandise such as Walters, the clothing sold by Burton's and The Fifty Shilling Tailors 'was not always necessarily acceptable for students', and if they did buy cheaper clothing, such as flannel trousers from Marks & Spencer, they did so surreptitiously (Ugolino 2000: 441 and 443). Moreover, the predilection for informal garments like flannels and plus fours over formal attire and suits among undergraduates and other men during the 1930s signalled a more relaxed and youthful attitude to modern codes of male dress.

In a More Relaxed Mode: Leisure and Pleasure in Advertising for Daks Simpson

The flagship men's clothing store Simpson of Piccadilly, designed by the modernist architect Joseph Emberton, opened in London on 29 April 1936. The original business had been established in 1894 by Simeon Simpson, who had set himself up as a bespoke tailor but subsequently wanted to ally the quality of craftwork to new methods of machine tailoring, such as the use of the band-knife that could cut through several layers of material simultaneously. Eventually, he opened three factories in London for the manufacture of ready-to-wear and bespoke garments and in 1917 his son Alec joined him in running a thriving business. It was Alec who opened the largest of the Simpson's factories at Stoke Newington in 1929 and who pioneered a new type of flannel sports trousers in 1932, which circumvented the need for wearing braces since they were held in place by rubber pads sewn into the waistband. These trousers, known as Daks because it rhymed with the words 'slacks' and 'vacs', short for 'vacations' (Havinden 1955b: 60), cost 30 per pair, nearly twice as much as '232' grey flannels, which retailed at a fixed price of 14s 11d between 1922 and 1930.[22] Stephens Advertising Service had masterminded an aggressive advertising campaign for the brand at this time, taking out the entire front page of the *Daily Mail* on no fewer than five occasions and buying space in the weekly *John Bull*; '232' could rightly claim that their advertising expenditure paid a handsome return in profits, attesting that after one front-page advertisement had appeared in the *Mail* in 1924, sales exceeded 5,000 pairs of flannels (*Advertiser's Weekly*, 9 June 1932: 334–5). Yet even though they had moved away from the stereotypical 'tailor's dummy' by representing how the garment looked during daily wear, nonetheless the overall layout of much of their advertising tended to appear cluttered with verbose reason-why copy and complementary illustrations.

By comparison, both the Daks product and publicity for it were conceived from the outset in terms of the highest quality; an advertisement in *Punch* in April 1934, for instance, proclaimed that Daks were the 'most beautiful trousers you have ever seen'. Initially sold in shades of grey, stone and white flannel, within the space of seven years Daks were available in various fabrics, including corduroy, whipcord and linen-woven tweed, and four new colours – biscuit, grey mixture, lovat and dungaree blue – and by 1952 they came in a range of fourteen different materials and forty-nine colours. Their publicity throughout this time was masterminded by Ashley Havinden and it did much to popularise the brand through its matching elegant style and economic layout. In 1940 Havinden himself affirmed that, 'whereas a few years ago a man would have one pair of grey flannel bags in his wardrobe, today he thinks nothing of having five or six pairs of Daks in different colours and materials . . . advertising has played a big part in this' (Havinden 1940: 66). While in the same year Tom Harrison of Mass-Observation commented in a lecture: 'In our recent investigation into the effect of fashion on the masses in this country, we found that the advertising for Daks trousers and Simpson's clothes has done more to change the working man's idea of clothes in this country than any one influence'.[23]

Havinden's entire career in advertising is associated with the agency William S. Crawford, established in 1914 and named after its owner. Joining the firm in 1922, he cut his teeth as a junior in the art department, earning £1 per week tidying up the artwork for promotions for Horne Brothers, but by 1929 he had been appointed art director, eventually becoming one of the managing directors by 1940. Crawford's was probably the pre-eminent agency in forging a new modern identity for advertising layouts during the interwar period, running accounts for Chrysler Motors, Enos Fruit Salt, Bass ale, Jaeger, Wolsey and Barratt Shoes, and employing commercial artists such as Zéró, Edward McKnight Kauffer and Terence Prentis. Prentis had trained as an artist at the Royal Academy Schools and worked in both Crawford's Berlin and London offices before co-founding the advertising agency Colman, Prentis and Varley in the mid-1930s (*Art and Industry* 1938d: 245).

The publicity for Simpson and Daks likewise involved a wide array of artistic talent. Between 1936 and 1937 Zéró and Feliks Topolski designed covers for some of their promotional booklets and Lázsló Moholy-Nagy, who had arrived in London as a refugee from Nazi Germany, contributed to the design of mail order brochures as well as merchandise display in the Piccadilly store. But Havinden and Max Hof were the two most prolific designers involved with promotions for the company. Hof (the alias of I.T. Pallas) was an Austrian-born artist, who started his career as an illustrator of theatrical costumes, and who was invited to visit London when Alec Simpson had seen examples of his designs in *International Textiles*.

After Hitler had annexed Austria in 1938, Hof moved to England permanently and his drawings of groups of impeccably dressed and homosocial male figures, virtually always depicted in a smiling and relaxed attitude, became the signature style of Simpson's men's wear press advertising right up until the early 1960s. But, as Havinden insisted, 'The idea of picture and words being complementary to each other is one of the most important developments of contemporary advertising presentation' (Havinden 1935–6: 15), and hence these promotions always incorporated the Simpson logotype that he had designed, and not infrequently his Ashley alphabet was used for the taglines (Figure 30). This calligraphic typeface, with sans serif capitals, was intended to give the appearance of a script that had been created with brush and ink, and also alternated with the modernist sans serif Condensed Gothic typeface for the taglines of Daks advertisements. In all promotions for the brand, however, the uppercase DAKS trademark that Havinden had devised in 1936 remained the same and the main copy was always printed in Gill Sans (Figure 31).

In their loose fit and use of natural fabrics the Daks brand have to be put into the wider context of debates concerning the need for healthier clothing. The chief organisation to promote this idea was the Men's Dress Reform Party (MDRP), founded in 1929 as an offshoot of the New Health Society that had been established in 1925 to campaign for a better awareness of the role of diet and environmental factors in everyday life. The MDRP had argued that tight clothing for males was the cause of rheumatism due to inefficient skin respiration and advocated that wool was the most proficient material for keeping the body temperature constant (Burman 1995; Bourke 1996). However, many of their proposals for men's clothing, such as the replacement of shirts by blouses, and trousers by shorts or breeches, were regarded as too outlandish for the daily attire of the average British male and their designs met with considerable opposition. After the BBC had televised an MDRP competition in 1937 for 'office, professional or other vocational wear' and 'ceremonial evening wear', for example, the *Listener* (14 July 1937) commented that: 'Whether man's lower limbs look their best encased in slightly flattened parallel tubes may be open to doubt, but at least there seems no great aesthetic advantage in cutting the tubes short at the knee' (Burman 1995: 281). Some men's wear retailers, however, were more sympathetic to the MDRP's aims, and Austin Reed had even offered a prize of five guineas' worth of reform clothing in 1931 (ibid.).

While there is no official record of Simpson's support for the MDRP, nonetheless Daks loose-fitting flannel trousers can be regarded as a more realistically acceptable response to the need for healthier clothing, and this message was connoted in publicity for the brand. Thus Crawford's advertising campaign imbricated health and sport, both in Godfrey Hope Saxon Mill's lapidary copy that crystallised the idea of 'comfort-in-action' and, most notably from 1935 onwards, in the trope of men's legs. All of the promotions, therefore, were based on a New Objectivity styled photograph by Geoffrey Morris that cropped off the body of a man wearing Daks just above the waist in order to underscore the casual fit of the trousers. In some advertisements the sport or activity in which he is engaged is denoted by a specific piece of equipment such as a tennis racket or golf club, but the image of a man standing with one leg crossed casually over the other, which first appeared in 1937, became the most recognisable and versatile symbol of Daks. The motif could be replicated in different advertisements in order to depict the availability of different cloths and shades, and a version with three pairs of legs/trousers that had appeared in *The Times* on 14 July 1954 (Figure 31) went on to win the Layton Trophy for best advertisement in 1955 (*Advertiser's Weekly*, 17 March 1955: 649).[24] Furthermore, the trope of the cut-off body seems much like a shop-window dummy and evinces the reversal of the Lacanian acephalic or incomplete real subject, who is 'devoid of the self', and the complete imaginary ego, which we have already identified at play in some of Tom Purvis's posters for Austin Reed. In common with them, therefore, the symbolism of Daks publicity seems to imply that it is the imaginary 'ego' that is 'devoid of self' and that consequently awaits fulfilment through the gaze of the spectator, who in this case is able to envisage not only his own face but also his body on top of the legs represented.

The image of the truncated body became highly iconic during the period, and we find it in a press advertisement for Guinea Guards slacks, which could also be worn without a braces or a belt (*Radio Times*, 28 June 1935: 66), as well as a poster promotion by Tom Purvis for Austin Reed flannels, which was on display between March and September 1937.[25] However, as much as wholesale bespoke was attacked for diluting standards of taste and class, so also did the trend for casual wear come under fire. At the start of the 1930s one critic writing in the *Advertiser's Weekly* found the dress codes of flannels or the lounge suit too lax, calling on retailers and advertisers to promote a return to the standards of 'the once immaculately dressed Englishman' and protesting that 'the lounge suit makes a lounge backbone, just as a stiff collar stiffens a man's neck, and a top hat lends him dignity' (Shaw 1932: 379 and 409). And by the end of the 1930s a similar point of view was still being expressed in some quarters. Thus in April 1939, an editorial in *Men Only* asserted that:

> Admitted, there are many men who think that an old tweed jacket and flannel trousers make an ideal kind of informal dress. But there are lots of others, who, while liking the style itself, consider it has become a great deal too popular; that it is almost off-duty 'uniform'; and that it has lost a lot of its appeal, so far as they are concerned, by getting too far down the social scale. Perhaps you feel the same way about it. It isn't a question of snobbery. Call it 'discrimination'.

Yet, within the space of six months or so of this comment being made, it was precisely uniformity in dress that took over as the Second World War was declared, and the pluralism of taste and class being advocated here were sacrificed to the redoubtable collective effort that Winston Churchill proclaimed would be required of the British people in order to 'defend our island home, ride out the storms of war, and outlive the menace of tyranny if necessary for years, if necessary alone'.[26]

Notes

1. The remaining City stores were located at Fleet Street, Queen Victoria Street, Cannon Street, Cheapside and Fenchurch Street.
2. The 2001 equivalents for four and eight guineas are £128.28 and £296.56 respectively. These figures and others cited in subsequent footnotes are from McCusker (2003).
3. See *Art and Industry* (1952) for an overview of Pritchard Wood's advertising; by 1941 their fashion accounts also included I&R Morley and Tenova hosiery, Luvisca shirts and pyjamas, and Saxone shoes.
4. Figures from Accounts Ledger for 1920–6 (PP 190 and PP 174) in Austin Reed Archive. Respective equivalents for 2001 are £684,393.84 and £2,203,525.
5. Respective equivalents for 2001 are £347.10, £606.05 and £115.70.
6. The 2001 equivalent is £120.12. Other examples of this kind of recycling in advertisements for the two-guinea raincoat in the *Radio Times* appeared on 7 October 1932 (p. 48), where an illustration by Purvis of a man with binoculars was used with the tagline 'You won't care if it snows', and on 4 November 1932 (p. 370) and 31 March 1933 (p. 835), where the same illustration had the respective captions 'Who minds about the weather?' and 'Who cares about the rain?' An advertisement in the *Radio Times* (23 June 1933, p. 777), entitled 'A Holiday Friend Indeed', featured an illustration of a man showing the lining of the raincoat, which was later used in an advertisement in *Punch* (17 March 1937, p. x) with the caption 'The Lining Too Is Weatherproof'.
7. Poster advertisements that promoted an entertainment, meeting, auction or sale were also exempt from restrictions, provided that they appeared in close proximity to the place where the activity was due to take place. Jantzen's poster campaigns were handled by the billposters David Allen and Sons from 1930 (*Advertiser's Weekly*, 30 June 1932: 449).
8. It is interesting to note that the figure of the walking man in the first panel of this underground promotion is similar in form to an earlier depiction of a man

caught in the rain in the double crown poster 'Grand Weather for An Austin Reed £2-2-0 Raincoat', which was bill-boarded between August and October 1935. A photocopy of this design is lodged with the Austin Reed Archive.

9. Purvis had obviously developed this commercial sense since his early career in advertising with Mather & Crowther. Writing in *Commercial Art* in 1927, Percy V. Bradshaw had also commented on Purvis's approach in this vein: 'In all his work there is personality, knowledge and vigour . . . He will talk over the client's problem with extreme care and thoroughness, and will then patiently search for the best method of illustrating the "personality of the product", and the purpose of a campaign. He never allows technique or pictorial mannerism to get between the product and the public' (Bradshaw 1927: 151–2).

10. A black and white reproduction of Hemberger's design appears in *Posters and Publicity*, 1928, p. 138.

11. Several other posters by Purvis also featured truncated heads. See photocopies of the following in the Austin Reed Archive: 'The Famous Two-Guinea Raincoat' (c. 1933), 'Austin Reed of Regent Street' (March–June 1938), 'Ready For You' (September–November 1938) and 'Austin Reed Service Weatherproofs' (November–December 1939). Another poster for flannel trousers (March–September 1937), meanwhile, represents a man's body cut off at the waist by the picture edge.

12. Sally Stein has demonstrated that in the United States by the late 1930s photomontage had also begun to appear in the commercial context of advertising. See Teitelbaum (1992: 141–8).

13. One of the first photographic advertisements for Barratts Shoes, representing a family taking a walk in the country, appeared in the *Radio Times* on 5 March 1937, p. 71, and for The Fifty Shilling Tailors a photographic image of a man and woman examining a shop window display appeared in the *Radio Times* on 13 March 1936, p. 26.

14. See Johnston (1997) for an exhaustive account of both photographic advertising in the United States and Steichen's role within it.

15. For an interesting overview of the development of this movement in Germany see Michalski (1994).

16. Two inclusive accounts concerning the impact of the New Objectivity on photography are Mellor (1978) and Hight (1996).

17. The 2001 equivalents of 45s in 1935 and 1936 are £119.43 and £113.21 respectively.

18. The 2001 equivalent is £773,373.91.

19. It is interesting to note that after a dispute at Rego's clothing factory early in 1929, the breakaway, communist-inspired United Clothing Workers' Union (UCWU) was set up on 7 March 1929. This was a short-lived affair, however, since the Communist Party had failed to remunerate striking members, who

were gradually forced to return to Rego, provided they renounced membership of the UCWU (Kershen 1995:175).

20. There were ten ads in all in the series and in addition to Lord Loch they featured the following individuals: Capt. Oswald Birley, an artist, Sir Harry Brittain, Frank Dobson, a sculptor, Sir Walter Gilbey, Earl Haig of Bemersyde, W. Nichols Marcy, an educational authority, John Powell-Jones, a City clerk, Capt. Sir Arthur Rostron, captain of the *Mauretania* and *Berengaria*, F.S. Smythe, author and Himalayan mountaineer, and Sir John Squire, poet and critic.

21. See Mort (1996: 140–3) on Burton's 1950s advertising policy.

22. Respective 2001 equivalents for 30s in 1922 and 1930 are £54.71 and £71.74, and for 14s 11d in 1922 and 1930 are £27.20 and £35.67. In Wainwright (1996: 4), another reason is given for the name DAKS, which is apparently a combination of Alec Simpson's initials, and the first and last letters of one of his business associates, Dudley Beck.

23. Mass-Observation TC22/1/A, lecture given by Tom Harrison, 'Advertising and the Public', Mass-observation Archive, University of Sussex.

24. The Layton Annual Awards in Advertising were inaugurated in 1955. The first set of judges included Havinden, James Holland (of the Society of Industrial Artists), Richard Guyatt (on behalf of the Council of Industrial Design), Beatrice Warde (for the Monotype Corporation) and Wilson Philip, president of the Society of Typographic Designers. DAKS won the trophy for best overall advertising campaign as well as being winners in Group B (textiles, clothing, furnishings, and store advertisements). Burton's, whose account was also handled by Crawford's, came third in Group B.

25. A photocopy of this poster is in the Austin Reed Archive.

26. Taken from Churchill's patriotic parliamentary speech of 4 June 1940 that was also included in 'Britain will ride out storms of war: "Never surrender"', *Daily Telegraph*, 5 August 1940.

–6–

'Business (Almost) As Usual'
Men's wear advertising, Utility and Rationing during the Second World War

'The first move is to combat by 'every means' the idea that it is 'patriotic' to be shabbily dressed.

Advertiser's Weekly, 14 November 1940

Make Utility clothes the fashion and all the male sex, with the exception of a few Irish eccentrics like the Duke of Wellington and Mr Shaw will love them. The truth is, men do not care about clothes.

Robert Lynd, *News Chronicle*, 7 March 1942

Writing in *Art and Industry*, John Gloag (1940), managing director of F.C. Pritchard Wood and Partners, the agency responsible for Austin Reed's advertising campaigns, observed how the First World War motto coined by Sir Herbert Morgan, 'Business as usual', was being rehabilitated by traders shortly after the start of the Second World War in September 1939. To this end, he inveighed how 'We are a trading nation. We live by trade, and we finance our war effort by trade', while acknowledging that for most manufacturers and retailers war was really more a case of 'Business *almost* as usual' (Gloag 1940:208). Given the economic hardships that the war demanded of business and civilians alike, it would be tempting to think that out of fiscal necessity most firms would have axed their advertising budgets entirely. Yet this was not to be the case and, although the level of spending on advertising was reduced in comparison to its heyday in the interwar period (by 1940, for instance, the advertisement revenue of the *Daily Express* stood at £229,155, less than half the total for 1938), companies such as Austin Reed, Simpson, Barratts and The Fifty Shilling Tailors continued to promote their goods, albeit subject to strictures such as paper and clothes rationing (*Advertiser's Weekly*, 12 July 1951:90), or industrial and creative personnel being away on active duty. (In addition to many factory workers and shop assistants being called up, the services of commercial artists like Ashley Havinden were also requisitioned for camouflage work in the army.)[1] Moreover, wartime advertising left very little manoeuvre for flights of fancy (F.H.K. Henrion's surrealist campaigns for women's overcoats by Harella that appeared in *Vogue* between 1941 and 1944 being a notable exception)[2] and, as we shall see, the messages contained in advertising campaigns for men's wear were framed as part of a wider propaganda machine that embraced entities as diverse as make-up and milk, and chocolate and clothing to promote not just the idea that quality mattered more than quantity but also the belief that constructive consumption was a strategic aspect of the war effort. As *Picture Post* expressed it at the start of the war: 'At a time like this, it is very natural that the minds of advertisers should be occupied with sterner things than advertising . . .Well . . . people still have a free choice, people still even buy delicacies' (*Picture Post*, 7 October 1939:8).

The Economics of Wartime Advertising and the New Patriotism

Of course it did not help that paper, the very material that advertisers relied on to get their messages into print, soon fell into short supply so that by July 1940 most newspapers (the chief advertising medium during the war) were cut down to six pages and had to include five rather than four columns on each page. This led the national dailies to charge more for each column inch of advertising. The new rate for the *Daily Mirror*, for example, had increased to £108 by 1 January 1940, and after the end of the war the advertising rates of five of the best-selling national dailies had more than doubled, and the per centage of space dedicated to advertisements had diminished in comparison to prewar values.[3] By contrast, the *Radio Times*, whose net sale was forecast to drop from 2 million to 1 million weekly copies in 1940, took the enterprising step of cutting its full-page advertising rate from £600 to £400, but had eventually settled on £490 by July 1940, in an attempt to entice more advertisers and thus make up for revenue lost from sales (*Advertiser's Weekly*, 23 November 1939: 130; 4 April 1940:4). Nonetheless, by 1939 both Austin Reed and The Fifty Shilling Tailors had ceased to advertise in the *Radio Times*, and after 8 September 1939 promotions for men's wear were totally absent from its pages. Instead, advertising for Austin Reed was concentrated in *Punch*, the *Evening Standard*, *Daily Mail* and *The Times*, as well as in posters on the London Underground. In contrast, The Fifty Shilling Tailors began to place advertisements in *Picture Post* (Figure 32), which emphasised the stoic sense of resilience and fair play endemic among the British people during the Second World War and went on to accrue a circulation of nearly 2 million copies every week (Hopkinson 1984: 110; Jobling and Crowley 1996:187–97).

Picture Post heralded itself as 'Britain's new advertising force' and, as we shall see, the patriotic tone of the men's wear publicity that appeared in its pages at this time compounded the magazine's general editorial bias. But throughout the war, its advertising rates were also very competitive, between £400 and £500 for a full page and around £100 per column. All of the advertisements that appeared in the magazine were printed in black and white (colour was not introduced until 1946) and no fewer than twenty-five different men's wear retailers were promoted in its pages between 1939 and 1945.[4] Only three of them, however, advertised consistently throughout the period of war, namely Barratt and Lotus shoes, and Maenson suits, overcoats and uniforms. The majority bought their advertising space either before the introduction of Utility and rationing in 1941, including Viyella socks, Swallow raincoats, and underwear by Aertex, Meridian, Morley and Wolsey, or as the cessation of hostilities in Europe drew nearer in the spring of 1944, including once more Aertex, Meridian, Swallow and Wolsey as well as Baracuta overcoats, K shoes and Radiac shirts. Austin Reed advertised only twice in the pages of the magazine; first in a special number on 29 July 1940 dealing with life in the United States, when it promoted itself as having 'an admiration for all things American' and looked forward to the day when it could once more sell its goods on board the transatlantic liners *Aquitania* and *Queen Mary*, and afterwards on 24 April 1945, when it mused on the return of carefree days playing sport and evenings in white tie and tails, for which 'The Austin Reed Service will be there'.

Whatever the cost of placing an advertisement, one upshot of the shortage of paper was that newspapers such as the *Daily Mail*, *Daily Express* and *The Times* began to allocate precious advertising space on a solus or quasi-solus basis. More often than not, however, in popular weeklies like *Punch*, and *Picture Post* between two and six advertisements for entirely different products vied for attention with each other on the same page. In the spring of 1940, several men's wear retailers circumvented this kind of promotion of disparate commodities in a series of novel composite advertorials entitled 'Britain: Leader of Men's Wear Styles' in *The Times*, which were intended to boost the home and export markets for male dress. Between 16 and 19 April 1940, the four full-page and half-page features focused consecutively on a different type of clothing – tailoring, woollens and knitwear, sportswear, shirts and accessories, and headwear and footwear. Breaking with the patriotic rhetoric of their independent wartime publicity, companies like Austin Reed, Daks Simpson and Wolsey (socks and pullovers) made no mention of the war in the advertisements that were included for them, while, in common with the *Times'* editorial, others like Celanese, Meridian, Lillywhite, Burberry, Gieves, Moss Bros. and Braemar all referred to their merchandise in the context of the war effort. Burberry, for example, promoted their weatherproofs as a sound investment in the face of a prolonged war, emphasising the garment's versatility and longevity, and Meridian's advertisement, 'the wheels of industry are "flying" too', made a symbolic link between their hosiery and underwear machine-production methods and the coordinated take-off of a battalion of RAF fighter planes. Battersby and Co., one of the manufacturers featured in *The Times* on 19 April 1940, also found that display advertising in shop stores and windows was a more effective way of shifting merchandise like their new Rockwell hat, since it enabled them to showcase their products from different angles and thereby attract the eye of the man who 'is probably reluctant to buy a hat at all, under present circumstances' (*Advertiser's Weekly* 1940a:64).

At the outset Churchill was opposed to government intervention in the production and consumption of clothes because he felt that it would lead to drabness in dress and thereby lower public morale (Sladen 1995:26; Reynolds 1999:149). Thus the consumer did not encounter any official restrictions in purchasing clothing during the first year of the war. Nonetheless fashion retailers tended to encourage the public to realise that if they spent their money wisely they could buy the clothing they needed and contribute to the war effort at the same time. As Gloag (1940: 211–12) argued: 'at a time like this, public opinion cracks down on mere fashion . . . So qualities like resistance to wear and tear, long life, and practical everyday use, are given particular prominence'. In 1940, for instance, Rego the tailors promoted a suit with the slogan 'Pay only 94/6 for this suit and put the rest into war savings', and Austin Reed's 'In these days of war' press campaign of 1939–40 in the *Evening Standard, Daily Telegraph* and *Sunday Times*, echoed Gloag by advising customers that fashionability must now be tempered by the 'new situation':

> In days of peace when people had money to spare, not all the clothes bought at Austin Reed's were given the full amount of wear that was in them. Now they will, in a National Cause, show what they are made of. A man needs clothes, and he must buy clothes. Let him therefore buy clothes that are good clothes, that are honest in price, faithful in wear and friendly to the very distant end.

The point of such advertising was to encourage more judicious spending through the purchase of fewer, better quality items of clothing. In actuality the reverse situation ensued with spending on fashion increasing exponentially during the first two years of the war as many people began to stockpile garments in order to avoid the clothing shortages that had occurred during the First World War. Added to this, spiralling inflation had resulted in the clothing price index rising by 66 per cent in the period between March 1938 and March 1941. Mindful of how the high price of clothing and profiteering had been the cause of considerable civil unrest among the working classes in 1918, therefore, Chancellor Kingsley Wood was forced to introduce several measures to stabilise the cost of clothing. In May 1940 the government was already the sole importer of 90 per cent of raw materials, including wool, which it distributed on a quota basis to registered manufacturers and wholesalers under the Limitation of Supplies (Miscellaneous) Order of 6 June 1940, and on 21 October 1940 it had also imposed purchase tax on clothing. But one year later, the two measures that were to have the most impact on fashion manufacture and retail were implemented – the Utility clothing scheme and clothes rationing – and by 1943 the Board of Trade came to control all aspects of civilian clothing through various statutory measures.

The Impact of Utility and Rationing

The Utility clothing scheme, which was masterminded by the Board of Trade in the spring of 1941, aimed to produce essential clothing using as little material and as few workers as possible. To this end, manufacturers were encouraged to produce longer runs of a smaller range of items, and under the Essential Works Order of January 1942 designated firms that agreed to devote not less than 75 per cent of their turnover to Utility clothing and other contract work such as service uniforms and exports were apportioned with at least 65 per cent of available stocks of Utility fabrics. By 1 June 1942, some 1,996 manufacturers had received designated status (Reynolds 1999: 130). The majority of them employed more than twenty workers and, like Burton's and The Fifty Shilling Tailors, produced items of clothing at the cheaper end of the market, but middle-market men's outfitters like Austin Reed and Simpson were also afforded designated status as producers of good quality service uniforms. In addition, the Goods and Services (Price Control) Bill of July 1941 ensured adequate supplies of working-class clothing, while from August 1942 all Utility garments were exempted from purchase tax provided they were not made from fur materials. There were no regulations concerning the design of garments until Austerity measures were introduced in mid-1942 restricting the amount of material that could be used for both Utility and non-Utility clothes destined for the home market.

On 21 January 1942, Sir Andrew Duncan, President of the Board of Trade, informed the House of Commons that men's suits bearing the CC 41 Utility label, which had been designed by Reginald Shipp, were beginning to appear in the shops (Figure 32), and in September 1942 Simpson's organised a display of winter Utility fashions (Sladen 1995: 31 and 50). The new suits were made from familiar woollen cloths but the jackets had a maximum of three pockets and buttons and were slightly shorter in length than usual, while trousers were cut more narrowly with a maximum leg length of 48 centimetres and turn-ups were abolished completely. The Central Price Regulation Committee estimated that the maximum price of men's Utility suits and overcoats would be 6–7 per cent less than the 'normal market' (PRO, BT 64/182), which in 1942–3 meant a top price of £5 3s 6d.[5]

Shortly after the inception of the Utility scheme, clothes rationing was also introduced on 7 June 1941. This meant that items of clothing had to be purchased with both cash and coupons. The standard issue to all British citizens, regardless of their class or income, was sixty-six coupons per annum until 1942, after which time it was reduced to forty-eight coupons, and by 1945 to thirty-six coupons. The coupon value was determined according to the amount and quality of cloth used in the making of any garment, such that in 1941 a man's three-piece suit was valued at twenty-six coupons, an overcoat at sixteen, a sweater at eight, a cotton shirt at seven, and underwear and shoes at four apiece. However, although the coupon value of any garment was static and the issue was standardised, this did not mean that all suits, for example, retailed for the same price. Non-Utility garments, though fewer in number than Utility garments, were usually made from better quality cloths and not exempt from purchase tax. Accordingly they cost more, but afforded those customers who had the wherewithal some choice in a limited market. At the same time, individuals could redeem their coupons in exchange for whichever items of clothing they preferred and in accordance with what type of garments were deficient in their prewar wardrobes. Thus Sir Henry Channon recorded in his diary, just after rationing had been announced, that he already had forty or more suits and that 'Socks will be the shortage. Apart from these, if I am not bombed, I have enough clothes to last me for years' (Rhodes-James 1967:307). Likewise, individuals were not prevented from stockpiling coupons from one year to the next, and nor was the pooling of coupons within a family unit illegitimate.

To a large extent, therefore, the introduction of Utility and rationing did manage to regulate the clothing industry, and according to research conducted in Bolton, Worcester and London by the Advertising Service Guild (f. 1939) for Mass-Observation (1941), both schemes found wide support with men from all classes. In turn, a survey by the Oxford Institute of Statistics in 1942 revealed that there were approximately 10,100 men's wear retailers in the United Kingdom with coupon accounts (*Advertiser's Weekly* 1944c:245). But by the same token spending on clothes had not increased appreciably – in the year 1 June 1941 to 31 May 1942, Board of Trade official figures recorded that the value of sales was not much higher than it had been two years before the outbreak of war (*Advertiser's Weekly* 1942b). By extension, as raw materials and the quantity of both clothing and coupons became scarcer, the volume of press advertisements for men's wear started to decline by 1942. On this level, for example, it is interesting to note how W.S. Crawford could promote the abundance of Wolsey socks and underwear in *Picture Post* on 9 November 1940, maintaining that, 'The very pick of [this] rich store comes to us at Wolsey', and how by the spring of 1941 it was forced to add the condition, 'If your favourite shop runs short of Wolsey – don't blame them. Remember, "there's a war on"!', at the bottom of a humorous campaign with rhyming couplets by G.H. Saxon Mills and cartoons by Nicholas Bentley (*Picture Post*, 3 May 1941). Short supply of materials was particularly troublesome for non-designated companies, yet many of those that did enjoy designated status also advertised less and less, as I have already indicated was the case in *Picture Post*. In fact, only two retailers – The Fifty Shilling Tailors and Simpson – chose to advertise their garments in *Picture Post* in the context of Utility and rationing, the former its civilian goods and the latter its uniform services.[6] Similarly, from the autumn of 1941 Austin Reed began to concentrate its publicity exclusively on the Summit shirt brand in the *Evening Standard*, *Punch*, *The Sphere* and in London Underground railway carriages.

Nor did or could Utility and rationing entirely erase the class distinctions that had existed in the interwar period when it came to earnings. As the war progressed, fewer people were embedded in the lower income thresholds. A White Paper on National Expenditure (Cmd 6623, 1945) had revealed that the number of those earning less than £250 per annum (Class E) had dropped from 17 million in 1938–9 to around 15 million by 1942, as well as an exponential rise in the number of those earning between £250 and £1,000 per annum (Classes C and D). However, the largest income group – 5.5 million individuals – earned between £250 and £500 at this time, and more people also began to earn between £1,000 and £10,000 per annum (Classes B and C).[7] This meant that during wartime men's wear retailers were still targeting more or less the same markets that they had in the interwar period – principally, Classes B, C and D. But the levelling effect of the coupon system made it paramount for individual retailers to promote similar items of clothing with regard to their difference in price and quality of materials. As the *Advertiser's Weekly* argued, 'There are two forms of currency now, and consumers with a lot of coupons are not usually those with a lot of money' (Frankel and Ady 1945:26). This distinction is much in evidence, for example, if we compare and contrast advertisements for Austin Reed and The Fifty Shilling Tailors.

As we saw in Chapter 5, there was considerable differential in the price of a three-piece suit produced by each of these companies, yet the rhetoric and style of advertising for The Fifty Shilling Tailors closely mimicked that of Austin Reed in order to suggest that their core market was more or less the same middle-class, white-collar male as their more upmarket competitors (Figures 14 and 29). Equally, both companies enjoyed designated status during the Second World War and were thus expected to dedicate at least 75 per cent of their turnover to the production of Utility garments and/or service uniforms. But whereas there was appreciable iconographical overlap in the interwar publicity of both companies, during the period of war there was as much divergence.

The Austin Reed campaigns of 1939–41, still conducted by Pritchard and Wood, stuck closely to prewar advertising in terms of class but were organised around heroic images of war officers in uniforms and greatcoats and civilians in overcoats. Suits were only occasionally part of their wartime campaign, principally between 1939 and 1940. Bodoni, in different weights and sizes, bold and italics, was still the preferred typeface for the verbal rhetoric of these advertisements, and interestingly the copy of some Austin Reed pre-Utility campaigns invoked austerity measures indirectly. A promotion in *Punch* (4 September 1940) for a single-breasted tweed lounge suit retailing for just over seven guineas, for instance, stated: 'Of course they obey the first principle of wartime economics – they are very hard-wearing'. After the Utility scheme was officially launched, however, the company's publicity overlooked austerity measures altogether and the idea of quality was expressed not in terms of coupon value but the intrinsic worth and cost of the garment itself. Hence, a promotion in *Punch* (12 November 1941) for greatcoats and overcoats stressed the point that civilian clothing and service personnel's uniforms shared the same high standards: 'Good clothes, faultless tailoring and absolute correctness of detail are in every Austin Reed coat, whether it be of the "great" or "over" variety'. Nonetheless such tailoring did not come cheap since service greatcoats retailed at ten guineas, and woollen Ulsters 'cost 8 guineas and upward'.[8]

By contrast, promotions by the agency Rumble, Crowther & Nicholas for The Fifty Shilling Tailors dealt with the company's relationship to Utility and rationing in entirely different terms, to the extent that they overtly proclaimed Utility had reinforced rather than altered in the least the original ethos of the company's rational tailoring scheme. Civilian suits and overcoats were the focus of the campaign – in 1942 the former retailed at 95s and the latter at 79s 6d – and the point of their advertising was to emphasise that these prices (around 50 per cent cheaper than those at Austin Reed) offered the best value for clothing coupons (Figure 32).[9] In some advertisements the dialogic/testimonial format that had been deployed to great effect in their prewar copy, was also exploited to convey how Utility measures had not led to a drop in quality in the garments produced by The Fifty Shilling Tailors. To this end, a paternalistic tone was adopted with the company's owner, Sir Henry Price, answering questions either from an anonymous interviewer or from professional types such as a draughtsman. In an advertisement in *Picture Post* (31 January 1942), for example, he attested that:

> Indeed, I might even go so far as to say that coupon tailoring is really an extension of Rational Tailoring to the whole nation . . . We know how to make a good suit at the lowest economic price. That is why I say with confidence that Rational Tailoring offers the best coupon value in tailoring today.

During the Second World War, therefore, the price of clothing by different retailers reinforced the class polarities that both coupon value was intended to disavow and interwar publicity for men's wear companies at the cheaper end of the market had connoted as being no longer important. Data on clothing expenditure garnered by the Board of Trade and reproduced in *Advertiser's Weekly* in June 1945 underscores this point. Figures cited for the average prices paid for particular items of clothing by different class groups, revealed that in 1941–2, men from income groups C, D and E were prepared to pay between £6 and £4 10s for a three-piece suit in 1941–2, and between £7 3s and £5 15s in 1943–4, whereas men in income groups A and B would have paid £9 15s in 1941–2 and £9 12s in 1943–44 (Frankel and Ady 1945:34).[10] On this basis, men from income classes C, D and E would have gravitated naturally toward garments from The Fifty Shilling Tailors, and men from classes A and B shopped at Austin Reed.

Moreover, the same marketing survey demonstrated considerable variation in the purchase of different types of male garments during the war period. With regard to class, men in Groups A and B maintained their purchases of raincoats, trousers, pullovers and underwear, Group C preferred to buy underwear, pullovers and nightwear, while Groups D and E devoted their coupons and income to socks, shirts and shoes (Frankel and Ady 1945: 30). But in general terms between 1941 and 1944, the most consistently popular garments were socks (on average every man purchased between two and four new pairs), shirts (one or two for every man), and boots and shoes (between one and two pairs for every man). By comparison other garments were in less demand: only 34 per cent of men bought a new suit in 1941–2, and less than 20 per cent in 1943–4, while less than 20 per cent bothered with a new raincoat or overcoat, pullover and nightwear (ibid: 28). It is interesting to note that the men's wear advertisements that appeared in *Picture Post* for the same period accord with this general trend. Hence, although we find promotions for suits by Maenson, we find many more promotions for footwear (Barratt and Lotus were the most consistent advertisers), socks (Viyella and Wolsey) and underwear (Wolsey, Viscana and Meridian) than we do for suits or knitwear. But the preferences of whatever Group A and B readers it had were also addressed: Swallow raincoats, which retailed at 30 shillings, for example, were advertised regularly throughout the war period, and between 1940 and 1941 a couple of promotions for Burberry and Aquascutum also appeared.[11]

'A walking – as well as a warring – nation': Men's Wear Advertising as Propaganda

Conducted in the spirit of wartime patriotism, men's wear advertising between 1939 and 1945 had much in common with the aims and objectives of government propaganda. This is not to say that the two state bodies that controlled official publicity during the Second World War, the Department of Propaganda and the Ministry of Information, intervened in the production and circulation of advertising campaigns by commercial companies and retailers, rather to argue that many men's wear promotions were imbued with the ideology of the 'people's war' and collective invincibility that had more directly been encoded in government-sponsored campaigns like 'Dig for Victory'.[12] We can observe this in operation in advertisements created by Willing's Press Service for Meridian socks and underwear in

1940, which mobilised belligerent iconography and slogans not only to promote their goods but also to link the production, and by extension the consumption, of them to the war effort. To this end, official discourse itself was occasionally incorporated into the rhetoric of some advertisements. Thus a Meridian campaign in *Picture Post* (16 March 1940, Figure 33) opened with the caption, 'Let us to the task to the battle and the toil', a fragment from one of Churchill's early wartime speeches,[13] while a series of eight advertisements created by the London Press Exchange for Radiac shirts in 1944 offered support for the Board of Trade 'Make Do and Mend' scheme, which had been launched in 1943, by including details of how to turn a frayed shirt cuff or collar.

By contrast, other manufacturers like Barratt Shoes hit a more topical note in their wartime publicity, referring to specific cultural and political events. Apart from a lull in 1942, following the introduction of Utility measures for footwear production on 30 June 1942, Barratt and Lotus were two of the most prolific companies to advertise during the Second World War; between November 1939 and 8 September 1945, for instance, no fewer than thirty advertisements for Lotus and seventy advertisements for Barratt appeared in *Picture Post*. Masterminded by W.S. Crawford, the 'Walk the Barratt Way' campaigns, many of them full or half-page in size, traded on the familiar interwar format involving Mr Barratt in conversation with his clients. But from the outset, actual figures like Hitler were woven into the rhetoric of the copy in order to portray the indomitability of the British under siege and the contribution of Barratt shoes to the moral, mental and physical health of the nation. References abound to the idea that the British were a 'walking – as well as a warring – nation' (*Picture Post*, 26 April 1941), and how Barratt shoes were enabling the ordinary citizen to perform his/her patriotic duty by keeping fit. Accordingly in one advertisement Mr Barratt expatiates: 'in war-time Barratts are a positive national asset! . . . it's an ill wind that blows no one any good – and though this wind from Germany is a bit uncomfortable, it *has* made us walk. And that saves us more than coal bills and fares. It saves doctor's bills as well' (Figure 34). On other occasions more specific historical references were invoked to portray a similar point concerning optimism in the face of adversity. The bad news that Greece and Crete had been occupied by the Nazis in May 1941, for example, could be ameliorated by 'trouble-free feet' (*Picture Post*, 27 September 1941), while even the Blitzkrieg tactics of 1940 formed the basis of puns in the 'My shoes are in blitz and pieces' campaign of the same year.

Thus the propaganda messages of Barratt advertising promoted shoes in a humanist context, to the extent that the British were portrayed as superior to the Germans because of their sense of humour and forbearance. While this kind of promotion clearly worked with popular stereotypes, however, it was of a different order to the crude stereotyping of the other as the 'Hun' and 'marauding ape' that had ensued during the First World War.[14] Instead of being emotionally heavy-handed in its effects, therefore, advertising by the likes of Barratt worked instead with what Barthes called 'depoliticised speech', in so far as this could be used to sell products by implying that historical events could always be overcome by human nature (Barthes 1973:142–5). Hence, the British could undergo any privation – even shortages in clothing (as underwear manufacturers like Wolsey, the subject of the next chapter, were quick to realise) – so long as they ended up both militaristic and moral victors.

Notes

1. See *Art and Industry* (1942).
2. For a thorough examination of the surrealist aspects of this campaign, orchestrated by the agency W.S. Crawford, see A. Lewis (2003).
3. *Advertiser's Weekly*, 21 March 1948, p.504 included details collated by *The Economist* of the respective 1937 and 1947 advertising rates and column space for the *Daily Express*, *Daily Mail*, *Daily Herald*, *Daily Mirror*, *Daily Telegraph* and *The Times*. Comparative ad rates for both the *Mail* and *Herald*, for example, were £6 and £15, while their dedicated space was 44 and 42 per cent, and 44 and 19–23 per cent respectively.)
4. Advertisements for the following companies appeared in *Picture Post* between 8 July 1939 and 29 September 1945: Aertex, Aquascutum, Austin Reed, Avenue shoes, Baracuta, Barratt, Burberry, Catesby, Coopers Y-fronts, Dunlop rainwear, The Fifty Shilling Tailors, K shoes, Lotus shoes, Maenson, Meridian, Morley, Norvic shoes, Radiac shirts, Simpson, Swallow raincoats, Viscana underwear, Viyella socks, John White shoes, Willerby the tailors, and Wolsey.
5. The 2001 equivalent is £148.10. This figure and those cited in the following notes are from McCusker (2003).
6. For Simpson ads, see *Picture Post*, 26 September, 10 October, 24 October, 7 and 28 November 1942. For The Fifty Shilling Tailors, see *Picture Post*, 31 January, 25 April and 20 June 1942, 29 May and 11 December 1943.
7. The White Paper (Table 26) estimated that in 1938–9 there were 1,745,000 individuals earning between £250 and £500, 500,000 between £500 and £1,000, 195,000 between £1,000 and £2,000, and 97,000 between £2,000 and £10,000. In 1942–3, the number of wage-earners in each income group had increased respectively to 5.5 million, 1.1 million, 295,00 and 102,000. The 2001 equivalents of these sums are as follows: £7,154.53 (£250), £14,309.07 (£500), £28,618.14 (£1,000), £57,236.27 (£2,000) and £286,181.37 (£10,000).

8. Respective 2001 equivalents are £358.69 and £286.95.
9. Respective 2001 equivalents are £135.94 and £113.96.
10. Respective 2001 equivalents for these sums are as follows: £171.71 (£6), £128.78 (£4 10s), £196.73 (£7 3s), £158.21 (£5 15s), £279.03 (£9 15s) and £264.14 (£9 12s).
11. Swallow raincoats were advertised on no fewer than thirty-eight occasions in *Picture Post* between 2 March 1940 and 1 September 1945. An ad for Burberry appeared on 13 January 1940, and one for Aquascutum on 8 March 1941.
12. Government expenditure on advertising between March 1940 and June 1945 totalled £9.5 million (Nevett 1982: 170).
13. The statement continues '– each to our part, each to our station'.
14. See Baker (1990) for an illuminating discussion of this type of symbolism.

–7–

'Nice Stuff Against the Skin'
Pleasure and Spectatorship in Men's Underwear Advertising

> Among the few products where a 'manly' advertising appeal is certainly required we can rank men's underwear.
>
> William Farringdon, *Advertiser's Weekly*, 5 April 1929

Most histories of fashion, including those devoted specifically to undergarments, tend either to marginalise the development of men's underclothing or ignore it altogether.[1] One of the chief reasons for this relegation lies in the comparative simplicity and utilitarian aspect of men's underwear itself, a point which is expressed by Willett and Cunnington (1981: 41) in *The History of Underclothes*: 'Man has never used provocative underclothing; its plain prose has been singular in contrast to the poetic allurements worn by women'. Yet this logic of 'out of sight, out of mind' also underplays the actual dynamics of technological and stylistic change that have taken place in the design of the garments themselves, particularly since the end of the nineteenth century, and the fact that every significant streamlining or reduction of outer garments has necessitated a corresponding modification in the amount and style of underwear worn both by women and men. Moreover, while men's underwear may often be regarded as prosaic, when we examine the various ways that it has been codified in advertising during the twentieth century, more than a certain 'poetic allure' becomes apparent. Thus Richard Martin, perhaps the only fashion historian to have dealt with the subject of men's underwear in a significant way, has argued that: 'The representation of underwear has always presented vexing problems of masculine cultural identity, definitions of male discretion, and the engineering principles of the underwear garments vis-à-vis the human body' (Martin 1992:19). This is probably most evident in the erotic appeal of advertisements for men's underwear produced since the early 1970s, such as those for Hom and, most notably, in various campaigns for Calvin Klein. The first of these tantalisingly voyeuristic promotions, produced by the In-House agency, appeared as a traffic-stopping bill-board in New York's Times Square in 1982, and subsequently in magazines like American *GQ*.

But it would be erroneous to regard this type of display of men's bodies as the exclusive concern of postmodern or late capitalist culture, as examples of men's underwear advertising in Britain as well as the United States earlier in the twentieth century reveal. Indeed, such promotions were ubiquitous, appearing in most daily newspapers as well as an eclectic spread of periodicals, including *Punch* and the *Radio Times*. At the same time, as the Figures in Table 3 demonstrate (see Chapter 3), amounts comparable to those spent on advertising tailoring and men's wear in general were expended on promotions for woollen underwear, particularly in October and November 1934.[2] While these sums include publicity for women's and children's underwear as well, even if we apportion them equally it has to be conceded that advertisers were prepared to spend considerable amounts of money on placing press promotions for men's underwear. Meridian and Morley, for instance, spent just over £4,000 and £6,000 respectively on placing press advertisements between October and December 1932.[3] Accordingly, in this chapter I want to uncover the mythology that it is only since the 1980s that men's underwear advertising in Britain became an economically potent force as well as visually provocative and erotic (as we shall see, many promotions of the interwar period were artfully executed). In this regard the visual and verbal rhetoric in publicity for several manufacturers during the 1920s and 1930s underscored the fetishistic nature of underwear, the feel of 'nice stuff against the skin' as an advertisement for Courtaulds in the *Radio Times* on 19 March 1937 proclaimed (Figure 37), while in their imbrication of pleasure, spectatorship and gender many advertisements also resorted to strategies of camp and sexual ambiguity. But first, it is necessary to raise once more the issue of advertising style to see how it related to the promotion of new materials and styles of underwear.

A Fitting Foundation: Underwear and Advertising Style

On both sides of the Atlantic the interwar period was crucial in the technological and stylistic development of both the men's underwear and advertising industries. On the basis of the advertisements that appeared in various magazines and newspapers between 1900 and 1939, for instance, at least fifty different men's underwear companies existed in the United States and Britain. Among them were several long-standing manufacturers of hosiery, who in the early twentieth century had also turned to the production of wool and cotton underwear. In the United States these included Fruit of the Loom, founded in 1856, B.V.D. (1876) and Coopers (1876), who pioneered Y-front briefs and jockey shorts in the 1930s; and in Britain, Wolsey (1753), I.R. Morley (1795), Allen Solly (1799), Peter Scott & Co. Ltd (1888), which produced the Pesco brand, and Two Steeples (1895). As these and other companies vied with each other for trade, they began not only to produce inventive lines of underwear in different styles and fabrics but also to promote them in more novel ways. Consequently, men's underwear was bound up in the debates concerning a new discourse for a modern, democratic form of advertising and its importance in attracting the most suitable target audience, which we have already addressed in Chapters 1 and 2. During the first ten years of the twentieth century, for example, Mather & Crowther's advertisements for Wolsey underwear, which usually foregrounded the manufacturer's symbolic trademark of Cardinal Wolsey's head, were frequently praised for their 'boldness in design, directness in wording, and . . . striking pictorial quality' (*Advertising World*, February 1907: 298). By contrast, promotions for Pesco tended to incorporate photographic imagery and copy in imaginative configurations, such as the press campaign for the autumn of 1907 which reproduced an aerial photograph of grazing sheep penetrated by a wedge-shaped space containing text that drew attention to the lightness and warmth afforded by woollen underwear. At the same time, it was realised that the evolution of striking publicity could contribute significantly to a company's financial success. Thus advertisements for Pesco underwear were distributed at the entrance to the National Scottish Exhibition in Edinburgh, held in the summer of 1908, in order to get people to visit its stall, and Peter Scott & Co. claimed that sales of the brand in 1909 had increased sixfold after nearly ten years of advertising in the general and trade press (*Advertising World* 1910).[4] As R.H. Currington commented: '"Pesco" advertising is a fascinating study in practical application . . . the "Pesco" policy has transformed a business that started in an old hand-frame establishment in a back lane of Hawick into the biggest underwear concern in Scotland' (Currington 1919:358).

Along with promotions for Horne Brothers' Cutuna brand of underwear, therefore, both and Wolsey and Scott were generally commended by the *Advertising World* for the standard of their publicity before the First World War. Nonetheless the magazine did conclude that British underwear advertising lagged behind promotions for American brands such as B.V.D. in terms of quality, character, form and symbolism (*Advertising World* 1913c). During the interwar period, however, advertising for men's underwear in Britain became more adventurous in terms of both style and content, and, in common with promotions for other items of male clothing, was transformed by the impact of modernist debates on the use of white space, asymmetrical layouts and appropriate forms of illustrations and typefaces that we discussed in Chapter 4. I have already cited how Cyril King singled out the harmonious interplay of text and image in an 1927 underwear promotion by Hope Brothers as the avatar of a new style of advertising to which other retailers should aspire (Figure 7), but several other underwear manufacturers also demonstrated a clear understanding of modernist principles of design in their publicity. In 1930, for instance, W.S. Crawford took over the Jaeger account, which they rejuvenated with figures drawn by Prentis of robotic men performing various movements and type set in Gill Sans. During the 1930s also promotions for I.R. Morley's Theta brand that were handled by Pritchard, Wood and Partners used Kabel light typography for the headlines alongside a contrasting Ambassador serif face for the main copy and illustrations with a strong sense of linear and tonal values (Figure 35), while under the art direction of Marjorie Marene (alias Marjorie Janko) several promotions for British Celanese were designed by Traus of Carlton Studios in a fashionably monumental *moderne* style (see front cover illustration).

But it was probably the interwar publicity for Wolsey underwear, which was in the hands of several different agencies at this time, that was the most stylistically varied. According to the *Advertiser's Weekly*'s 'Quarterly Analysis of Press Advertising' for the period April to September 1933 Wolsey's average monthly budget of £1,400 for press advertising space was the largest of the nine manufacturers of woollen underwear listed.[5] During the 1930s full-page promotions for Wolsey's goods could be found in the *Daily Mail* and *Daily Express*, and half-page advertisements in the *Daily Mirror* and *Daily Herald*. Under Pritchard, Wood and Partners, the hallmark of Wolsey advertising between 1930 and 1932 was a clean layout, usually incorporating the company's trademark alongside an illustration of a male figure, with headlines set in Erbar bold, one of the new German sans serif typefaces designed in the early 1920s (Harrison 1930a:280). By contrast, in the spring of 1934 the London Press Exchange introduced a sense of humour to Wolsey advertising with the Walrus-moustached and monocled character of Colonel Blimp. Conceived by the cartoonist David Low, who worked principally for Lord Beaverbrook's *Evening Standard* between 1927 and 1950, and first introduced on 21 April 1934, Blimp was the corpulent militaristic gas-bag who Low used to symbolise both right- and left-wing political incompetence. In the context of Wolsey's advertising campaign the political side of his personality does not surface; instead in promotions such as 'Rather winsome, my dear', where he is depicted proudly showing off his new vest and shorts to his wife as she eats her breakfast in bed, he is set up as an object of mirth in order to make athletic forms of underwear appealing to older and more portly males. Two years later, Arks Publicity began to use photographs in some of their promotions for Wolsey underwear and hosiery, such as the cards that were displayed on the escalators of the London Underground. It must be noted, however, that photographic advertising for underwear was the exception at this time in Britain and did not become the norm until the 1960s. Only three further advertisements using photographs were found, for instance, in the research conducted for this chapter and, probably on the grounds of decorum, they appeared in the trade journal *MAN and his Clothes* rather than the general press.[6] Furthermore, according to an anonymous reviewer in *Advertiser's Weekly* on 5 November 1936, hand-drawn illustrations of undergarments were favourable to the realism of photographs since, 'To show them [undergarments] on the masculine form is to reveal it in its most undignified and ridiculous garb' (p. 214). And in any case, the author argued, that 'Men's underwear advertising isn't inspiring stuff for the artist. No glamour about it. To show the garments themselves is not only dull, but useless, for one brand looks much the same as another'.

In common with other men's wear retailers and manufacturers, therefore, the advertisers of male underwear faced a twofold challenge at this time – how to transcend the apathy or resistance of the male customer, and how to combat the idea that men don't care what underwear looks like as long as it keeps them comfortable. Essentially, as G.F. Curtis wrote in 1927, the overriding task was to convince the public that 'there is more in underwear than has met the eye' (Curtis 1927: 28). And, as far as Cyril King was concerned, this meant allying atmospheric advertising to 'reason why' or factual advertising. 'Men's wear advertising', he admonished manufacturers, 'must be subtle and at the same time must contain facts about the merchandise you are selling' (King 1927: 28).

A Material World: Underwear, Health and Sport

One of the most common ways that this double impetus was codified in men's wear advertisements for several manufacturers during the first half of the twentieth century was by framing health and comfort in terms of sporting ability. In 1927, for example, promotions for both British Celanese and Aertex emphasised respectively the versatility of their rayon and cellular cotton underwear to keep you cool or warm, depending on the weather, by representing men at the top of their game in sports as diverse as golf, cricket and tennis. This athletic context was continued in their publicity during the 1930s, by which time a similar message was being connoted in advertisements for Irmo (manufactured by Morley), Meridian and Courtaulds (Figures 36 and 38).[7]

Hence, on one level the rhetoric of these promotions clearly overlapped with the discourse of reform for better hygiene and living conditions that had grown apace in Britain, Europe and the United States since the late nineteenth century. By the 1920s and 1930s the culture of the fit and healthy body was central to such debates and, as we have already seen, organisations such as the British Men's Dress Reform Party (1929–37), in which J.C. Flugel was a leading figure, began to address the issue of restrictive clothing. In this respect, research was also under-taken into the efficacy of different materials for underwear, and usually centred on the relative merits of wool and cotton. In 1893, for example, a series of articles by Dr Gustav Jaeger, Professor of Zoology and Physiology at the University of Stuttgart, in *Aglaia* (published by the Healthy and Artistic Dress Association, which had been founded in 1890) had extolled the virtues of wool, since its porous nature would allow 'noxious inhalations to disperse' (Wilson 1985: 213–14). This point of view had been compounded after the experiences of army personnel during the First World War, when woollen underwear by the likes of Pesco had been issued to conscripts from October 1917 onwards (Currington 1919: 357). By contrast, Dr Lahmann, who ran a sanatorium in Dresden, insisted in 1938 that cotton mesh underwear was the most versatile since it was warm in winter and cool in summer (*MAN and his Clothes*, November 1938: 25). And in 1935 George Spencer of Cheapside devised a *juste milieu* in male underwear that pandered to both tastes, producing a range called Tuplex, which was made of botany wool but had an internal lining of superfine cotton. A contemporaneous advertisement in the national press claimed that the product had been widely tested among a range of professional types including doctors, actors, army officers and school teachers, and that over 99 per cent of them had liked wearing it (*MAN and his Clothes*, January 1935:10).

The question as to which material was the most suitable for underwear for the modern man was likewise analysed in articles in *MAN and his Clothes*, where support was given to the idea that lighter-weight fabrics and closer-fitting garments could be worn the whole year round on the grounds of style and health, witness this comment: 'When we take into consideration the fact that fully half the autumn underwear sold today is cut on athletic lines, there seems to be a plain indication that men in this country are getting healthier' (*MAN and his Clothes* 1937:26). In fact, the first half of the twentieth century witnessed considerable experimentation and ingenuity in the design and manufacture of more athletic and minimal forms of underclothing for men, such that many of the prototypes we are used to buying today were established. B.V.D. was one of the first companies to pioneer popular athletic styles of underwear in the United States and Britain with the introduction of the one-piece union suit in 1914. Modelled on an athlete's outfit, this was a loose-fitting combination of shorts and a sleeveless vest with an adjustable waistband that was initially made from lightweight cottons such as nainsook but by the 1920s was available in knitted cotton, silk, rayon and poplin. By the early 1920s, individual boxer shorts and vests had begun to supplant the one-piece union suit. The T-shirt had been available in North America since 1909, while boxer shorts had been issued to US servicemen during the First World War as summer attire and proved to be so popular that many men continued to wear them afterwards. Boxer shorts and vests with '*v*' or round necks also became available in Britain during the late 1920s, alongside French and American shorts in ribbed cotton or cashmere with fancy patterns and elasticated waistbands or adjustable side straps (Albemarle 1932). Styles of vests and trunks by Meridian in lightweight knitted lastex yarn, a mixture of wool and elastic originated in 1933–34, retailed in the region of 3s to 5s between 1927 and 1935, which meant that they would also have been within the pocket of the average working-class man, who earned typically £3 10s per week during the early 1930s. More expensive at this time was underwear by Aertex in knitted cellular cotton, which cost between 5s and 8s 6d, and underwear by British Celanese in rayon, an artificial cellulose silk first developed in 1905, which cost between 10s 6d and 15s 6d.[8]

After 1935, the Union Suit and boxer shorts were both largely superseded by the advent of Y-fronts, pioneered by Coopers Inc. of Kenosha, Wisconsin. In 1911 Coopers had devised the KKK (Kenosha Klosed Krotch) brand of underpants, which had two flaps of fabric at the front overlapping in a X-formation – a proto-type that was modified by Wolsey in Britain with their X-fold underpants in 1951. The first experimental Y-front briefs, called Model 1001, were patented in August 1935 in knitted mesh fabric and based on the swimming trunks with a front pouch as worn by men on the French Riviera. Initially these were viewed with great scepticism by the underwear industry and men's wear retailers alike but became an immediate success with the buying public – 12,000 pairs were purchased during the first week of promotion alone. At the same time *MAN and his Clothes* (August 1935: 46) commented that the new jockey shorts had been inspired by the 'spell of Tarzan and the Apes' and predicted that the style would also revolutionise the underwear market in Britain and Europe. Indeed, Lyle and Scott became the main franchiser of the brand for Britain, France and Denmark in 1938, manufacturing an average of 60,000 garments per week in their purpose-built factory in Hawick, Scotland from June 1939 onwards. The name 'Y-front' went on to become a generic term for other brands of men's underwear and greatly democratised the market. In Britain, for example, the basic range of Cooper Y-front jockey wear retailed at 3s 6d, which stood comparison with the price of knitted underwear by Meridian.

Significantly, the promotion of athletic underwear as a desirable garment was achieved not just in terms of class or income but of age as well, and *MAN and his Clothes* noted considerable polarisation in the British market for the new under-wear styles on this level. Sales surveys were revealing that colourful boxer shorts, for instance, were mostly being bought by a 'younger set of men', with brands in pale blue, silver grey, pale pink and green being much in demand (Albemarle 1931). The association of these kinds of shorts with fashionable young males is evident in an advertisement that appeared in *Punch* on 29 May 1929. This com-prised an illustration of a man wearing a button-top vest with coloured stripe trunks and a tagline affirming: 'Aertex in colour adds to the gaiety of nations'. While the word 'gay' had probably come into currency in the United States by the 1920s to refer to homosexuals, it is unclear whether the term was being used simultaneously in Britain in entirely the same way (Dynes 1990:456). Nonetheless, it is interesting to note that by this time pale blue had been designated the 'trade mark' of gay men according to the recollections of several correspondents in a Mass-Observation survey into sexual behaviour conducted in 1949, and to discern also the way that the male figure illustrated in the Aertex promotion crooks his wrist limply on his hips.[9] In this regard, we seem to have a more indeterminate codification of mascu-linity that trades on camp sensibility, a point that I shall return to in more detail.

Pleasure, Fetishism and Sexuality

The advertisements from the interwar period are not just instructive in the way they reveal the considerable variation that was available in cut, materials and styles, for they also connote the psychological momentum to be had in purchasing and wearing underwear. The haptic and sensory pleasures that could be attained from the touch and feel of soft, contour-revealing fabric, for example, is connoted in both the verbal and visual rhetoric of several of the underwear promotions reproduced here. Thus, the copy in the advertisements for 'Celanese' and Courtaulds stress the comfort and luxury of rayon underwear in terms of the 'clean, fresh feel of the fabric' and feel of 'nice stuff against the skin' respectively (Figures 36 and 37), while the texture of knitted wool is described as 'smooth and soft' in the publicity for Meridian, and 'silky smoothness' in that for Morley (Figures 39 and 35).[10] At the same time, the fact that the new styles of garments cling to and caress the skin – the idea of being 'snug inside' expressed in one Morley Theta campaign in 1935 – is represented in the way that the underpants fit snugly around the buttocks of the man viewed from behind (Figure 35). Such a fetishistic desire for soft, figure-hugging fabric is also expressed in an article that appeared in *MAN and his Clothes*, which stated: 'Once a man has experienced the psychological stimulus of fine underwear, he will never go back to an inferior quality' ('Stylus' 1927:14).

It is instructive to note the editorial referring to the nexus of psychological stimulus and fine underwear, and in this respect it seems to frame sensory pleasure in the context of Freud's thinking on fetishism. Freud had alluded to this in his 'Three Essays on the Theory of Sexuality' (1905), and in his psychoanalytic study of Leonardo in 1911, but discussed the idea in more detail in an essay published in the autumn of 1927, which appeared in an English translation by Joan Riviere in the *International Journal of Psycho-analysis* the following year. In the 'Three Essays' he had postulated that fetishism is an aberration, which arises when an individual fixates on an object – a part of the body such as the foot or hair, or a piece of material or clothing – as a replacement for normal sexual behaviour (Freud 1977a: 65–6). By 1910, however, he had added a footnote to his original text stating that, 'The shoe or slipper is a corresponding symbol of the *female* genitals' (Freud 1977a: 67), an idea that is compounded one year later in 'Leonardo da Vinci and a Memory of his Childhood', and reinforced in 'Fetishism' in 1927 where he maintains that the fetishised object was specifically, 'a substitute for the woman's (the mother's) penis that the little boy once believed in and . . . does not want to give up' (Freud 1977b: 352). Thus, as Freud has it, the fetish becomes a way of warding off the threat of castration.

Accordingly, underclothing has a special place in this economy of pain and pleasure since it crystallises 'the moment of undressing, the last moment in which the woman could still be regarded as phallic' (Freud 1977b: 354–5). By extension, men's underwear could be regarded in parallel terms, both as a way of concealing the phallic power of the male subject, and as a form of protection from his own (potential) unveiling and castration. It is interesting in this regard that the male in the advertisement for 'Celanese' does not even model the advertised brands of underwear but is represented playing tennis fully clothed (Figure 36). Moreover, the figure-hugging underpants represented in the Morley advertisement appear to align with the scopophilic drive and the play on concealing and revealing that is also evinced by Freud (Figure 35). In the 'Three Essays' he maintains: 'The progressive concealment of the body which goes along with civilisation keeps sexual curiosity awake. This curiosity seeks to complete the sexual object by revealing its hidden parts' (1977a: 69).

A Haze of Smoke: the Ambiguities of Pleasure and Spectatorship

Rather than being portrayed as something that should be kept out of sight, then, the undergarments in the majority of British advertisements in the twentieth century are implicated in a double-edged act of conspicuous consumption. Given that women were the largest purchasers of men's underwear – a survey by George Smith & Co. revealed that by the early 1950s they were buying 85 per cent of men's socks and underclothing – it is hardly surprising to find some advertisers making an overt appeal to them.[11] The 1937 Courtaulds advertisement 'Confidential – To Wives and Mothers' is one such that interpellates women as active agents in the consumption of men's undergarments, but it does so in patriarchal terms (Figure 37). Thus the copy objectifies women not only as the natural purchasers but also as the launderers of men's underwear. By contrast, the illustration by Tisdall Carter of two men in their shorts and vests sharing a drink, ostensibly in a ship's cabin, portrays an exclusive homosocial atmosphere, something which appears to be the norm in publicity for men's underwear until after the Second World War, by which time women were not just referred to but sometimes actually or symbolically included in certain advertisements. During the interwar period, therefore, the males in such advertisements were frequently represented as solipsistic narcissists, while their bodies were also put forward for the spectatorial pleasure of others, by which I mean men as well as women. Furthermore, as the campaign for Aertex in 1929 reveals, male sexuality and masculine identity could be connoted in somewhat transgressive and queer terms, a suggestion that is amplified in underwear promotions for the likes of 'Celanese', Chilprufe, Irmo and Meridian, all of which represent men in their underwear and smoking cigarettes in intimate surroundings such as the bedroom or dressing room (front cover and Figures 38–40).[12]

Of course, one would not want to overdetermine the gayness of some of these texts, which like Figure 37, could be regarded as innocently homosocial. But, the camp gestures and poses portrayed in them also nod in the direction of queer desire, and trade on the irony that those in the know will recognise such codes while those on the outside will remain oblivious to them.[13] While Christopher Isherwood and others have rightly argued that camp 'is terribly hard to define' and by no means exclusive to male homosexuals (Isherwood 1954:126; Dynes 1990: 189), nonetheless these advertisements seem to function on the level of camp that Richard Dyer argues is, 'A way of poking fun at the whole cosmology of restrictive sex roles and sexual identifications which our society uses to oppress its women and repress its men' (Dyer 1979: 67–8). Particularly suggestive in these promotions is the trope of smoking. Once again, an idea from Freud's 'Three Essays' (1977a: 98–9) springs to mind here, inasmuch as he argues that smoking can signify a deep-seated desire to recuperate the pleasure of contact with the mother's breast, encountered as an erotogenic zone during breastfeeding. But Freud is speaking of obsessive smoking rather than the social activity that appears to take place in the advertisements. Nor can or should we regard the communal act of smoking in these advertisements as being as straightforward in terms of normative masculine identities as the solitary act of smoking connoted, for instance, in many tobacco campaigns of the period. Rather, a compelling and evidential reason for decoding these texts in terms of homosexual desire is furnished by the gay American author Edward Irenaeus Prime Stevenson, who wrote under the nom-de-plume of 'Xavier Mayne'. In *The Intersexes: A History of Similisexualism as a Problem in Social Life* (1908), Mayne not only describes how the use of cigarettes was a common overture to sexual contact between men, but also pinpoints how certain furtive or keen looks were a 'signal and challenge everywhere current and understood among homosexuals' (Mayne 1908: 427–8). Furthermore, as George Chauncey Jnr's illuminating analysis of sexual practices between 1919 and 1920 among naval officers at Newport, Rhode Island reveals, these camp in-codes were not the exclusive province of gay men or 'queers' but had also been assimilated by straight men seeking casual sex with other males (Chauncey 1985).

David B. Boyce (2000) identifies this kind of sexual intimacy in a 1926 promotion for Chesterfield cigarettes captioned 'I can tell that taste in the dark', where two men dressed in tuxedos and top hats stare into each other's eyes as one lights the other's cigarette. While it is one thing to observe such semiotic 'in-codes' in advertising for tobacco and quite another to see them mobilised in publicity for underwear, nonetheless I would proffer that this is precisely the kind of cruising that is connoted in the Irmo, Celanese and Meridian campaigns (front cover and Figures 38–9); a point that is further compounded in the phallic symbolism of Tony Castle's illustration for Irmo, where we observe the seated figure glance knowingly at the man standing behind him as he holds erect his golf club/'penis'.[14]

In fact, the 'in' codes of such advertising could have been intentional. Boyce, for example, in assessing the iconography of J.C. Leyendecker (who had been employed by Calkins & Holden and was reputed to be gay) and other advertising artists working in the United States during the early twentieth century, attests: 'What is clear is that a number of artists and admen of the day were homosexual, so it would not be unexpected for their affectional desires to have seeped into their ads' (Boyce 2000: 26). Judging from many of the advertisements for underwear and other items of clothing that appeared during the same period in Britain, it is probably safe to argue that there must also have been a parallel – though clandestine – gay presence in the British advertising industry. One such was painter Keith Vaughan, who between 1931 and 1939 worked as a trainee in the art department of Lintas, the ad agency of the soap manufacturer Unilever. Unlike Leyendecker, however, he was not identified as gay at the time and I have not been able to trace any discernible homoerotic or homosocial tropes in publicity for their products during this period. Similarly Traus, the illustrator of the 1932 'Celanese' advertisement on the cover of this book, had sometimes included images of heroic and homoerotic male bodies in his work (such as the working-class man holding up a glass of beer in an advertisement for Carlton Studios in *Advertising Display*, November 1928), but it has not been possible to ascertain any details about him as an artist let alone his sexuality. It is not for nothing, therefore, that Jeffrey Weeks has contended: 'The Oscar Wilde débâcle and the successive controversies and scandals of the 1890s made the public avowal and defence of homosexuality a perilous project' (Weeks 1977: 115). Noel Coward's play *Semi Monde*, for example, which overtly portrays the bitchiness and unbridled sexuality of several gay characters, was censored in 1926 and not performed in public until 1977. Hence, in common with other cultural producers in Britain during the interwar period, advertising artists and agencies were made to tread a fine line in dealing candidly with gay desire and queer identities.

Yet, even though at this time homosexuality remained illegal and was rarely spoken about or represented overtly, the visual – if not the verbal – rhetoric of advertisements such as these appeared at least to sublimate gay desire and to make an appeal to prospective gay customers, without either alienating those who weren't or incurring censorship, by mobilising camp irony and inbetweenism that was efficiently ambiguous ('The happy medium', as the tagline in Figure 39 aptly phrases it). As ambiguous, in fact, as the normative masculine appearances that many gay men themselves adopted in order not to be immediately identified as being gay by straights or straight by gays.[15] Thus the strategy of camp in these promotions offered a point of identification between producer and consumer that, as Eve Kosofsky Sedgwick puts it, reveals the opportunity for projective fantasy; a way of negotiating ambiguity by asking *what if?* – not only 'what if whoever made this was gay too?' but also, 'what if the right audience for this were exactly me?' (Sedgwick 1990:156). Moreover, Alan Sinfield argues that in male homosexual subcultures, camp is not only a strategy for negotiating sexual identities but also one that mimics 'leisure-class mannerisms and upward class mobility' (quoted in Healy 1996: 30). This much is evident in the *moderne* aesthetic and the haughty mien of the males represented in both the Irmo and Celanese campaigns, who seem to have much in common with the artistic and queer dandies described in works such as Terence Greenidge's *Degenerate Oxford?* (1930) and Caroline Ware's *Greenwich Village, 1920–1930* (1935).

By extension, the 1935 press promotion for Morley objectifies the male body in an entirely different way, representing a man from the rear (Figure 35). This was not the first advertisement to depict men's underwear from such a perspective. In 1914, for example, J.C. Leyendecker coined the emblematic 'Man on the Bag' illustration for S.T. Cooper & Sons (now Jockey International), representing a man in a KKK union suit from the back. At the same time, however, he is depicted pressing the weight of one leg on top of a leather bag as he tightens the strap with his hands. The pose is deliberate since it enables the spectator to see the way that the KKK garment had been engineered to enable freedom of movement with its asymmetrical closing and single button, positioned for comfort high up on the right buttock, but as Richard Martin also argues: 'In granting action and plausible context to the figure, Leyendecker invented a man who could be seen from the rear without capitulation to the anal anxieties in male depiction' (Martin 1992: 21). The male figure drawing the curtains in the Morley advertisement has likewise been placed in a situational context, yet the way that we see underwear not only worn from behind but also clinging to and defining his own behind is exceptional for the period and seems to register anal desire on a completely different level to Leyendecker.

Guy Hocquenghem has propounded in *Homosexual Desire* (1993) that, in comparison to the phallus, which is social, the anus is private. But, in keeping with Freud, he also maintains that the sublimated anus forms the bedrock of the individual's identity, that it is only through privatising the excremental and antisocial body part that we can progress to the clean, social order. Thus he argues that the anus has liminal status, and 'only exists as something which is socially elevated and individually debased; it is torn between faeces and poetry' (Hocquenghem 1993: 100). The Morley advertisement, however, can be seen to transgress and transmute these binary codes. Here, the body part that is regarded in social terms as the most private and most unclean is made visible, and veiled in tight-fitting underpants and bathed in seductive lighting that emphasises its pert and rounded contours, it is elevated to the status of fetishistic desirability and spectatorial pleasure, for women and men, and straights and gays alike. Thus the advertisement certainly appears to be more daring and deviant than other underwear promotions during the interwar period in the way it encodes feelings of comfort and pleasure. Yet like many of them, it also highlights the ambiguities of putting the male body on display and the way that such publicity intersects with both commodity and corporeal fetishism. It is in this respect, then, that the rhetoric of underwear advertising exceeds the advertising of the garment itself, just as much as the publicity addressed in the previous chapters is more than merely advertising for suits, shirts and shoes.

Notes

1. For instance, Carter (1992) writes at the outset that she will mention men's (and children's) underwear only when they have a 'bearing on developments in women's underwear' (1992: 9), while neither Ewing (1978) nor Steele (1985) go as far as this.
2. In October and November 1934 £38,708 and £28,799 were spent respectively. The 2001 equivalents are £2,150,496 and £1,599,983. These figures and others cited in subsequent footnotes are from McCusker (2003).
3. *Advertiser's Weekly* (1932d, 1933a); 2001 equivalents are £242,000 and £347,000 respectively.
4. Pesco advertisements appeared in the *Daily Mail, Daily Mirror, Daily Telegraph, Tatler, Country Life* and *Strand Magazine*.
5. The 2001 equivalent is £77,133. The cumulative figure that Wolsey spent for the six months was £8,402 (2001 equivalent £462,908). The remaining underwear manufacturers included in the 'Quarterly Analysis of Press Advertising' were Chilprufe, Comfortex, Jaeger, Kosiclad, Meridian, Morley, Pesco and Vedonis.
6. The three advertisements in *MAN and his Clothes* were for Allen Solly (March 1933:41), Lastex (September 1934:60) and Courtaulds (April 1938:11).
7. See, for example, the full-page promotion, 'This is Aertex Week', in the *Daily Mail* (16 June 1927: 6), which extolled the virtues of the Aertex brand as the healthiest and most natural type of underwear for men, women and children alike, and also the following advertisements in the *Radio Times*: Courtaulds, 'Their clothes are different' (15 June 1934: 864), 'More play in Meridian' (24 May 1935: 75) and Aertex, 'Cultivate Health' (3 July 1936: 37).
8. See the following advertisements: Meridian (*Radio Times*, 24 May 1935:75), Aertex (*Daily Mail*, 16 June 1927:6; and *Radio Times*, 3 July 1936:37) and 'Celanese' (*Daily Mail*, 22 July 1927:9). The 2001 equivalents of these prices are £167 (£3 10s), £7.17 (5s), £11.96 (8s 6d), £25.11 (10s 6d) and £37.06 (15s 6d).
9. Mass-Observation (1949) *1949 Sex Survey, Sexual Behaviour* (Box 4, File E, Appendix 1, 'Abnormality', 6 July 1949), housed in the University of Sussex Library, special collections.

10. These manufacturers spent the following sums on advertising their goods between 1932 and September 1933. In *Advertiser's Weekly*'s 'Quarterly Analysis of Press Advertising', for example, the Willing Advertising Service spent £4,234 on buying space in the press for Meridian, and Service Advertising Co. £6,081 for Morley between October and December 1932 (*Advertiser's Weekly* 1933a). Respective 2001 equivalents are £242,189 and £347,839. Between January and September 1933 the respective figures for Meridian and Morley were £9,834 and £302 (*Advertiser's Weekly* 1933b, 1933c, 1933d). Respective 2001 equivalents are £541,804 and £16,639.

11. See *Advertiser's Weekly*, 28 February 1952:325. This figure was based on the response to a questionnaire that Smith & Co. had in *Men's Wear* and *Outfitter*. Martin (1995) also addresses the appeal to women made in underwear advertisements in the United States during the 1950s.

12. Chilprufe had been founded in 1905, initially to manufacture children's underclothing. See Hughes (1930). Represented by Muller, Blatchly & Co., Chilprufe spent £4,641 on buying space in the press between July and December 1932 (*Advertiser's Weekly*, 10 December 1932: 29–30) and £779 between January and September 1933 (*Advertiser's Weekly* 1933b, 1933c, 1933d). Respective 2001 equivalents are £265,470 and £4,2919.

13. As early as 1878, for example, in *The Draper and Haberdasher: A Guide to the General Drapery Trade*, J.W. Hayes had alluded to the idea that male shop assistants working in hosiery stores could run the risk of being regarded effeminate since they should 'be redolent of lavender water or eau de cologne rather than tobacco smoke' (quoted in Breward 1999:111).

14. Tony Castle had also been involved with promotions for London Transport in the 1920s and 1930s. See, for example, his poster 'Zoo by Tram to Camden Town', in the collections of Leicestershire County Council. It is interesting to observe how the pair of toucans represented in the poster is stylistically close to the men in the Irmo ad.

15. Turbin (2002: 479–80) also deals with this kind of ambiguity in her assessment of J.C. Leyendecker's 'Arrow Collar' campaigns, executed for Cluett, Peabody & Co. between 1907 and 1931.

Bibliography

Adams, H.F. (1916), *Advertising and its Mental Laws*, New York: Macmillan.

Adquisitor (1930a), 'Style – Is Advertising Creating it Today?', *Man and his Clothes*, September: 24–5.

—— (1930b), 'Does Men's Wear Advertising Mislead?', *Man and his Clothes*, October: 22–3.

—— (1931a), 'Where Tailoring Advertising Goes Wrong', *Man and his Clothes*, January: 18–19.

—— (1931b), 'How Much Should Advertising Cost Us?', *Man and his Clothes*, May: 30–1.

—— (1931c), 'Is the "Saving Factor" the Only One?', *Man and his Clothes*, July: 22–3.

—— (1931d), 'When, Why and How Posters Pay their Way', *Man and his Clothes*, September: 32–3.

—— (1931e), 'Get Men's Thoughts Back to Style', *Man and his Clothes*, December: 26–7.

—— (1932a), 'What are the Essentials of a Good Advertisement?', *Man and his Clothes*, January: 18–19.

—— (1932b), 'Round Britain in Search of an Advertising Policy', *Man and his Clothes*, March: 24–5.

—— (1932c), 'How Shall We Climb Out of the Slough of the Depression?', *Man and his Clothes*, April: 30–1.

—— (1932d), 'Why Talk to the Man Who Won't Listen?', *Man and his Clothes*, May: 24–5.

—— (1937), 'Advertising Analysis', *Man and his Clothes*, February: 52–3.

Advertiser's Weekly (1913), 'Clever Local Advertising', *Advertiser's Weekly*, 26 July: 44–5.

—— (1927), 'All about Accounts', *Advertiser's Weekly*, 9 December: 414.

—— (1928), '£25,000 Scheme for Serge Publicity', *Advertiser's Weekly*, 13 July: 50.

—— (1930a), 'Are Newspaper Rates Too High?', *Advertiser's Weekly*, 15 August: 182.

—— (1930b), 'Advertising has Not Slumped', *Advertiser's Weekly*, 3 October: 8.

—— (1932a), 'What 53,932 People Read', *Advertiser's Weekly*, 9 June: 336.

—— (1932b), 'Mayfair Copy Sells Aquascutum to Upper Tooting', *Advertiser's Weekly*, 15 September: 363.

—— (1932c), '34-year-old Men's Wear Chain Starts', *Advertiser's Weekly*, 6 October: 5.

—— (1932d), 'Quarterly Analysis of Press Advertising', *Advertiser's Weekly*, 10 November: 29.

—— (1933a), 'Quarterly Analysis of Press Advertising', *Advertiser's Weekly*, 2 February: 30.

—— (1933b), 'Quarterly Analysis of Press Advertising', *Advertiser's Weekly*, 4 May: 23.

—— (1933c), 'Quarterly Analysis of Press Advertising', *Advertiser's Weekly*, 3 August: 15.

—— (1933d), 'Quarterly Analysis of Press Advertising', *Advertiser's Weekly*, 9 November: 14.

—— (1934a), 'Women Can't Write Fashion Copy', *Advertiser's Weekly*, 8 February: 166.

—— (1934b), 'Reactions to Advertisements and Editorial Features of 8,296 Readers', *Advertiser's Weekly*, 7 June: 270 and 318.

—— (1935), 'They were Starving . . . The Advertising Saved Them', *Advertiser's Weekly*, 21 November: 282.

—— (1936a), 'Sales of 45s. Suits Jumped 63% after One Week's Advertising', *Advertiser's Weekly*, 11 June: 351 and 354.

—— (1936b), 'I.S.B.A. Research Converts "Circulation" into "Spending Power"', *Advertiser's Weekly*, 27 August: 276–7, 282 and 284.

—— (1936c), 'More Facts and Conclusions from the I.S.B.A. Survey', *Advertiser's Weekly*, 3 September: 310–12.

—— (1936d), 'I.S.B.A. Hit Back at Circulation Report Critics', *Advertiser's Weekly*, 8 October: 41, 57–8, 60 and 63.

—— (1936e), 'How Shall I Use the I.S.B.A. Report?', *Advertiser's Weekly*, 29 October: 151.

—— (1936f), '6 Years . . . 60 Shops . . . Appropriation Increased from £600 to £6,000', *Advertiser's Weekly*, 3 December: 356.

—— (1937), 'Which are the Paying Appeals in Selling to Men?', *Advertiser's Weekly*, 29 July: 170.

—— (1940a), 'Battersby's Not Only Carry On – They Launch a New Hat!', *Advertiser's Weekly*, 25 January: 64.

—— (1940b), 'Govt. Will Support £10,000 Men's Wear Export Advg. Plan', *Advertiser's Weekly*, 22 February: 139.

—— (1940c), '6-Page Papers Put Most Ads into Near-Solus Positions', *Advertiser's Weekly*, 4 July: 4.

—— (1940d), 'Men's Wear Trade Plans Big Drive to Expand Home Market', *Advertiser's Weekly*, 14 November: 103.

—— (1941), 'New Survey Gives the Facts on Clothes Rationing', *Advertiser's Weekly*, 4 September: 178 and 190.

—— (1942a), 'What Concentration of Retail Trade Means to Advertising', *Advertiser's Weekly*, 2 July: 3–4.

—— (1942b), 'Clothes Rationing has Affected Whole of Retail Sales', *Advertiser's Weekly*, 9 July: 56.

—— (1943), '"Make Do and Mend" Campaign Adopts New Angle', *Advertiser's Weekly*, 16 September: 340.

—— (1944a), 'I. and R. Morley "Ring the Bell" with a Long-Term Campaign', *Advertiser's Weekly*, 11 May: 180.

—— (1944b), 'Radiac Shirts Advertise Advertisements', *Advertiser's Weekly*, 13 July: 101.

—— (1944c), 'Britain has 86,150 Clothing Shops', *Advertiser's Weekly*, 17 August: 245 and 254.

—— (1947), 'How Newsprint Cuts and Raised Costs Hit Press Advertising', *Advertiser's Weekly*, 6 November: 362.

Advertising Display (1932a), 'The New Law for Outdoor Advertising', *Advertising Display*, June: 246 and 255.

—— (1932b), 'Mr Punch's Cavalcade', *Advertising Display*, October: 136–7.

—— (1933), 'The Song of the Shepherd Shirt', *Advertising Display*, January: 12–13.

Advertising Review (1938), 'The Development of the Modern Advertising Service Agency', *Advertising Review*, 19 November.

Advertising World (1902a), 'Ads of the Month', *Advertising World*, November: 356.

—— (1902b), 'Ads of the Month', *Advertising World*, December: 74.

—— (1903a), 'Ads of the Month', *Advertising World*, January: 142.

—— (1903b), 'Note for the Advertisement Manager', *Advertising World*, February: 214.

—— (1904a), 'Interesting Interviews – J & H Ellis, the Smart Set Tailors', *Advertising World*, January: 126–9.

—— (1904b), 'Advertising Literature', *Advertising World*, April: 318.

—— (1904c), 'In the Dailies', *Advertising World*, July: 91.

—— (1904d), 'Advertising Literature', *Advertising World*, July: 104.

—— (1904e), 'Association of Advertising Agents – An Organisation Formed', *Advertising World*, December: 34–6.

—— (1904f), 'A Sound Idea', *Advertising World*, December: 92.

—— (1906a), 'Advertising in the Magazines', *Advertising World*, April: 529.

—— (1906b), 'The Monthlies', *Advertising World*, May: 666–8.

—— (1906c), 'In the Dailies', *Advertising World*, November: 542.

—— (1906d), 'Suits by Post', *Advertising World*, November: 562–4.

—— (1907a), 'Boot and Shoe Advertising', *Advertising World*, May: 631–3.

—— (1907b), 'In the Magazines', *Advertising World*, October: 490.

—— (1908a), 'Lower Grade Underwear', *Advertising World*, July: 202 and 204.

—— (1908b), 'London's Advertising Area', *Advertising World*, July: 206.

—— (1909a), 'Dailies and Weeklies', *Advertising World*, May: 753.

—— (1909b), 'Retailing Men's Wear', *Advertising World*, July: 161–6 and 168.

—— (1910), 'The "Pesco" Campaign', *Advertising World*, August: 149–52.

—— (1911a), 'Advertising as a Career', *Advertising World*, February: 194.

—— (1911b), 'Women and Advertisements', *Advertising World*, June: 673–4.

—— (1911c), 'Current Ads Reviewed', *Advertising World*, June: 704.

—— (1911d), 'Irreverent Criticism – Mr Punch Finds a Weak Spot', *Advertising World*, September: 281–2.

—— (1911e), 'An Outstanding Advertisement', *Advertising World*, October: 442.

—— (1912a), 'Selling Men's Clothes', *Advertising World*, July: 37–8, 42–4 and 46.

—— (1912b), 'A Notable Campaign', *Advertising World*, December: 722, 724 and 726.

—— (1913a), 'Selling Power, Artistic Effect and Excellence in Printing', *Advertising World*, January: 43–4.

—— (1913b), 'The Travelling Public', *Advertising World*, February: 228.

—— (1913c), 'In the Magazines', *Advertising World*, July: 100 and 102.

—— (1914a), 'First International Advertising Exhibition, Holland Park', special issue, *Advertising World*, May.

—— (1914b), 'The Man about Town', *Advertising World*, June: 907–8.

—— (1914c), 'British Advertising at Toronto Convention', *Advertising World*, June: 1,018.

Aitken, A.J. (1923), 'Selling Talk that Succeeds with Men', *Advertiser's Weekly*, 30 November: 269–70.

Albemarle, G. (1931), 'Flashes of Fashion', *Man and his Clothes*, February: 29.

—— (1932), 'Flashes of Fashion', *Man and his Clothes*, January: 46.

Artad (1923), 'Humour in Advertising', *Commercial Art*, April: 122–3.

Art and Industry (1937), 'Simpson Advertising – A Campaign of Ideas', *Art and Industry*, June: 245–52.

—— (1938a), 'The Story of an Agency – Calkins and Holden', *Art and Industry*, February: 65–8.

—— (1938b), 'Creative Men of the Agencies No. 2 – W.D.H. McCullough', *Art and Industry*, October: 152–5.

—— (1938c), 'Creative Men of the Agencies No. 3 – Ashley', *Art and Industry*, November: 191–8.

—— (1938d), 'Creative Men of the Agencies No. 4 – Terence Prentis', *Art and Industry*, December: 244–8.

—— (1941a), 'The Work of Eckersley Lombers', *Art and Industry*, June: 153–8.

—— (1941b), 'The Eagle Stirs', *Art and Industry*, July: 1–9.

—— (1941c), 'Pearl Falconer, Fashion Designer and Magazine Illustrator', *Art and Industry*, November: 133–6.

—— (1941d), 'Coupon Advertising', *Art and Industry*, November: 137–41.

—— (1942), 'The Artist in Uniform', *Art and Industry*, April: 90–3.

—— (1944a), 'Whitehall as a National Advertiser', *Art and Industry*, February: 34–9.

—— (1944b), 'It's Time I Got a New Hat', *Art and Industry*, February: 40–1.

—— (1944c), 'The Woman in the Queue', *Art and Industry*, February: 49–51.

—— (1952), 'Advertising that Advertises', *Art and Industry*, September: 88–93.

Baker, S. (1990), 'Describing Images of National Self: Popular Accounts of the Construction of Pictorial Identity in the First World War Poster', *Oxford Art Journal*, 13(2): 24–30.

Barbey D'Aurevilly, J. (1988 [1897]), *Of Dandyism and of George Brummell*, trans. D. Ainslie, New York: PAJ Publications.

Barraclough Paoletti, J. (1985), 'Ridicule and Role Models as Factors in American Men's Fashion Change, 1880–1910', *Costume*, 19: 121–34.

Barthes, R. (1967), *Système de la mode*, Paris: Editions du Seuil.

—— (1973), *Mythologies*, London: Paladin.

—— (1994 [1963]), 'The Advertising Message', in his *The Semiotic Challenge*, trans. R. Howard, Berkeley, CA: University of California Press.

Beckford, F. (1928), 'Where the Daily Newspapers Go Wrong', *Man and his Clothes*, June: 26–7.

—— (1932), 'Establish Still More Strongly London's Style Supremacy', *Man and his Clothes*, February: 14–15.

Betjeman, J. (1940), 'Current Advertising – A Commentary', *Penrose Annual*, 42: 17–20.

Bogart, M.H. (1995), *Artists, Advertising, and the Borders of Art*, Chicago: University of Chicago Press.

Bordo, S. (1999), *The Male Body: A New Look at Men in Public and Private*, New York: Farrar, Straus & Giroux.

Bourdieu, P. (1977), *Outline of a Theory of Practice*, trans. R. Nice, Cambridge: Cambridge University Press.

Bourke, J. (1996), 'The Great Male Renunciation: Men's Dress Reform in Interwar Britain', *Journal of Design History*, 9(1): 23–33.

Boyce, D.B. (2000), 'Coded Desire in 1920's Advertising', *Gay and Lesbian Review*, Winter: 26–9.

Bradshaw, P.V. (1927), 'The Art of Tom Purvis', *Commercial Art*, April: 151–6.

Braun, A.A. (1924), 'Artists Who Help Advertisers No. 15: Tom Purvis', *Commercial Art*, October: 129–31

—— (1928), 'An Analysis of Foreign Types', *Penrose's Annual*, 30: 50–60.

Braun, J.F. (1933), 'The Success of the Symbol in Advertising', *Penrose's Annual*, 35: 111–13.

Braun, R. (1927), 'Type v. Lettering', *Commercial Art*, April: 167–9.

Breward, C. (1999), *The Hidden Consumer: Masculinities, Fashion and City Life 1860–1914*, Manchester: Manchester University Press.

Bulwer Lytton, E. (1849), *Pelham, or, Adventures of a Gentleman*, London: Chapman and Hall, reprinted Kila, MT: Kessinger.

Burman, B. (1995), 'Better and Brighter Clothes: The Men's Dress Reform Party, 1929–1940', *Journal of Design History*, 8(4): 275–90.

Butler, W.H. (1928), 'The Types We Use', *Advertiser's Weekly*, 10 August: 205.

—— (1933), 'Has the Sans Come to Stay?', *Advertising Display*, January: 16–17.

—— (1936), 'Here are the World's New Type Faces of 1935', *Advertiser's Weekly*, 23 January, supplement, iv and vi.

—— (1939), 'Typefaces in the Nationals in War Time', *Advertiser's Weekly*, 28 December: 234.

—— (1945), 'The Types We Use', *Advertiser's Weekly*, 1 March: 290–1.

Calkins, E.E. (1915), *The Business of Advertising*, New York: D. Appleton.

—— (1927), 'Beauty the New Business Tool', *Atlantic Monthly*, August: 145–56.

Carter, A. (1992), *Underwear: The Fashion History*, London: Batsford.

Cassandre, A.M. (1930), 'A.M. Cassandre Describes his New "Bifur" Type', *Commercial Art*, January: 31–3.

Chauncey, G.F., Jnr (1985), 'Christian Brotherhood or Sexual Perversion? Homosexual Identities and the Construction of Sexual Boundaries in the World War 1 Era', *Journal of Social History*, 19: 189–212.

Chenoune, F. (1993), *A History of Men's Fashion*, Paris: Flammarion.

Chisholm, C. (ed.) (1936), *Marketing Survey of Great Britain*, London: Business Publications.

Clothes Show (1997), 'Traffic Stoppers', *Clothes Show*, March: 30.

Cole, S. (2000), *Don We Now our Gay Apparel*, Oxford: Berg.

Collier, R. (1931), 'The New Movement in Commercial Art', *Advertising Display*, April: 226 and 228.

Commercial Art (1924a), 'Artists Who Help the Advertiser – Aldo Cosomati', *Commercial Art*, February: 377 and 379.

—— (1924b), 'Artists Who Help the Advertiser – The Work of the Baynard Press', *Commercial Art*, June: 36–9.

—— (1926a), 'Artists Who Help the Advertiser', *Commercial Art*, March: 62–3.

—— (1926b), 'Artists Who Help the Advertiser', *Commercial Art*, March: 66.

—— (1927a), 'Humorous Advertisement Drawings by Fougasse', *Commercial Art*, July: 24–5.

—— (1927b), 'Men Who Create Advertising – I. The Advertiser', *Commercial Art*, September: 97.

—— (1927c), 'Men Who Create Advertising – III. The Designer', *Commercial Art*, November: 193.

—— (1927d), 'Men Who Create Advertising – IV. The Printer', *Commercial Art*, December: 241.

—— (1927e), 'The Work of the Bassett Gray Studio', *Commercial Art*, December: 282–5.

—— (1929), 'The Spirit and the Letter of Modern Advertising Design', *Commercial Art*, October: 142–6.

—— (1931), 'The Atmosphere of Fashion', *Commercial Art*, January: 27–8.

Cook, G. (1992), *The Discourse of Advertising*, London: Routledge.

Costain, H.H. (1935–6), 'Advertising Parade', *Modern Publicity*, 20–1.

Coster, H. (1934), 'Photographic Advertising for Men's Wear', *Commercial Art and Industry*, 17(July–December): 92–8.

Crawford, W.S. (1928), 'The Artist in Advertising: Stating the Problem', *Commercial Art*, 5(July–December): 146–51.

—— (1930), 'What Gives our Dreams their Daring is that They Can be Realised', *Modern Publicity*, 16–19.

—— (1931), *How to Succeed in Advertising*, London: World's Press News.

—— (1937), 'London 1937', *Gebrauchsgraphik*, March: 25–9.

Currington, R.H. (1919), 'Scientific Selling of Branded Underwear, *Advertiser's Weekly*, 16 May: 357–8.

—— (1921), '"We Kept Up Advertising during the Darkest Days" and Now – !', *Advertiser's Weekly*, 8 July: 37–8.

Curtis, G.F. (1927), 'Little Things that Matter', *Man and his Clothes*, May: 6–8.

Daley, P.V. (1930), 'British Printers and Foreign Advertising', *Penrose's Annual*, 32: 113–15.

Degen, F.A. (1913), 'The Future of the Woman Advertising Specialist', *Advertiser's Weekly*, 2 August: 68.

Dempsey, M. (1978), *Bubbles: Early Advertising Art from A&F Pears Ltd.*, London: Fontana.

Dennis, P. (1992), *Daring Hearts: Lesbian and Gay Lives of 50s and 60s Brighton*, Brighton: Queenspark.

Donald, D. (2002), *Followers of Fashion – Graphic Satires from the Georgian Period*, London: Hayward Gallery Publishing.

Dunbar, D.S. (1977), 'Estimates of Total Advertising Expenditures in the U.K. before 1949', *Journal of Advertising History*, 1: 9–11.

Dwiggins, W.A. (1928), *Layout in Advertising*, New York: Harper & Bros.

Dyer, F.W. (1914), 'Talks to Retailers – Tailor's Advertising', *Advertiser's Weekly*, 30 May: 216–17.

—— (1915), 'War Talks to Retailers – Footwear Advertising to Create Business', *Advertiser's Weekly*, 2 January: 280–1.

Dyer, R. (1979), *Stars*, London: British Film Institute.

Dynes, W.R. (ed.) (1990), *Encyclopedia of Homosexuality, 1*, Chicago: St James Press.

Encyclopaedia Typographica (1954), Part One, London: Encyclopaedia Typographica Publishing Co.

Ewing, E. (1978), *Dress and Undress: A History of Women's Underwear*, London: Batsford.

Farringdon, W. (1929), 'The Daily Dozen Sells Underwear', *Advertiser's Weekly*, 5 April: 16.

Fearon, K.O. (1927), 'Terence Prentis', *Commercial Art*, 3(July–December): 84–8.

Firm, J. (1917), 'Advertising Hosiery', *Advertiser's Weekly*, 27 January: 50.

Foster, E.D. (1934), 'Negroes Still Buy Banjoes from Mr. Barratt', *Advertiser's Weekly*, 26 July: 95.

Frankel, H. and Ady, P. (1945), 'The Wartime Clothing Budget', *Advertiser's Weekly*, 21 June: 26–8, 30, 32, 34, 36, 38 and 40.

Freud, S. (1977a [1905]), 'Three Essays on the Theory of Sexuality', in *On Sexuality*, trans. J. Strachey, Penguin Freud Library, vol. 7, pp. 31–169, Harmondsworth: Penguin.

—— (1977b [1927]), 'Fetishism', in *On Sexuality*, trans. J. Strachey, Penguin Freud Library, vol. 7, pp. 345–57, Harmondsworth: Penguin.

—— (1985 [1911]), 'Leonardo da Vinci and a Memory of his Childhood', in *Art and Literature*, trans. J. Strachey, Harmondsworth: Penguin.

Frith, W.P. (1889), 'Artistic Advertising', *The Magazine of Art*, 421–7.

Furst, H. (1934), 'Tom Purvis', *The Artist*, October: 55–8.

Games, A. and Henrion, F.H.K. (1943), 'The Poster Designer and his Problems', *Art and Industry*, July: 17–26.

Gardner, J. (1993), *James Gardner – The ARTful Designer*, London: Lavis Marketing.

Garland, M. (1941), 'Co-relation of Various Sections of the Fashion Industry', *Art and Industry*, March: 65–9.

Garland, S.T. (1919), 'Advertising Causes an Evolution in Men's Wear', *Advertiser's Weekly*, 4 July: 5–6.

Gloag, J. (1940), 'Business (Almost) as Usual', *Art and Industry*, December: 208–21.

—— (1941), 'Commercial and State Propaganda in Wartime, *Modern Publicity in War*, 9–27.

—— (1959), *Advertising in Modern Life*, London: Heinemann.

Gluck, C. (1968), *World Graphic Design – Fifty Years of Advertising Art*, London: Studio Vista.

Goodall, A. (1906), 'The Advertising of Men's Clothing, *Advertising World*, September: 314 and 316.

Goodall, G.W. (1914), *Advertising: A Study of a Modern Business Power*, London: Constable.

Gossop, R.P. (1926), 'Design in Press Advertisement', *Commercial Art*, March: 79.

Gowing, M. (1943), 'Quo Vadis Eve . . . ?', *Advertiser's Weekly*, 29 April: 110.

—— (1947), 'Can Good Art be Bad Propaganda?', *Art and Industry*, July: 8–13.

Grant, M. (1994), *Propaganda and the Role of the State in Inter-war Britain*, Oxford: Oxford University Press.

Greenfield, J., O'Connell, S. and Reid, C. (1999), 'Gender, Consumer Culture and the Middle-Class Male, 1918–1939', in A. Kidd and D. Nicholls (eds), *Gender, Civic Culture and Consumerism: Middle Class Identity in Britain, 1800–1940*, Manchester: Manchester University Press.

Greenidge, T.L. (1930), *Degenerate Oxford? A Critical Study of Modern University Life*, London: Chapman and Hall.

Greenly, A.J. (1927), *Psychology as a Sales Factor*, London: Sir Isaac Pitman.

Gruber, L.F. (1937), 'Four Miniatures', *Gebrauchsgraphik*, March: 35–55.

Hallowell, J.W. (1924), 'How a Humorous Cartoon Created Big Sales', *Advertiser's Weekly*, 19 September: 636.

Hamilton, P. (1939), *Impromptu Moribundia*, London: Constable.

Hammond, A.E. (1939), *Store Interior Planning and Display*, London: Blandford Press.

Hammond, G. (1921), 'Advertising to Protect an Industry', *Advertiser's Weekly*, 15 April: 65.

Harford, W.H. (1929), 'Can We Still Learn from America?', *Advertiser's Weekly*, 2 August: 148.

Harrison, J. (1927), *Posters and Publicity: Fine Printing and Design*, London: The Studio Ltd.

—— (1930a), 'The New Simplicity in Press Advertising', *Commercial Art*, December: 276–80.

—— (1930b), 'What Modern Types to Use', *Commercial Art*, December: 281–2.

Havinden, A. (1935–6), 'Pictorial Advertising', *Modern Publicity*, 15–16.

—— (1938–9), 'Great Britain', *Modern Publicity*, 53–61.

—— (1940), 'Men's Fashions in England and America', *Penrose Annual*, 42: 63–6.

—— (1955a), 'E. McKnight Kauffer', *Art and Industry*, February: 38–43.

—— (1955b), 'The Importance of "Company Handwriting"', *Penrose Annual*, 49: 58–61.

—— (1956), *Advertising and the Artist*, London: Studio Publications.

—— (1959), 'Tom Purvis', *Journal of the Royal Society of Arts*, October: 780–1.

—— (1962), *Posters 1890–20*, London: Lord's Gallery.

Havinden, M. (1941), 'London as a Fashion Centre', *Art and Industry*, March: 61–3.

Haworth-Booth, M. (1971), 'E. McKnight Kauffer', *Penrose Annual*, 64: 83–96.

—— (1979), *E. McKnight Kauffer: A Designer and his Public*, London: Gordon Fraser.

Hayes, J.W. (1878), *The Draper and Haberdasher: A Guide to the General Drapery Trade*, Houlston's Industrial Library, no. 28, London: Houlston.

Healy, M. (1996), *Gay Skins: Class, Masculinity and Queer Appropriation*, London: Cassell.

Heber Smith, M. (1910), 'Is England Ready for Half-Ready Clothes?', *Advertising World*, April: 421–4.

Heideloff, N. and Ackermann, R. (1949 [1794–1802]), *Gallery of Fashion*, vols I–IX, London: Batsford.

Heller, S. and Fili, L. (1998), *British Modern – Graphic Design between the Wars*, San Francisco, CA: Chronicle Books.

Hennessy, P. (1992), *Never Again*, London: Cape.

Henrion, F.H.K. and Stone, H. (1944), 'Artist and Art-Direction', *Art and Industry*, December: 179–84.

Herrick, J. (1913), 'The Week's Advertisements', *Advertiser's Weekly*, 26 April: 41–4.

Hewitt, J. (1992), 'The "Nature" and "Art" of Shell Advertising in the Early 1930s', *Journal of Design History*, 5(2): 121–39.

—— (1995), '*East Coast Joys*: Tom Purvis and the LNER', *Journal of Design History*, 8(4): 291–311.

—— (1996), *The Commercial Art of Tom Purvis*, Manchester: Manchester Metropolitan University Press.

—— (2000), 'Posters of Distinction: Art, Advertising and London, Midland and Scottish Railways', *Design Issues*, 16(1): 16–35.

Higham, C.F. (1916), *Scientific Distribution*, London: Nisbet.

Hight, E.M. (1994), *Picturing Modernism, Moholy-Nagy and Photography in Weimar Germany*, Cambridge, MA: MIT Press.

Hobson, I. (1961), *The Selection of Advertising Media*, 4th edn, London: Business Publications.

Hocquenghem, G. (1993), *Homosexual Desire*, Durham, NC: Duke University Press.

Hodgkin, E. (1935), 'The Onlooker Hits Back', *Art and Industry*, April: 145–9.

Hollander, A. (1994), *Sex and Suits: The Evolution of Modern Dress*, New York: A.A. Knopf.

Holme, G. (ed.) (1926), *Posters and Publicity: Fine Printing and Design*, London: The Studio Ltd.

Honeyman, K. (1993), 'Montague Burton Ltd: The Creators of Well-Dressed Men', in J. Chartres and K. Honeyman, *Leeds City Business 1893–1993: Essays Marking the Centenary of the Incorporation*, Leeds: Leeds University Press.

—— (2002), 'Following Suit: Men, Masculinity and Gendered Practices in the Clothing Trade in Leeds, England, 1890–40', *Gender and History*, 14(3): 426–46.

Hopkins, C.C. (1998), *My Life in Advertising and Scientific Advertising*, Chicago: NTC Business Books.

Hopkinson, T. (ed.) (1984), *Picture Post 1938–50*, London: Chatto & Windus – Hogarth Press.

Horn, F.A. (1935), 'The Modern Trend in Fashion Presentation', *Penrose's Annual*, 37: 56–9.

—— (1936), 'After Functionalism – Surréalism?', *Penrose Annual*, 38: 48–51.

Horn, S. (1932), 'Sell it by Photography', *Man and his Clothes*, February: 43.

Hughes, H.A. (1930), 'Underwear Manufacturer's War of Independence', *Advertiser's Weekly*, 7 March: 363.

Huxley, A. (1931), 'I Look at Modern Advertising', *Advertising Display*, August: 68.

Isherwood, C. (1954), *The World in the Evening*, London: Methuen.

Jackson, J.A. (1928), 'Potentialities of Textile Advertising', *Advertiser's Weekly*, 9 March: 403.

Jeal, N. (1989), 'Back to Basics', *Observer, Living*, 26 November: 36.

Jobling, P. (1999), *Fashion Spreads – Word and Image in Fashion Photography since 1980*, Oxford: Berg.

—— (2003), 'Underexposed: Spectatorship and Pleasure in Men's Underwear Advertising in the Twentieth Century', *Paragraph*, 26(1–2): 147–62.

Jobling, P. and Crowley, D. (1996), *Graphic Design: Reproduction and Representation since 1800*, Manchester: Manchester University Press.

Johnston, P. (1997), *Real Fantasies: Edward Steichen's Advertising Photography*, Berkeley, CA: University of California Press.

Kershen, A.J. (1995), *Uniting the Tailors: Trade Unionism amongst the Tailors of London and Leeds, 1870–39*, Ilford: Frank Cass.

Kidwell, C.B. and Christman, M.C. (1974), *Suiting Everyone: The Democratisation of Clothing in America*, Washington, DC: Smithsonian Institution Press.

King, C.H. (1927), 'Do Men *Read* Men's Wear Advertisements?', *Man and his Clothes*, October: 28–9.

Kinross, R. (1992), *Modern Typography*, London: Hyphen Press.

Kirkwood, J.C. (1911), 'The Retailer and the Press', *Advertising World*, February: 133–7.

Knight, A. (1917), 'A Campaign for Woollens', *Advertiser's Weekly*, 20 October: 228.

Knight, C. (1917), 'One Month's Advertising Campaign for Outfitters', *Advertiser's Weekly*, 15 September: 150.

Kodak Ltd (1957), *Photography in Advertising and Selling*, London: Kodak Ltd.

Kuchta, D. (2002), *The Three-Piece Suit and Modern Masculinity: England 1550–1850*, Berkeley, CA: University of California Press.

Kudwell, W. (1906), 'Photographic Art in Advertising: A Plea for its Larger Use', *Advertising World*, May: 680, 684 and 686.

Lacan, J. (1977), *Ecrits: A Selection*, trans. A. Sheridan, London: Tavistock.

—— (1978), *Four Fundamental Concepts of Psycho-Analysis*, trans. A. Sheridan, New York: Norton.

—— (1988), *The Seminar of Jacques Lacan, Book I: Freud's Papers on Technique, 1953–54*, trans. J. Forrester, Cambridge: Cambridge University Press.

Laird, P.W. (1998), *Advertising Progress – American Business and the Rise of Consumer Marketing*, Baltimore, Md: Johns Hopkins University Press.

Larkin, G. and Pon, L. (2001), 'The Materiality of Printed Words and Images', *Word and Image*, 17(1–2): 1–6.

Le Corbusier (1978), *Towards a New Architecture*, trans. F. Etchells, London: Architectural Press.

Leech, F. (1966), *English in Advertising*, London: Longman.

Le Mahieu, D. (1988), *A Culture for Democracy: Mass Communication and the Cultivated Mind in Britain between the Wars*, Oxford: Oxford University Press.

Lever, E.A. (1947), *Advertising and Economic Theory*, Oxford: Oxford University Press.

Lewis, A. (2003), 'Surrealism, Advertising and British Graphic Design in the 1930s and 1940s: F.H.K Henrion's Advertisements for Harella International', unpublished MA thesis, University of Brighton.

Lewis, L. (1926), 'Small Spaces Create Atmosphere', *Advertiser's Weekly*, 13 August: 201.

Loeb, L.A. (1994), *Consuming Angels – Advertising and Victorian Women*, Oxford: Oxford University Press.

London Magazine (1902), 'Beauty in Advertising – The Development of Photographic Art in Business', *London Magazine*, December.

'Longshoreman' (1927), 'More Money Will Be Spent on Bathing Suits', *Man and his Clothes*, February: 22–3.

Lund Humphries Gallery (1935), *The Work of E. McKnight Kauffer*, London: Lund Humphries.

McCullough, W.D.H. (1929), 'A Successful Art Policy', *Commercial Art*, 6 (January–June): 52–63.

—— (1936), 'In Defence of Prestige', *Penrose Annual*, 38: 39.

McCusker, J.J. (2003), 'The Purchasing Power of the British Pound 1264–2002', Economic History Services, http://www.eh.net/hmit/ppowerbp/

McKay, W. (1918), 'High Standard of War-time Advertising', *Advertiser's Weekly*, 5 December: 578.

McKenzie, D.F. (1986), *Bibliography and the Sociology of Texts*, London: British Library.

Mackenzie Brown, D. (1928), 'How to Organize your Advertising', *Man and his Clothes*, June: 13 and 15.

McKnight Kauffer, E. (1924), 'The Poster and Symbolism', *Penrose's Annual*, 24: 41–5.

MAN and his Clothes (1927a), 'Bigger Part Played by Rayon in Summer Underwear', *Man and his Clothes*, March: 16–17.

—— (1927b), 'A New Form of Advertising that Sells Clothes', *Man and his Clothes*, March: 18.

—— (1927c), 'Display Ideas from the Display Convention', *Man and his Clothes*, November: 37.

—— (1927d), 'How Autumn was Ushered in', *Man and his Clothes*, November: 39.

—— (1928a), 'How This Magazine Can Help You, No. 5, The Advertising Pages', *Man and his Clothes*, February: 61.

—— (1928b), 'Pre-Easter Advertising Emphasises Style', *Man and his Clothes*, May: 35.

—— (1928c), 'The Diary of a Fashionable Young Man', *Man and his Clothes*, June: 17.

—— (1931), 'First Thing Every Morning, Last Thing Every Night', *Man and his Clothes*, June: 22–3.

—— (1932), '"Something a Little Different" Will Bring Underwear Sales', *Man and his Clothes*, February: 28.

—— (1933a), 'Underwear Ranges Styled for Ready Selling', *Man and his Clothes*, February: 24–5.

—— (1933b), 'Underwear', *Man and his Clothes*, June: 17.

—— (1934), 'The "Song of the Shirt" Becomes an Anthem', *Man and his Clothes*, June: 22–3.

—— (1937), 'Mesh is the Next-to-the-Skin Weave for Autumn', *Man and his Clothes*, July: 26–7.

—— (1953), 'Focus on Underwear', *Man and his Clothes*, November: 12–13.

Marshall, E.J. (1925), 'Artists Who Help the Advertiser – Dillon McGurk', *Commercial Art*, June: 151–3.

Marshall, P. (1924), 'Making the Advertising Pages Look Good', *Commercial Art*, October: 137–9.

Marteau, F.R.A. (1925), 'How These Tailors Use Advertising – And Why', *Advertiser's Weekly*, 13 March: 435–6.

Martin, R. (1992), 'Fundamental Icon: J.C. Leyendecker's Male Underwear Imagery', *Textile and Text*, 15(1): 19–32.

—— (1995), '"Feel Like a Million!"': The Propitious Epoch in Men's Underwear Imagery, 1939–1952', *Journal of American Culture*, 18(4): 51–8.

—— (1996), 'J.C. Leyendecker and the Homoerotic Invention of Men's Fashion Icons, 1910–1930', *Prospects*, 21: 453–70.

Mass-Observation (1941), *Clothes Rationing Survey by Mass-Observation, Change No. 1*, London: Advertising Service Guild Bulletin.

—— (1949), *1949 Sex Survey, Sexual Behaviour* (Box 4, File E, Appendix 1, 'Abnormality', 6 July 1949), University of Sussex Library (special collections).

Maxwell, G. (2000), 'Trapped in Miss America's Boudoir', *London Review of Books*, 27 April: 34.

Mayne, X. (1908), *The Intersexes: A History of Similisexualism as a Problem in Social Life*, Rome (privately printed).

Mazur Thomson, E. (1994), 'Early Graphic Design Periodicals in America', *Journal of Design History*, 7(2): 113–26.

—— (1996), '"The Science of Publicity": An American Advertising Theory, 1900–20', *Journal of Design History*, 9(4): 254–72.

Meerloo, E. (1913), 'Women in Advertising', *Advertiser's Weekly*, 14 June: 282.

Mellor, D. (ed.) (1978), *Germany, the New Photography, 1927–33*, London: Arts Council of Great Britain.

Men's Wear (1956), 'The Influence of the Woman Shopper', *Men's Wear*, 12 May: 18–20.

Mercer, F.A. (1941), 'Blue Prints for Tomorrow', *Art and Industry*, March: 57–9.

Michalski, S. (1994), *New Objectivity*, Cologne: Taschen.

Mills, G.H.S. (1923), 'The New Idea in Advertising', *Commercial Art*, November: 298.

—— (1934), 'Colour War', *Penrose's Annual*, 35: 8–12.

—— (1948), 'Advertising is Largely a Matter of Words', *Art and Industry*, December: 209–11.

—— (1954), *There is a Tide*, London: Heinemann.

Modern Publicity (1930), 'Introduction', *Modern Publicity*, 9–11.

—— (1937–8), 'Foreword by the Editors', *Modern Publicity*, 7–10.

Moholy-Nagy, L. (1927), 'Die Photographie in der Reklame', *Photographische Korrespondenz* (Vienna), 9, September: 257–60, reprinted in C. Phillips (ed.) (1989), *Photography in the Modern Era, European Documents and Critical Writings, 1913–1940*, New York: Metropolitan Museum of New York.

—— (1936), 'A New Instrument of Vision', *Telehor*, 1 February: 34–6, originally published (1933) 'How Photography Revolutionizes Vision', *The Listener*, 1 February: 688–90.

—— (1969), *Painting, Photography, Film*, London: Lund Humphries.

Moran, C. (1905), *The Business of Advertising*, London: Methuen.

Morison, E. (1924), 'The British Bibliography of Advertising', *Advertiser's Weekly*, 21 March: 398.

—— (1928), 'Bibliography of British Advertising', *Advertiser's Weekly*, 20 January: 92.

Mort, F. (1996), *Cultures of Consumption: Masculinities and Social Space in Late Twentieth-Century Britain*, London: Routledge.

—— (1999), 'The Commercial Domain: Advertising and the Cultural Management of Demand', in B. Conekin, F. Mort and C. Waters (eds), *Moments of Modernity: Reconstructing Britain 1945–1964*, London: Rivers Oram Press.

Mulvey, L. (1989), 'Visual Pleasure and Narrative Cinema', in her *Visual and Other Pleasures*, London: Macmillan.

Murray Allison, J. (1906), 'Textiles – The Advertising Opportunity of Today', *Advertising World*, March: 396–401.

Nemo (1923), 'A Pun that Grew into a Policy', *Advertiser's Weekly*, 23 November: 241–2.

Nevett, T.R. (1982), *Advertising in Britain*, London: Heinemann.

Newton, F. (1943), 'The Poster in War-time Britain', *Art and Industry*, July: 2–16.

Nicoll, J.S. (1929), 'The Advertising of K Shoes', *Commercial Art*, 6 (January–June): 102–7.

Notley, C.D. (1942), 'The Advertising Guild', *Art and Industry*, May: 140.

Orwell, G. (1965 [1937]), *The Road to Wigan Pier*, Harmondsworth: Penguin.

Osgerby, B. (2001), *Playboys in Paradise – Masculinity, Youth and Leisure-style in Modern America*, Oxford: Berg.

Page, A. (1941), 'British Fashions', *Art and Industry*, March: 77–86.

Parrish, L.G. (1925), 'Why Good Layouts Sometimes Fail', *Commercial Art*, April: 109–10.

Paterson, A. (1911), *Across the Bridges, or Life by the South London Riverside*, London: Edward Arnold.

'Pelican' (1923), 'The Month on the Hoardings', *Advertiser's Weekly*, 5 October: 25.

'Penguin' (1922), 'Branded Footwear Advertising Reviewed', *Advertiser's Weekly*, 20 October: 463–4 and 485.

Penwarden, C.B. (1908), 'Hats for Men', *Advertising World*, April: 578.

Pettit, F.W. (1903), 'The Power of Thought and its Relation to Advertising – A Psychological Study Which Makes Profitable Reading for Publicists', *Advertising World*, August: 180 and 182, September: 242–3.

Pevsner, N. (1936), 'The Psychology of English and German Posters', *Penrose Annual*, 38: 36–8.

Phillips, C. (ed.) (1989), *Photography in the Modern Era, European Documents and Critical Writings, 1913–1940*, New York: Metropolitan Museum of New York.

Phillips, M. (1925), 'An Unusual Layout Simplifies a Complicated Advertising Story: How the Van Heusen Checkerboard Came into Being', *Printer's Ink: A Journal for Advertising*, 125: 33–6.

Picture Post (1939a), 'Unemployed!', *Picture Post*, 21 January: 5–13.

—— (1939b), 'Employed!', *Picture Post*, 11 March: 57–9.

Pincus Jaspert, W., Turner Berry, W. and Johnson, A.F. (2001), *Encyclopaedia of Typefaces*, London: Cassell.

Powe, H. (1929), 'What is Advertising? Science or Sympathy?', *Commercial Art*, 6 (January–June): 200–4.

Presbrey, F. (1929), *The History and Development of Advertising*, Garden City, NY: Doubleday, Doran.

Printer's Ink (1910), 'Selling Men's Wear to Business Men', *Printer's Ink*, 11 May: 12–16.

'Publicitas' (1927), 'An Interview with Joseph Binder – Poster Designer', *Commercial Art*, December: 242–8.

Punch (1911), 'The Age of Specialisation', *Punch*, 9 August: 95.

Purvis, T. (1930), 'To the Young Designer', *Advertising Display*, November: 306 and 308.

—— (1932), 'Tom Purvis Attacks Plagiarism in Publicity', *Advertising Display*, November: 162 and 168.

Raffé, W.G. (1929), *Poster Design*, London: Chapman and Hall.

Repford Ltd (1932), *Investigated Press Circulation*, Rugby: Albert Frost and Sons Ltd.

Reynolds, H. (1999), 'The Utility Garment: Its Design and Effect on the Mass Market 1942–45', in J. Attfield (ed.), *Utility Reassessed – The Role of Ethics in the Practice of Design*, Manchester: Manchester University Press.

Rhodes-James, R. (ed.) (1967), *Chips: Diaries of Sir Henry Channon*, London: Weidenfeld & Nicolson.

Ritchie, B. (1990), *A Touch of Class – The Story of Austin Reed*, London: James & James.

Roche, D. (1994), *The Culture of Clothing: Dress and Fashion in the Ancien Regime*, Cambridge: Cambridge University Press.

Russell, T. (1919), *Commercial Advertising*, London: G. Putnam and Sons.

Sadler, A. (1954), *Men's Wear Display*, London: Blandford Press.

Schorman, R. (1996), 'The Truth about Good Goods: Clothing, Advertising and the Representation of Culture', *American Studies*, 37(1): 23–50.

Scott, P. (1994), 'Learning to Multiply: The Property Market and the Growth of Multiple Retailing in Britain, 1919–39', *Business History*, 36(3): 1–28.

Scott, W.D. (1904a), 'The Psychology of Advertising – Beauty of Symmetry and Proportion', *Advertising World*, January: 113–19.

—— (1904b), 'The Psychology of Advertising – Sympathy', *Advertising World*, February: 181–5 and 188.

—— (1904c), 'The Psychology of Advertising – Sympathy for Joy versus Sympathy for Sorrow', *Advertising World*, March: 245–50.

—— (1904d), 'The Psychology of Advertising – Deliberation', *Advertising World*, April: 308–12.

—— (1904e), 'The Psychology of Advertising – The Survival of the Fittest', *Advertising World*, May: 372–5.

—— (1904f), 'The Psychology of Advertising – The Habit of Reading Advertisements', *Advertising World*, June: 17–21.

—— (1904g), 'The Psychology of Advertising – Summation of Stimuli', *Advertising World*, September: 232, 234, 236 and 238.

—— (1904h), 'The Psychology of Advertising – Reflex and Instinctive Actions', *Advertising World*, October: 298, 300, 302 and 302.

—— (1904i), 'The Psychology of Advertising – Some Instincts which Affect Advertising', *Advertising World*, November: 376–8, 380 and 383.

—— (1905), 'The Psychology of Advertising – A Helpful Classification of Instincts', *Advertising World*, January: 148–54.

—— (1908), *The Psychology of Advertising*, Boston, MA: Small Maynard.

Searle Austin, E. (1938), 'The £. s. d. of Advertising Photography', *Advertising Monthly*, January: 37.

Sedgwick, E.K. (1990), *The Epistemology of the Closet*, Harmondsworth: Penguin.

Selby, H.L. (1930), 'In Eight Years – ', *Advertiser's Weekly*, 12 December: 416 and 431.

Settle, A. (1948), 'The Fashion Artist in Advertising', *Art and Industry*, December: 212–19.

Shaw, D.K. (1932), 'Swat that Lounge Lizard!', *Advertiser's Weekly*, 17 March: 379 and 409.

Sheldon, C. (1916), *Billposting: A Practical Handbook and Work of Reference for the Use of Advertisers*, Leeds: Sheldons Ltd.

—— (1927), *Poster Advertising*, Leeds: Sheldons Ltd.

Sigsworth, E. (1990), *Montague Burton: The Tailor of Taste*, Manchester: Manchester University Press.

Simmonds, C.C.J. (1933), '" . . . Just Part of the Austin Reed Service"', *Commercial Art and Industry*, 14(January–June): 130–2.

Simpson (1937), 'Piccadilly', *News for Spring*, London: Simpson Ltd.

—— (1939a), *Autumn Glimpse*, London: Simpson Ltd.

—— (1939b), *Christmas Presents for Men*, London: Simpson Ltd.

—— (1940), *Uniforms*, London: Simpson Ltd.

Simpson, M. (1994), *Male Impersonators*, London: Cassell.

Sladen, C. (1995), *The Conscription of Fashion – Utility Cloth, Clothing and Footwear 1941–42*, London: Scolar.

Somerford, G.W.W. (1919), 'Advertising Men's Wear on a Colour Scheme', *Advertiser's Weekly*, 14 November: 426.

Sphinx Club of London (1904), *Supplement to The Advertising World*, June.

Spiers, E.A. (1910), *The Art of Publicity*, London: T. Fisher Unwin.

Stabiner, K. (1982), 'Tapping the Homosexual Market', *New York Times Magazine*, 2 May: 34.

Stanley, H. (1906), 'To Sell More Collars', *Advertising World*, October: 410–12.

Steele, V. (1985), *Fashion and Eroticism: Ideals of Feminine Beauty from the Victorian Era to the Jazz Age*, Oxford: Oxford University Press.

'Stylus' (1927), 'Sell Better Underwear', *Man and his Clothes*, May: 13–14.

Swann, J. (1982), *Shoes*, London: Batsford.

Teague, W.D. (1931), 'The Eastman Kodak Shop', *Architectural Forum*, April: 449–54.

Teitelbaum, M. (ed.) (1992), *Montage and Modern Life 1919–1942*, Cambridge, MA: MIT Press.

The Adman (1929a), 'More Originality in Men's Wear Advertising', *Man and his Clothes*, February: 43.

—— (1929b), '"Something Different" Advertises Men's Clothes', *Man and his Clothes*, October: 36.

The Advertising Register (1927), London: Rolls House Publishing.

The Look-Out Man (1931), 'Austin Reeds Sells Shirts for Meakers', *Advertiser's Weekly*, 29 October: 144 and 168.

—— (1934), 'Review of the Week's Advertising', *Advertiser's Weekly*, 5 April: 18.

—— (1936), 'Swopping Sex Appeals', *Advertiser's Weekly*, 3 December: 350.

The Merchandise Man (1929), 'The Underwear World Needs Retail Encouragement', *Man and his Clothes*, December: 30–1.

—— (1930), 'Sport Influences Underwear Styles More than Ever', *Man and his Clothes*, July: 28–9.

The Onlooker (1927), 'NO Shop is Barred from Advertising', *Man and his Clothes*, August: 11–12.

—— (1928a), 'How American Shops Advertise Men's Clothes', *Man and his Clothes*, May: 6–7.

—— (1928b), 'Sport – And the Men's Wear Business', *Man and his Clothes*, July: 23.

The Outfitter (1910), *Publicity: A Practical Guide for the Retail Clothier and Outfitter to All the Latest Methods of Successful Advertising*, London: The Outfitter.

Thorp, J. (1927), 'The Work of the Clement Dane Studio', *Commercial Art*, November: 220–3.

—— (1928), 'The Adventurous Trend of Modern Advertising Design', *Penrose's Annual*, 30: 40–3.

Timmers, M. (1998), *The Power of the Poster*, London: V&A Publications.

Tregurtha, C.M. (1926), 'Photography for Publicity – E.O. Hoppé's Posters', *Commercial Art*, January: 27–31.

—— (1927), *Types and Typefaces*, London: Sir Isaac Pitman.

—— (1931), 'The Ways of the Modern Advertisement', *Penrose's Annual*, 33: 49–52.

Tschichold, J. (1930), 'The New Typography', special issue, *Commercial Art*, July.

—— (1995 [1928]), *The New Typography: A Handbook for Modern Designers*, trans. R. McLean, Berkeley, CA: University of California Press.

Turbin, C. (2002), 'Fashioning the American Man: The Arrow Collar Man, 1907–1931', *Gender and History*, 14(3): 470–91.

Tyler, O. (1928), 'Making a Collar Known among Men', *Man and his Clothes*, February: 30–1.

Ugolino, L. (2000), 'Clothes and the Modern Man in 1930s Oxford', *Fashion Theory*, 4(4): 427–46.

Underwood, L. (1906), 'Neckties as a Proposition, the Opportunities and the Possibilities', *Advertising World*, April: 503–4.

Valotaire, M. (1927), 'Fashion Advertising in France', *Commercial Art*, December: 254–61.

Wadman, G. (1936), 'Mechanism or Humanism? Current Design in Publicity Printing', *Penrose Annual*, 38: 40–3.

Wainwright, D. (1996), *The British Tradition: Simpson – A World of Style*, London: Quiller Press.

Wainwright, S.B. (1927), 'Art and Commerce, Austin Reed Ltd.', *Commercial Art*, January: 11–14.

Waldman, G. (2002), *Who's a Dandy?*, London: Gibson Square Books.

Walsh, C. (2000), 'The Advertising and Marketing of Consumer Goods in Eighteenth Century London', in C. Wischermann and E. Shore (eds), *Advertising and the European City*, London: Ashgate.

Warde, B.L. (1935), 'Is There Room for "Modern" Typography?', *Art and Industry*, April: 141–4.

—— (1936), 'What Does "Modern" Mean in Typography?', *Penrose Annual*, 38: 44–8.

Ware, C.F. (1935), *Greenwich Village 1920–1930: A Comment on American Civilization in the Post-war Years*, Boston, MA: Houghton Mifflin.

Warrington, G. (1916), 'Things that Matter in Advertising', *Advertiser's Weekly*, 16 December: 234.

Weber, H. (1931), 'The Modern Shop', *Annual of American Design*, 11–13.

Weeks, J. (1977), *Coming Out: Homosexual Politics in Britain from the 19th Century to the Present*, London: Quartet.

Wildman, A.S. (1930), 'A Note on Some Types Used in Current Advertisements', *Penrose's Annual*, 32: 110–12.

Wilkinson, H. (1997), '"The New Heraldry": Stock Photography, Visual Literacy, and Advertising in 1930s Britain', *Journal of Design History*, 10 (1): 23–38

Willett, C. and Cunnington, P. (1981), *The History of Underclothes*, London: Faber & Faber.

Williams, A.H. (1912), 'Illustrating Men's Dress', *Advertising World*, June: 672 and 674.

Williams, J.G. (1932), 'The Why and Wherefore of Shrinkage', *Man and his Clothes*, June: 44–5.

Willis, A.G. (1932), 'Photography in Advertising', *Journal of the Royal Photographic Society*, April: 164–5.

Wilson, E. (1985), *Adorned in Dreams: Fashion and Modernity*, London: Virago.

Wilson, R. (1930), 'These Moderns are Ruining Advertising Art', *Advertiser's Weekly*, 6 June: 360.

Wingrave, J.H. (1927), *Poster Publicity*, London: Sir Isaac Pitman.

Woolman Chase, E. and Chase, I. (1954)*, Always in Vogue*, London: Gollancz.

Yochelson, B. (1983), 'Clarence White Reconsidered: An Alternative to the Modernist Aesthetic of Straight Photography', *Studies in Visual Communication*, 9 (4):26–44.

Yoxall, H.W. (1931), 'Don't Sell by the Yard – Habits have Changed', *Advertiser's Weekly*, 1 October: 6.

—— (1937), 'Development in Fashion Photography', *Penrose Annual*, 29–33.

Archives, Annuals and Periodicals

Advertiser's Weekly, 1913–70.

Advertising Display, 1926–35.

Advertising Monthly, 1937–40.

Advertising Review, 4 January 1936–13 April 1940.

Advertising World, 1901–40.

Advertising World Year Book (London: Ewart, Seymour & Co.), 1908.

Art and Industry, 1936–58.

Art and Publicity (London: The Studio Ltd), 1925.

The Artist, 1930.

Atlantic Monthly, 1927.

Austin Reed Archive, Sackville Street, London, W1.

Board of Trade Documents BT 64/182, Public Records Office (now known as the National Archives), Kew, London.

Bibliography

Commercial Art (London: The Studio Ltd), 1922–31.

Commercial Art and Industry (London: The Studio Ltd) 1932–6.

Companies House, Cardiff.

Daily Express, occasional numbers, 1925–45.

Daily Mail, occasional numbers, 1901–45.

Daily Mirror, occasional numbers, 1920–45.

Evening News, occasional numbers 1923–39.

Gebrauchsgraphik, 1930–9.

History of Advertising Trust, Raveningham, Norfolk – W.S. Crawford Archive and London Press Exchange Archive.

James Gardner Archive, Design History Research Centre, University of Brighton.

Man and his Clothes, 1926–59.

Mass-Observation, University of Sussex.

Mather & Crowther, *Practical Advertising: A Handy Guide for Practical Men* (London: Mather & Crowther), annually 1890s onwards.

Men's Wear, 1932, 1956.

Modern Publicity (London: The Studio Ltd), 1930–70.

Penrose's Annual (London: Percy Lund Humphries and Co. Ltd) 1895–1935.

Penrose Annual (London: Percy Lund Humphries and Co. Ltd) 1936–40 and 1949–82.

Picture Post, September 1938–September 1945.

Posters and Publicity (London: The Studio Ltd), 1926–9.

Posters and their Designers (London: The Studio Ltd), 1924.

Printer's Ink, 1910, 1938.

Public Records Office (now known as the National Archives), Kew, London.

Punch, 1902–45.

Radio Times, 1923–45.

Smith's Advertising Agency, *Successful Advertising: Its Secrets Explained* (London: Smith's Advertising Agency), 1880s onwards.

The Times, occasional numbers 1911–45.

Index

Index